Human Rights, Refugee Protest and Immigration Detention

Lucy Fiske

Human Rights, Refugee Protest and Immigration Detention

palgrave
macmillan

Lucy Fiske
University of Technology Sydney
Australia

ISBN 978-1-137-58095-5 ISBN 978-1-137-58096-2 (eBook)
DOI 10.1057/978-1-137-58096-2

Library of Congress Control Number: 2016940666

Cover illustration: © epa european pressphoto agency b.v. / Alamy Stock Photo
Cover design by Samantha Johnson

Printed on acid-free paper

This Palgrave Macmillan imprint is published by Springer Nature
The registered company is Macmillan Publishers Ltd. London

For Dad

Acknowledgements

Writing a book can, at times, be a solitary and isolating task, but it is never undertaken alone. The first to be acknowledged must be the men who shared their stories and insights with me. I wish I could name you all, as your courage, creativity, commitment to principles and sometimes sheer endurance deserve public acknowledgement.

It is impossible to thank my mentor and colleague, Linda Briskman, enough. Linda's knowledge of the field, shared passion for the topic, contacts, insights, feedback and unwavering support have been crucial in this project. I am particularly grateful though, for her wicked sense of humour, love of life and valued friendship.

Mary Anne Kenny first introduced me to working with asylum seekers in detention and we have worked together at every opportunity since. She has a brilliant mind and a great, big heart. Kiran Grewal has read several chapters and provided helpful feedback, but more importantly, has helped further enrich my thinking around human rights, refugees, southern theories and ethics.

My colleagues at the Centre for Human Rights Education at Curtin University and at the UTS Cosmopolitan Civil Societies Research Centre are 'fellow travellers' and contribute greatly to my thinking and love of the work we do. Caroline Fleay (Curtin) must be singled out for a special mention for her generosity, friendship and reassurance throughout. I am also very grateful to Nina Burridge at UTS for believing in this and helping to make space and time in my workload to complete the book. I am personally and academically grateful to Rita Shackel who does excellent work in women, children and the law and from whom I have learned a great deal.

My colleagues at Murdoch University, Sydney University, ASeTTS, CARAD and CASE for Refugees, who I have had the great pleasure of working with over many years, do great work to make human rights real. Thomas Crofts, Adam Kamradt-Scott, Andrew Jakubowicz, Devleena Ghosh, Fausto Buttá, Vicki Sara and Mary Spongberg have all contributed to my thinking. They make work a pleasure and represent what academia can be at its best. Anne Shields has read every word, proofed every comma, chased down legal citations and much more—thank you!

Jim Ife has been a key figure in shaping my politics and thinking over many years. My father, John Fiske, instilled in me a strong sense of social justice from an early age. His influence cannot be overstated. His feedback on drafts was both affirming and extending.

I am grateful to Harriet Barker at Palgrave Macmillan for seeing the potential of this book.

Finally, to Anne, Finbar and Perry, thank you for your love, support and understanding.

Contents

Abbreviations

ACM	Australasian Correctional Management
AFP	Australian Federal Police
AHRC	Australian Human Rights Commission (see also HREOC)
ASIO	Australian Security and Intelligence Organisation
BID	Bail for Immigration Detainees (UK)
CERT	Critical Emergency Response Team
CIE	Centre for Identification and Expulsion (Italy)
CoE	Council of Europe
CPT	European Committee for the Prevention of Torture
DHS	(United States) Department of Homeland Security
DIBP	(Australian) Department of Immigration and Border Protection
DIMIA	(Australian) Department of Immigration, Multicultural and Indigenous Affairs
DIMA	(Australian) Department of Immigration and Multicultural Affairs
DIAC	(Australian) Department of Immigration and Citizenship
EMDD	Electro Muscular Disruption Device
EC	European Council
ECtHR	European Court of Human Rights
EU	European Union
GSL	Global Security Ltd
HCA	High Court of Australia

HREOC	Human Rights and Equal Opportunity Commission (see also AHRC)
IAAAS	Immigration Advice And Assistance Scheme
ICCPR	International Covenant on Civil and Political Rights
ICE	(United States) Immigration and Customs Enforcement
IDAG	Immigration Detention Advisory Group (Australia)
IDC	Immigration Detention Centre
IDF	Immigration Detention Facility
IND	(United Kingdom) Immigration and Nationality Directorate
IRA	Irish Republican Army
IRC	Immigration Removal Centre
IRPC	Immigration Reception and Processing Centre
JRS	Jesuit Refugee Service
JSCFADT	Joint Standing Committee on Foreign Affairs, Defence and Trade
JSCM	Joint Standing Committee on Migration
MEDU	Medici per I Diritti Umani (Doctors for Human Rights)
MSF	Médecins Sans Frontières (Doctors Without Borders)
NAACP	National Association for the Advancement of Coloured People
NACCD	(United States) National Advisory Commission on Civil Disorders
NGO	Non-Government Organisation
RRT	Refugee Review Tribunal
UKBA	United Kingdom Border Agency
UNHCR	United Nations High Commissioner for Refugees
UNOHCHR	United Nations Office of the High Commissioner for Human Rights
UNWGAD	United Nations Working Group on Arbitrary Detention
WAICS	Western Australian Inspector of Custodial Services

1

Introduction

* * *

Especially after a protest, I would feel proud of myself. Cos I did something that every free man would do. You know? You are not dead body. You are human, you have got dream. So when you do those things and you come back to your room and think 'Oh that was good.' Even if we didn't achieve what we wanted, like talking with Immigration or bring Immigration to see us, but at least you feel like the things inside your chest come out. It's better than inside, you get sick. You feel a little bit open and relax, until the next action.

Osman, detained 3 years and 4 months

* * *

... in detention we had very well educated people. We had politicians, we had pilots and they knew how to deal with protests and everything. So there were the people that says 'Okay. We do it peacefully. We sit here,' and there were the people who said 'Peacefully doesn't answer anything because there is no journos here. We need to get journos here.' And how we can do it just go to a town and sit in there until journos gets here. Or just burn the place down and the smoke will bring journalists, you know? ... We had lots

L. Fiske, *Human Rights, Refugee Protest and Immigration Detention*,
DOI 10.1057/978-1-137-58096-2_1

> of well educated people who could get their heads around policies and politics and everything. They played it well. We played it like politicians. … So all the demonstrations and all the protests we did, there was a great reason behind it. It wasn't just like 'we are bored and let's break something.'
>
> Issaq, detained 3 years and 11 months

* * *

As the use of immigration detention has proliferated around the globe, so too has the academic literature addressing the practice. Immigration detention has generated a broad and rich body of literature spanning law (Goodwin-Gill 1986; Hailbronner 2007; Hamilton 2011; Kalhan 2010; Stevens 2013), sociology (Marfleet 2006; Nethery and Silverman 2015; Story 2005), criminology (Grewcock 2009; Malloch and Stanley 2005; Pickering 2005), psychology and psychiatry (Robjant et al. 2009; Steel and Silove 2001), politics (Nethery et al. 2012; Sampson and Mitchell 2013) and cultural studies (Pugliese 2007; Wolfram Cox and Minahan 2004) to name a few. Much of this literature focuses on the practices of the state and considers 'the refugee' in abstract form, as a passive, interchangeable object caught in an extraordinary exercise of state power. The refugee is at once a concern as the victim of human rights violations, yet is not present in any distinct or recognisable form. While there is a discernible consensus among writers, advocates and human rights bodies that immigration detention presents serious challenges to human rights (in law, ethics and politics), very few turn to those subjected to detention as a means of furthering our understanding of the troubling practice. Very few works engage with detained refugees as agents in the exercises of power or the challenges to human rights that immigration detention entails.

This book takes accounts of formerly detained refugees as the entry point for analysis of the detention of refugees and its implications for human rights. It looks at immigration detention at a specific and localised level. It examines the daily individual interactions and social relations occurring within detention centres in Australia, taking formerly detained refugees as key sources of knowledge. By taking a detailed approach to immigration detention and refugees' resistance to it, I hope to generate new insights into understandings of the global figure of 'the refugee' and human rights. Refugees occupy a critical position in human rights theory and practice, both exemplifying why human rights remain utterly necessary and exposing the failings of modern human rights institutions. Through in-depth interviews with refugees who protested against their incarceration in immigration detention centres, this book moves between the micro (daily relations inside detention) and the macro (political, legal and theoretical frameworks which enable or contest detention) to stimulate new ways of thinking about detention, refugees and human rights.

The use of immigration detention is on the rise globally. More than one million people pass through immigration detention centres in the USA, Canada, Australia, and Europe each year. They may be held in over-crowded, dilapidated detention centres or in modern, purpose-built facilities designed as 'super-max' prisons, allocated an identification number, subjected to arbitrary rules and sometimes arbitrary and excessive use of force, distanced from legal protections by their incarceration, lack of knowledge, little political voice and their status as non-citizens, non-people. Life inside immigration detention centres is precarious, filled with uncertainty and monotony and, too often, with degrading treatment. As the use of immigration detention has risen, so too has detainee protest. When detainees go on hunger strike or riot or occupy the roofs of detention centres, their actions are usually narrated by governments keen to discredit them and their actions as criminal, manipulative and evidence of 'their' barbarity and difference. A secondary, counter narration is provided by detainee supporters who explain the actions as evidence of detainees' distress and deteriorating mental health. The voices of the actors themselves, people held in detention and taking protest action, are rarely heard in any depth.

The separation of detained refugees' narrations from their actions rests upon a distancing of the refugee from the citizenry. The less contact that 'ordinary citizens' have with detained refugees, the less likely they are to have access to refugees' own explanations of their actions. Indeed, governments practicing immigration detention often go to great lengths to obstruct, if not entirely prohibit, contact between detained refugees and citizens, thereby retaining greater control over the narrative used to frame asylum seeking and the need for immigration detention. Detention both enables, and is itself enabled by, the distance between asylum seekers and citizens.

The dominant narrative surrounding refugees and asylum seekers in the UK, Europe, Australia and North America is one in which the refugee is viewed either as a victim or as a villain. Possible responses are consequently narrowed to charity or hostility. Most commonly, the (real) refugee appears in fund-raising campaigns as a familiar image of a poor, visibly needy, brown-skinned woman or child (e.g., see Malkki 1996 or Rajaram 2002), whereas asylum seekers are more commonly represented as lawless, unknown and threatening males (e.g., see Aas 2007; Pickering 2005 or Philo et al. 2013). The dominant hegemony provides only a simplistic binary for understanding a complex and dynamic phenomenon involving real people. This hegemony needs to be challenged and unsettled; it has philosophical, ideological and moral limitations and, further, it is a worldview which results in material harm and injustice—for asylum seekers and others 'here' as well as for refugees in lands far away.

Both humanitarian and criminalising discourses draw upon archetypal figures and, as established discourses, easily overwhelm the voices of refugees in detention centres. Refugees are popularly seen as passive victims, and any display of agency or assertion of political identity risks their being recast as suspect—the 'cheating, conniving, manipulative, dishonest person out to subvert the aid system' (Harrell-Bond 1999, 153). The power of these archetypes effectively precludes any chance of detained refugees' protest actions being read as legitimate responses to injustice. In addition to governments' and refugee supporters' greater public voice and access to media, explanations for refugee protest against detention that reduce actions to simple criminality or despair are readily digested by the nation's population. As demonstrated by Issaq and Osman earlier, however, protest holds many layers of significance: deliberate actions aimed at particular goals, existential functions to express agency and, sometimes, catharsis to relieve the pressure of detention. Most importantly, their testimony reveals conscious agents analysing their situation and disputing the ethics and efficacy of possible actions. All of which are obscured in external narrators' explanations of refugee protest.

This book attempts to intervene in the dominant hegemony surrounding refugees and to unsettle the polarised discourse in which asylum seekers and refugees are to be either feared or saved. The work is based on a series of lengthy, in-depth interviews with fifteen refugees who had been previously detained in Australian detention centres. The fifteen participants were all men and came from Iran, Iraq, Afghanistan and Jordan. One person was stateless. The men had been held in detention for periods ranging from seven months to six years, and between them, had been held in every detention centre on Australian territory operating between 1999 and 2005. Most had been held in multiple detention centres during their periods of detention. All had found the experience of detention profoundly offensive and dehumanising and had engaged in protest against it. Beyond agreement on the injustice of detention, the men did not hold a consensus view about protest, as the following chapters reveal. The men were all interviewed after their release from detention, primarily as gaining permission to access detained populations for research of this nature was unlikely to be granted. The research draws on a relatively small sample of formerly detained refugees as it seeks rich qualitative understandings of the experience of immigration detention and the social relations produced there. This book does not make any claims to a new truth, but rather presents previously unexamined experiences and perspectives that enrich our understanding of just how detention works and challenges us to rethink refugees, detention and human rights.

Why This Book?

This book has three aims. First, it provides a platform for refugees subject to immigration detention to speak for themselves, to explain what their experiences of detention were and, particularly, to explain their protests against detention. This leads to the second purpose, to better understand a phenomenon that has grown over the last two decades and is set to become more frequent and more widespread as the use of immigration detention spreads. The use of immigration detention has grown at an alarming rate in the last two decades. As recently as the 1990s, immigration detention was used by only a few states and almost entirely as a last resort, whereas in 2015, almost all states practice immigration detention, creating a global carceral web (Silverman and Nethery 2015, 6). Finally, this book considers what immigration detention, and refugees' use of human rights in their protest against it, means for human rights—theoretically and practically.

At the time of writing, the world is experiencing the largest refugee flows since World War II. Almost sixty million people are currently displaced from their homes and if gathered together would form the twenty-fourth most populous nation on earth (UNHCR 2015, 2). Some have been refugees for years or decades, such as Afghans and Burmese, but newer conflicts in Syria, Burundi and Ukraine, and escalations of existing conflicts in the Democratic Republic of Congo, South Sudan and the Central African Republic have produced millions of newly displaced people. While it continues to be true that the vast majority of refugees remain close to home in neighbouring countries, over one million people entered Europe in 2015, and all except a little more than 50,000 have lodged claims for refugee status (BBC 2016). The numbers of people entering Europe have overwhelmed sophisticated border protections and Europe's extensive immigration detention capacity. It is difficult to conceive of a world in which there are no refugees, with no one crossing borders without prior authorisation and proper travel documents.

Extra-judicial, administrative immigration detention has been the ascendant trend in response to unauthorised crossing of borders throughout *Refugee Convention* signatory countries. Chapter 7 outlines the rapid expansion of immigration detention in Europe, the UK, North America and Australia, including the more recent phenomenon of extraterritorial detention—intercepting and detaining would-be asylum seekers before they reach a signatory country. The EU funds detention centres in Ukraine, the USA in Mexico and Australia in Indonesia, interrupting refugee journeys and holding them outside the potentially protective embrace of western liberal democratic states' legal systems. Immigration detention is an administrative practice deployed against non-citizens. It is not subject to the same oversight, monitoring and protections as judicially ordered detention, the resulting regimes and conditions of detention very often fall short of standards set for judicial detention (Silverman and Nethery 2015, 3). In addition to the sometimes deplorable physical conditions of detention, people typically do not know how long they will be detained, rules and punishments are often meted out arbitrarily and there are frequent allegations of physical and sexual abuse of detainees (ACLU n.d.; Elliot and Gunasekera 2016, 9; Shaw 2016, 22).

Who is targeted for detention varies somewhat in different states. Immigration detainees may be refugees, asylum seekers, people who have over-stayed their visas, unauthorised migrants or people who were in a state lawfully but had their visa cancelled. This book focuses in particular on refugees and asylum seekers held in detention, partly because they are the largest group that Australia detains, but more importantly because, while administrative immigration detention is problematic in and of itself, the detention of refugees and asylum seekers is especially so. Refugees and asylum seekers are of particular concern as they have no state to claim them or to advocate for their release and so are in a profoundly asymmetrical relationship with the detaining state. They are a key concern of international human rights regimes and present particular challenges to human rights, both practically—how to respond to people falling outside the nation-state-territory structure of the world since at least the Treaty of Westphalia? (Haddad 2008); and theoretically—refugees embody the tension between citizenship (sovereign) and universal human rights and expose deep fissures in a body of knowledge that insists that human rights are universal, inalienable and inabrogable. Immigration detention centres are becoming notorious as sites where human rights violations are most likely to occur in liberal democracies. That refugees and asylum seekers are principal targets of detention regimes raises compelling ethical and theoretical challenges.

It is not uncommon for detained refugees to resist or protest against their incarceration. Resistance may take the form of non-compliance with directives or work 'go-slows,' actions that can be difficult to police and which rarely come to public light, but which nonetheless aim to subvert, frustrate or directly challenge immigration detention, through to more explicit protests such as hunger strikes, escapes or riots. Many messages coming from inside detention centres in Australia and around the world use a language of human rights to articulate the wrongs of detention and the claims of the detained. The cry, variously formulated, 'We are human! We need our rights' is made over and over in detainee correspondence from detention, through emails, letters, protest banners and phone calls. So too, the former detainees who participated in this research frequently expressed their critique using a language of human rights. At the same time, Western governments have repeatedly assured the domestic and international communities that they are adhering to their human rights obligations. 'Human rights' is disputed terrain, carrying different meanings for different actors referring to quite different points of reference. What then, in light of such divergent claims, are 'human rights?'

The third aim of this book is to think through some of the challenges that detained refugees' use of human rights language present to human rights, and to do so from a perspective that focuses more on the human subject of rights than the juridical and institutional mechanisms. Drawing on the experiences and opinions of people who have been subject to immigration detention, I hope to enable readers to think about immigration detention and human rights from a perspective not often accessible in depth. Foucault articulated the subtle and expansive ways in which hierarchies of knowledge work to reinforce power relations—to legitimise and 'naturalise' certain sources of knowledge as authorities, while simultaneously marginalising, silencing and discrediting other sources of knowledge. Invariably, 'the knowledge of the psychiatrised, the patient . . . the delinquent' is disregarded as anecdotal, self-serving, non-conceptual and ultimately as hierarchically inferior, if not false, knowledge (Foucault 1997, 7). Yet people subject to immigration detention have expansive, intimate experiential knowledge of human rights, and specifically of the tensions between legally based, institutionalised rights and moral and ethical dimensions of human rights.

Human rights, particularly when discussing refugees and immigration detention in Western liberal states, is likely to lead one to think about human rights law—the bodies of jurisprudence at national, regional and international levels pertaining to the movement of refugees across borders and their treatment by the states engaged. Indeed, it is to this body of law that asylum seekers present their claims for formal recognition as refugees and the range of protections and guarantees that come with this recognition. Human rights also exist beyond legal positivism; they have power as an idea, a set of values and ethics, and provide a language with which to articulate wrongs and legitimise opposition to lawfully enacted injustices. While human rights in this sense do not carry the same enforceability as legally based rights, they can be powerful nonetheless. Serena Parekh posits that essentialist positions are particularly useful for social movements in that they establish a good base from which to claim rights which do not yet exist in law and are not recognised by institutions (Parekh 2007, 768–769). While a 'right' is interpreted in legal discourses as the claim of an individual made against a state, 'right' has layers of meaning. 'Right' makes an appeal to conscience, each person's capacity to make judgements and discern ethical actions (Parekh 2008). In this sense, human rights are the responsibility of us all, and one does not need a degree to form a significant opinion and participate in public debate. Because human rights exist beyond legal frameworks in philosophical and moral domains, these claims can continue to exist even where there are no legally encoded rights protected. Through a language of human rights, it may be possible for refugees to lay their claims not only at the feet of the state, but also to fellow humans through an appeal to conscience. A language of human rights can appeal for political, legal and human responses all at the same time.

The refugees interviewed for this book spoke about human rights both as laws and as a philosophical or ethical framework. While this book draws on positivist and essentialist approaches to human rights, it relies principally on a constructivist approach in which human rights come into being through human decision and action. Hannah Arendt (1976) famously stated that universal and inalienable human rights are nonsense, as any stateless person or refugee can attest (the bounded nature and alienability of rights is discussed in more detail in Chap. 2). Arendt's perspective argues that human rights are essentially a contract between members of a political community and that they only exist to the extent that members agree to guarantee those rights to one another and are therefore constructed, contested and contingent. The task for humans is to decide what rights we want (and therefore are willing to guarantee others) and to whom we are willing to extend this guarantee or with whom we share a political community (Parekh 2007). This approach is useful in a number of ways. It is sufficiently broad to enable space for legal, ethical and strategic approaches to human rights—whichever ways human rights are being conceived or used, and the interaction between these approaches can be considered and thought through. Secondly, and perhaps more importantly, it places actual human beings and the contestations and alliances between them as the central object of study, rather than an abstract principal or the legality (or otherwise) of policies and practices of states to non-citizens. Maintaining specificity (and specific humans) in discussions of human rights sheds unsettling light on the absurdity of states proclaiming the importance of human rights generally and affirming their continued commitment to refuge, while systematically violating the rights of people within their territory. Finally, a constructivist approach gives more scope to the agency of people in defining and shaping human rights.

The second major conceptual challenge that refugee protest presents is forcing a rethinking of 'the refugee' and agency. Humanitarian approaches construct and portray refugees as inherently dependent, helpless and passive (Harrell-Bond and Voutira 1992; Harrell-Bond 1999; Malkki 1996; Soguk 1999), a portrayal difficult to maintain when refugees go in search of their own solutions and impossible when they set fire to detention centres. The practice of immigration detention is an extraordinary exercise of state power, exempt from many of the limitations placed on the detention powers of the state over its own citizens (Gibney 2004, 256; Silverman and Nethery 2015, 2). It is unsurprising then that much writing on immigration detention focuses on the sources, justifications, deployments and effects of this power, and in doing so, quietly rests on a presumption of the powerlessness of detainees (Maley 2003; Tazreiter 2006; Wilsher 2012). Indeed, it is indisputable that detainees have far less power than the sovereign states which detain them. Refugee protests against detention, however, reveal that detainees are not passive recipients of state power. Asylum seekers, through their own movement both away from their homelands, and particularly at the moment of their unauthorised entry into a state, are initiating the relationship with the receiving state. The state's actions are in *response* to the agency of refugees. The relationship between the state and the refugee is marked by a cycle of struggle, power and resistance. This book seeks to rehabilitate the figure of the refugee into something more closely resembling the actual people to whom the label is ascribed, not only for the purpose of definitional accuracy, but more importantly because the embedded passivity and powerlessness of 'the refugee' plays an important role in enabling governments to criminalise asylum seeking, thereby allowing the continuation of the broad range of punitive practices that are increasingly deployed against refugees.

A Brief Note on Terminology

The use of language is critically important. Through the careful use of words and positioning of ideas, subjects are constructed and positioned and meanings and values are conveyed. Some key terms are explained here.

Refugee, Asylum Seeker or Detainee?

The UNHCR, in its *Handbook on Procedures and Criteria for Determining Refugee Status*, makes it clear that a refugee is made by events in their home countries and not by receiving governments' decisions:

> A person is a refugee within the meaning of the 1951 Convention as soon as he fulfils the criteria contained in the definition. This would necessarily occur prior to the time at which his refugee status is formally determined. Recognition of his refugee status does not therefore make him a refugee but declares him to be one. He does not become a refugee because of recognition, but is recognized because he is a refugee. (UNHCR 1992, para 28)

The term asylum seeker is a relatively recent invention of Western governments. It refers to the status of a person who has applied to a government for protection under the *Refugees Convention* and is awaiting a determination of that application. It is a term that creates a layer of suspicion around refugees. Until verified by a government body, even if a person already holds a refugee card issued by the United Nations High Commission for Refugees (UNHCR), the person is placed in the unstable category of 'asylum seeker.' This enables governments to cast the arrival of refugees (needing protection) as a security threat and is essential for the many regressive policies employed by Western governments to deter and repel refugees from their nations.

Initially, I wanted to use the term refugee because almost everyone interviewed in this work had been found to be a refugee by the Australian government, but also as a political statement. However, the use of refugee to refer to people at various stages of the refugee journey and at various stages of government processing of claims became confusing and cumbersome. Consequently, I have used both the terms refugee and asylum seeker, according to the context.

The term 'detainee' is used to refer to asylum seekers and refugees held in detention throughout most of this book. The term is less pejorative than asylum seeker and enables a distinction between refugees recognised or not recognised by the Australian government. It is a descriptor of the situation that people were in. It was also the fact and conditions of people's detention that underpinned much of the protest. 'Detainee' proved to be a mobilising identity, one which could, in particular moments, transcend other identities (such as linguistic, religious, political, ethnic or gender) and unite people in protest against detention. The power of being a 'detainee' is evident in Osman's pledge to help any who needed it:

> Anyone! Anyone who are detainee. It doesn't matter if you are Iraqi, Afghan, No No. We are detainee. We are detainee!

Identifying Individuals

Most of the men who spoke with me about their time in detention and protest against it are identified by pseudonyms. Three men are identified by their real names: Farshid Kheirillapour, Shahin Shafaei and Aamer Sultan. Farshid has been an outspoken critic of immigration detention in the years since his release and believes that detainees need to be encountered as real people in the struggle against detention. Accordingly, he wanted to appear in this book as an individual with his real name. Shahin is a playwright, actor and college lecturer. Upon his release from detention he wrote and performed *Refugitive*, a play about hunger strikes in detention centres. Shahin has spoken publicly about his journey as a refugee and about detention and also in his capacity as an activist for other refugees' rights. A quick internet search of his name will uncover many of his post-detention activities. He could not be de-identified, nor did he have any wish to be.

Similarly, Aamer Sultan is a medical doctor who has also spoken publicly about detention. He is most well known for co-authoring a journal article published in the *Australian Medical Journal* while he was still in detention. The article identifies and outlines the progressive deterioration of a large sample of detainees over a long period of time and proposes a depressive disorder called 'Immigration Detention Stress Syndrome.' He is also well known in Australia for his role in smuggling out of detention, footage of a young boy, Shayan Badraie, which was aired on national television and proved to be a catalyst in challenging the detention of children. Aamer has also spoken frequently with the media, community groups and in other public forums since his release. Again, it would not be possible to talk about Aamer's activism without identifying him.

Bureaucratic Terms

Australia's Department of Immigration has undergone several name changes over the last fifteen years, many of which reflect the shifting discourse surrounding asylum seeking. Farshid was detained in 1999 by the Department of Immigration and Multicultural Affairs, whereas today it is the Department of Immigration and Border Protection. For ease of reading, Department of Immigration is used throughout.

There are a range of classifications of immigration detention centres in Australia, such as Immigration Detention Centre (IDC), Immigration Reception and Processing Centre (IRPC), Alternative Place of Detention (APOD), Immigration Detention Facility (IDF) and more. Each facility is classified differently by the Department of Immigration and has particular features. When referring to a specific detention centre, I use the correct classification for it, and when referring to multiple centres or detention in general I use the term 'detention centre' or 'immigration detention centre.' I am unable to discern any meaningful differences between different classifications of detention centres. As Mohammed said after being moved to a 'better' detention centre, 'doesn't matter golden cage, it's a cage.'

Structure of the Book

The book begins by using the words and actions of refugees protesting against detention as a framework for rethinking human rights, power and human agency and arguing for a revisiting of the difficult questions of what it means to be human and what the detention of humans from other countries seeking protection raises in terms of human rights. Chapter 2 considers detainees' plea, 'We are human,' and discusses Hannah Arendt's theoretical framework of human rights and the human condition. In doing so, it proposes that ontological paradoxes within contemporary human rights theories need to be addressed and that refugee experiences and opinions are vital in this project. The argument is made that, post-World War II, attention to the juridical development of human rights has institutionalised and buried these important paradoxes and that greater attention needs to be paid to the human subject of human rights. From there, the book explores the power relations at work in the relationship between asylum seekers and receiving states. In particular, it explores a range of analytical perspectives presented by detainees, some of the many ways in which detainees resisted the omnipotent power of detention on a daily basis, as well as the material, semiotic and existential effects of resistance.

The following three chapters are organised around specific protest actions: escape (both in order to simply evade detention and also as a deliberate act of civil disobedience), hunger strike, lip sewing and self-harm and riots. In each of these, the work uses accounts by formerly detained refugees to explore how certain protests came about, conflicting opinions between different people in detention about the ethics and efficacy of different actions, the interplay between actions of the state and of detainees and the implications for how we think about human rights and refugees. While the primary material presented in the book is Australian, I contend that the Australian experience, while having some specificities in the local context, has many more structural similarities with immigration detention in Europe, the USA and elsewhere. Many of the dynamics of detention and the theoretical and ethical arguments addressed here will find resonance beyond Australia. The final substantive chapter of the book provides a broad survey of the use and nature of immigration detention in Australia, Europe and the USA.

References

Aas, K. F. (2007). Analysing a world in motion. Global flows meet "criminology of the other". *Theoretical Criminology, 11*(2), 283–303.

ACLU. (n.d.). Sexual abuse in immigration detention facilities. Sexual abuse complaints since 2007 from ACLU Freedom of Information Act documents. *ACLU*. Retrieved February 8, 2016, from https://www.aclu.org (home page).

Arendt, H. (1976). *The origins of totalitarianism*. Orlando: Harcourt Publishing.

BBC. (2016). Migrant crisis: Migration to Europe explained in graphics. *BBC Online*, January 28. Retrieved February 7, 2016, from http://www.bbc.com/news/world-europe-34131911

Elliot, E., & Gunasekera, H. (2016). *The health and well-being of children in immigration detention. Report to the Australian Human Rights Commission. Monitoring Visit to Wickham Point Detention Centre, Darwin, NT. October 16th–18th 2015*. Sydney: Australian Human Rights Commission.

Foucault, M. (1997). *Society must be defended. Lectures at the College de France 1975–76* (D. Macey, Trans.). London: Penguin Books.

Gibney, M. (2004). *The ethics and politics of asylum. Liberal democracy and the response to refugees*. Cambridge: Cambridge University Press.

Goodwin-Gill, G. (1986). International law and the detention of refugees and asylum seekers. *International Migration Review, 20*(2), 193–219.

Grewcock, M. (2009). *Border crimes: Australia's war on illicit migrants*. Sydney: Sydney Institute of Criminology Press.

Haddad, E. (2008). *The refugee in international society. Between sovereigns*. Cambridge: Cambridge University Press.

Hailbronner, K. (2007). Detention of asylum seekers. *European Journal of Migration and Law, 9*(2), 150–172.

Hamilton, K. R. (2011). Immigrant detention centers in the United States and international human rights. *Berkley La Raza Law Journal, 1*(4), 93–132.

Harrell-Bond, B. (1999). The experience of refugees as recipients of aid. In A. Ager (Ed.), *Refugees: Perspectives on the experience of forced migration*. London: Continuum.

Harrell-Bond, B., & Voutira, E. (1992). Anthropology and the study of refugees. *Anthropology Today, 8*(4), 6–10.

Kalhan, A. (2010). Rethinking immigration detention. *Columbia Law Review, 110*, 42–58.

Maley, W. (2003). Asylum-seekers in Australia's international relations. *Australian Journal of International Affairs, 57*(1), 187–202.

Malkki, L. H. (1996). Speechless emissaries: Refugees, humanitarianism, and dehistoricization. *Cultural Anthropology, 11*(3), 377–404.

Malloch, M., & Stanley, S. (2005). The detention of asylum seekers in the UK. Representing risk, managing the dangerous. *Punishment & Society, 7*(1), 53–71.

Marfleet, P. (2006). *Refugees in a global era*. Basingstoke: Palgrave Macmillan.

Nethery, A., Rafferty-Brown, B., & Taylor, S. (2012). Exporting detention: Australia funded immigration detention in Indonesia. *Journal of Refugee Studies, 26*(1), 88–109.

Nethery, A., & Silverman, S. (Eds.) (2015). *Immigration detention. The migration of a policy and its human impact*. Abingdon: Routledge.

Parekh, S. (2007). Resisting "dull and torpid" assent: Returning to the debate over the foundations of human rights. *Human Rights Quarterly, 29*(3), 754–778.

Parekh, S. (2008). Conscience, morality and judgement: An inquiry into the subjective basis of human rights. *Philosophy and Social Criticism, 34*(1–2), 177–195.

Philo, G., Briant, E., & Donald, P. (2013). The role of the press in the war on asylum. *Race & Class, 55*(2), 28–41.

Pickering, S. (2005). *Refugees and state crime*. Annandale: Federation Press.

Pugliese, J. (2007). The event-trauma of the carceral post-human. *Social Semiotics, 17*(1), 63–86.

Rajaram, P. M. (2002). Humanitarianism and representations of the refugee. *Journal of Refugee Studies, 15*(3), 247–264.

Robjant, K., Hassan, R., & Katona, C. (2009). Mental health implications of detaining asylum seekers: Systematic review. *British Journal of Psychiatry, 194*, 306–312.

Sampson, R., & Mitchell, G. (2013). Global trends in immigration detention and alternatives. *Journal on Migration and Human Security, 1*(3), 97–121.

Shaw, S. (2016). *Review into the welfare in detention of vulnerable persons. A report to the home office*. London: UK Home Office.

Silverman, S., & Nethery, A. (2015). Introduction. In A. Nethery & S. Silverman (Eds.), *Immigration detention. The migration of a policy and its human impact*. Abingdon: Routledge.

Soguk, N. (1999). *States and strangers. Refugees and displacements of statecraft*. Minneapolis: University of Minnesota Press.

Steel, Z., & Silove, D. (2001). The mental health implications of detaining asylum seekers. *Medical Journal of Australia, 175*, 596–599.

Stevens, D. (2013). Asylum seekers, detention and the law: Morality in abeyance? In S. Juss (Ed.), *The Ashgate research companion to migration law, theory and policy*. Farnham: Ashgate.

Story, B. (2005). Politics as usual: The criminalisation of asylum seekers in the United States. *Refugee Studies Centre, Working Paper Series, 26*. Oxford: University of Oxford.

Tazreiter, C. (2006). Security and the use of state violence. Justifications and limits in the treatment of asylum seekers. In J. Madeira & I. Gozaydin (Eds.), *Evil, law and the state*. Oxford: Inter-Disciplinary Press.

United Nations High Commissioner for Refugees (UNHCR). (1992). *Handbook on procedures and criteria for determining refugee status under the 1951 convention and the 1967 protocol relating to the status of refugees*. Document HCR/IP/4/Eng/REV.1. Retrieved November 30, 2011, from http://www.unhcr.org/ 3d58e13b4.html

United Nations High Commissioner for Refugees (UNHCR). (2015). *Global Trends 2014*. Geneva: UNHCR. Retrieved February 2, 2016, from http://unhcr.org/556725e69.html

Wilsher, D. (2012). *Immigration detention. Law, history, politics*. Cambridge: Cambridge University Press.

Wolfram Cox, J., & Minahan, S. (2004). Unravelling woomera: Lip sewing, morphology and dystopia. *Journal of Organizational Change Management, 17*(3), 292–301.

2

'We Are Human.' Re-humanising Human Rights

* * *

> Respect. Just respect. When someone respect me I respect him, because the respect it's belong just to human. Animal won't respect you, animal will obey you, because you feed them. They don't know the respect. They walking with you, dog walking with you, suddenly without 'excuse me' he just pee in the road. But a human, it's the respect between each other. So when we say that we are human – show some respect. That's it.
>
> Osman detained 3 years, 4 months

* * *

A recurring theme among refugees interviewed was the desire to be recognised as human. Embedded in these calls was both an appeal to a shared or universal humanity and an implied belief that human status entails a guarantee of a minimum standard of treatment and an implicit acknowledgement of a human rights framework. Sometimes, respondents made overt pleas to human rights as a means to improve their situations, while at other times the inference of human rights was less explicit. Although some participants in this research did have extensive knowledge of formal human rights systems, the discussion of humanity

L. Fiske, *Human Rights, Refugee Protest and Immigration Detention*,
DOI 10.1057/978-1-137-58096-2_2

and rights by most of the participants seldom arose from a substantive knowledge of international human rights laws and systems. Detainees nonetheless found human rights to be a powerful language for articulating matters of injustice. Every person interviewed in the course of this research complained of feeling dehumanised and unrecognised in detention, with some comparing their status to that of animals, inanimate objects or death. Osman expressed his frustration at being reduced to a status lower than an animal:

> When officer call me '0276,' I said 'Oh God! I've got name. Your donkey, er your dog and your cat has name. I'm a human like you. Don't call me by number.' (Osman)

While detainees' physical survival needs were met in detention through the provision of shelter, food and clothing, the testimony of former detainees supports a position that human life entails more than mere physical survival. Human life entails an existential aspect that cannot be reduced to mere biology and that distinguishes humans from animals. Detainee cries of 'we are human' were appeals for recognition of these existential aspects of humanity. Former detainees interviewed for this research, regardless of the extent of their knowledge of formal human rights systems, shared an unshakeable belief that to be human, at least morally if not legally, entitled them to certain rights.

This chapter uses Hannah Arendt's work on the human condition and human rights to explore the understandings of human rights evident through detainees' protests and narratives.

Dehumanising Categories

> They could call me Sam or whatever, but they call me ERA23. OK, it's me. They wrote the number when we were in Ashmore Reef, the first day, the navy, the soldiers, that's what they have done. That was the first thing we seen on the Australian soil. They came to us and wrote the number here on the left hand side *(points to his left upper arm)*. So the first day we been in Australia we been numbered. (Ibrahim)

The project of modernity seeks to know the world. It rests upon a belief that the world is knowable and that certainty can be established through the systematic application of reason. According to Bauman (1990, 1991), a central aim of the project of modernity is the eradication of ambivalence. Categorisation, which refers to the identification, labelling and classification of all earthly matter, is perhaps the one key strategy in this eradication of ambivalence. Ambivalence, or the 'possibility of assigning an object or event to more than one category' (Bauman 1991, 1) causes discomfort and anxiety and so is experienced as disorder. The drive to categorise the world is a drive to 'know' the world and to increase our feeling of being in control and to feel safe in the world. 'To classify, in other words, is to give the world a *structure*: to manipulate its probabilities' (Bauman 1991, 1 [emphasis in original]) and to increase human mastery. Ambivalence, Bauman (1991, 2) contends, reminds us of the impossibility of complete mastery and so is experienced as threat, and 'everything that could or would not be defined' must be 'suppressed or eliminated' (Bauman, cited in Parekh 2004, 42–43). Asylum seekers are perfect instantiations of the strangers that Bauman identifies as particular threats to the world's logical order—not tourists, diplomats, friends or enemies, but 'that "third element" which should not be. … They unmask the brittle artificiality of division—they destroy the world … and must be tabooed, disarmed, suppressed, exiled physically or mentally' (Bauman 1990, 148–149). Asylum seekers are not known at the place and time of their arrival, their arrival is unregulated, out of order (it is perhaps no coincidence that Australia's official term for asylum seekers arriving by boat is 'irregular maritime arrivals') and not only produces an ambivalent situation, but threatens the very framework of order and, thus, risks exposing the fallacy of an entirely knowable world.

The process of labelling and categorising is a necessary step in turning the ambivalent into the certain, and so the Australian government's first response to the arrival of a boat has been to label it, usually using three letters (such as DON, or ANA), and the people on board using numbers. Then each person is allocated an identification sequence. This sequence started with the first three letters of the government-ascribed labelling of the boat on which they arrived, thereby identifying a sub-category within the larger category of 'unlawful entrant,' and was followed by two to four numbers to identify the individual within the sub-category, without recognising his or her individuality in any meaningful way. Asylum seekers were subsequently treated according to this categorisation of 'what' they were, which was unlawful entrants. For instance, the government proceeded to publicly announce the arrival of '73 unlawful entrants,' categorising the people on board into a clear definition of 'what' they are (unlawful entrants). The use of figures and bureaucratic language is intended to reassure the Australian polis that the world remains certain, organised into manageable categories and safely under bureaucratic control. This 'reception' and categorisation then framed all treatment that followed, until the person was able to win reallocation to another category, that of 'refugee.' This process of categorisation, which numerically identifies each separate body (akin to samples in a scientific laboratory), while simultaneously denying any individual distinction, is explained by Baha'adin: 'It was numbers. We had numbers, we were just numbers. No names, nothing.'

Hannah Arendt makes a distinction between 'what' and 'who' a person is (Arendt 1958, 179). A person may be identified and placed into certain categories, such as woman, Jew, Muslim, or boatperson, from externally observable characteristics, such as dress, appearance or context in which he or she is encountered, such as on a small, overcrowded boat off Australia's northern coastline. However, that person can only reveal *who* he or she in particular is, through their own speech and action, including their unique biography and opinions, hopes, fears, loves and beliefs. The individual characteristics that distinguish each person can only be discerned through the revelations of that person, gained inter-subjectively through interaction and engagement on a basis of equality. The 'what' of a person can only ever be an approximation of humanity, consisting of stereotypes or categories into which individuals are grouped with little or no regard to the uniqueness of each specific person. To treat a person according to 'what,' rather than 'who,' he or she is dehumanises the person. They are denied the opportunity to reveal their unique self to the world and denied entry to the public sphere as an initiating and equal person, *vita activa*, and reduced to a representative sample of the category into which he or she has been placed:

> If a Negro in a white community is considered a Negro and nothing else, he loses along with his right to equality that freedom of action which is

specifically human; all his deeds are now explained as 'necessary' consequence of some 'Negro' qualities; he has become some specimen of an animal species called man. (Arendt 1976, 301–302)

It is, according to Arendt, a distinguishing human characteristic to be able to reveal a unique and distinct self to the world. When treated primarily or only as a representative of a group, in this case 'boatpeople,' a person's humanness is not recognised, their ontological equality is denied and they are reduced to a state of animal biology. If a person is recognised in the common world (public sphere) merely as a representative of her group, as a specimen, she holds no specific value as an individual and her life becomes unimportant and potentially superfluous. Detainees interviewed in this research understood and felt this lack of individual recognition keenly. Dr Aamer Sultan commented:

That's one of the arguments I used to leave with many Australians outside, that the government are doing that now to people who are in detention, outsiders, migrants, Arab, Muslim, it doesn't matter. What guarantee that they won't do the same to someone else outside? Started with the homeless people, the Aborigines in a way. (Aamer)

Aamer could see that when experienced only as a representative of a group, such as 'Arab, Muslim,' he didn't matter and was interchangeable with 'homeless people' or 'Aborigines.' They were all individually unrecognised and therefore superfluous.

Emad expressed a similar concern. He complained that in detention there was no attempt made by the authorities to discern any individuality, but that instead 'detainees' were treated as just that—detainees—regardless of any individual distinction:

Not all people are the same. Mentally, some of the people can cope with the circumstance there. Some of them, the majority of them – especially kids and women – cannot. So the management and the immigration didn't take into consideration that the people are different. They behaved in a one rough manner, one rough standard towards all of the people, and that's completely wrong. You're being tough to everyone. You have to understand every person's need – or try to understand. Even if you fail, try to understand. Try to take some effort to understand. That we couldn't see, we

> didn't see at all actually. We just saw some, a very hard-line treatment and it was typical every day, every morning, every night. *They didn't try to investigate what's in our hearts or mind. And we believed that humans can, actually can, reach to the hearts and minds of the other humans* [emphasis added]. But unfortunately it wasn't the case at that time. (Emad)

Ibrahim expressed similar frustration when he said, 'It's wrong. But for us, we been just all same. Refugee or criminal or whatever—you the same. Like the children, women, anyone.' Ibrahim complained that any individual speech or action in detention was not recognised and had no impact on the way in which he or his fellow detainees were treated. He, and those detained with him, had been categorised as 'unlawful entrants' and would be treated accordingly until a Department of Immigration official advised of his re-categorisation as 'refugee.' The sameness about which Ibrahim, Emad and Aamer complain is defended by the Department of Immigration as 'equality before the law' and non-discrimination; that all people who arrive by boat will be detained until a determination is made about their claim, and that the same process is applied to all. Yet this principle, designed to protect the equal dignity and worth of all individuals regardless of status, birth, achievement or other characteristics, functions in this setting to dehumanise through the aggregation of individuals into categories and the application of the same rules to all regardless of individual health, biography, fears, resilience or need.

At heart, it was this bureaucratic dehumanisation, the strategies and practices of detention and refugee assessment, during which time people were not recognised as unique individuals, but treated according to their categorisation as boat people, that the insistent cries of 'we are human' struggled against.

Some Problems with Human Rights in Modernity

Human rights are commonly spoken of as a body of jurisprudence—laws, treaties, declarations, legislation, judicial decisions and official comments of national, regional and international bodies. Following World

War II, these formal legal human rights systems have grown in scope and depth as the Western world, in particular, has sought to overcome the horror and shame of two world wars that caused unprecedented destruction and the Holocaust, in which modernity's eradication of ambivalence was taken to its logical extreme. In a well-intentioned, but perhaps too hasty, effort to ensure such events would 'never again' occur, the world, dominated by Western victor nations, developed the United Nations and a series of declarations and treaties to create legal human rights protections. Too hasty because, in the determination to build systems aimed at preventing a recurrence, some fundamental paradoxes and tensions within human rights discourse were left unaddressed. Principal among these tensions is that human rights are conceived of universally, but international systems are built upon national sovereignty.

The global human rights system constructs human rights as claims belonging to the individual and made against the state in which they were born or hold citizenship. Paradoxically though, it is precisely at the moment when the relationship between individual and state ruptures, or when the state itself collapses, that human rights are both most needed and cease to exist in any enforceable, tangible form of protection for human life (Arendt 1976, 302). Arendt considered that this paradox (and others) may well be irresolvable, but she saw a protection in the effort of active engagement with the *idea* of human rights, as well as in wrestling with the dilemma and the ontological issues made evident in times of crisis.

Serena Parekh notes that, since World War II, 'the ontological dimensions of human rights have been ignored largely in favour of the juridical' (2008, 12). This has two particularly important effects relevant for this study. The first is that human rights become the field of the expert, such as the lawyer, diplomat and bureaucrat. Technical and expert juridical knowledge is required for an opinion to carry weight and the voices of the non-expert, including those most at risk of human rights violations, are relegated to the margins, devalued and discredited as personal opinion (Foucault 1997, 7). The second is that the process of institutionalising human rights has imported fundamental and unresolved paradoxes while simultaneously divorcing human rights from its philosophical and historical roots. The result is that human rights takes on the status of legal orthodoxy and 'common sense,' assuming a place in the 'natural order of things' and becoming protected from critique. Protecting human rights from critique, however, does not help the human subject of human rights in the moment of rupture between citizen and state, when someone becomes simply and only a human being and must look to the international human rights system for protection (Arendt 1976, 293–297). It is at this moment that the 'human' (rather than human-citizen) realises the material implications of a purportedly universal system enacted through state sovereignty. A continued focus on institutional rights, without a critical reappraisal of its philosophical, human roots is unlikely to lead to systems which better achieve their well-intentioned universal aims. Protecting human rights from critique does nothing to protect *human* rights.

Human rights are, for Arendt, a human construction and, thus, continued human engagement with the concepts, limitations and possibilities of human rights enliven them and create a political space based on plurality, which can be understood as incorporating difference, equality and inter-subjectivity. It is also in this space that hitherto subjugated and discredited voices, which represent the many rather than the experts, can enter the public debate as political equals because pluralistic knowledge is valued (Arendt 1958, 1976; Baldissone 2009; Foucault 1997).

Arendt called for a revived attention to the human subject of human rights, asking whom it was that human rights seek to protect. There is a risk of fixing and essentialising humans in any attempt to identify what features or characteristics are the 'human' ones that distinguish humans from other species. Anyone who is deemed not to possess or display these characteristics can be classified as non-human, pseudo-human, quasi-human or some other lesser category (Ife 2010; Rorty 1999). Any list of human characteristics will necessarily reflect the subjectivities of the compiler, privileging a particular viewpoint at high risk for all others. Those categorised as pseudo- or lesser-humans can then be treated with disregard and violence without implicating the fully human perpetrators in any ethical wrongdoing. Richard Rorty (1999) points to Serb torture and murder of Bosnians, to the holding of slaves by the drafters of the US Declaration of Independence, and to the continuing subjugation of women the world over as examples of the dangers of attempts to define 'human.'

An increased awareness of the subjectivities involved in such an exercise may account, in part at least, for the avoidance of such dangerous philosophical territory in modern human rights frameworks. A converse risk, however, is that abandoning discussion of 'human' entirely does not result in universal human rights, but leaves a system of human rights which continues to rest upon a foundation of the autonomous, rational Enlightenment man. Human rights then inherit the subjectivities and limitations arising from a global system based on this temporally, culturally and geographically specific abstraction of 'man,' while also precluding discussions with ontological implications resulting in a collective blindness to important paradoxes. Arendt (1976) warned that continuing to speak of human rights as universal and inalienable, when they are in fact national and contingent, seriously undermines any modern human rights regimes. Her challenge and her contribution, having shown the clear alienability of rights, was to stimulate and participate in a political discussion (in the Ancient Greek manner) about the human condition and human rights (Arendt 1958, 1976).

And so it is with an awareness of the problems and dangers in such an exercise, but compelled by detainees' cries of 'we are human,' that I now turn to a discussion of Arendt's theories of 'the human condition' and human rights and map detainee testimony alongside her thoughts, in order to argue for fluid and un-institutionalised conceptions of some universal human traits which can be helpful in forming a basis for human rights beyond nationality and other constructed divides.

The Right to Have Rights

Arendt conceived of human rights in two groups. Civic rights are 'all those rights which require the protection of a government' (Parekh 2004, 41), which includes all the rights contained in international human rights treaties, such as the right to adequate food and shelter, the right to vote, to education, to freedom of movement and so on. Prior to this group of rights, however, is the right to have rights, which she defined as the right to 'a place in the world which makes opinions significant and actions effective' (Arendt 1976, 296). Speech and action, Arendt contended, are fundamental dimensions of the human condition and distinguish us from other animals. We work because we must eat and have shelter, or we can escape work by compelling others to work for us, such as in the case of a slaveholder, without losing any fundamental aspect of our humanity (Arendt 1958, 176). But if we are deprived of the opportunity to speak and act, and to engage with other human beings on a basis of political equality, we are denied an essential aspect of our humanity. Speech and action become meaningful only when they are recognised by others, and this recognition of our words and deeds conveys and constitutes our equality and our membership of a polis.

Conversely, when our speech and actions are ignored by those around us, we become a non-person. We have no impact on the common world, which is the political world beyond the private sphere of family and close personal relationships that makes up our political selves. In this case, one's self as an equal member of human society is denied. It was precisely this non-existence that Farshid referred to when he said that 'people's situation in detention was that you were the lost person, the forgotten person, you don't exist, you cannot change anything and you have no power over anything.'

Arendt termed this status, people existing outside any polis which recognised and claimed them, as 'absolute rightlessness' (Arendt 1976, 295). The right to have rights arises from and is entirely contingent upon acknowledged membership of a political community and the fundamental recognition which comes with this. A person may have certain civic rights such as freedom of belief or speech or movement, but still remain fundamentally rightless:

> There is no question that those outside the pale of law may have more freedom of movement than a lawfully imprisoned criminal or that they enjoy more freedom of opinion in the internment camps of democratic countries than they would in any ordinary despotism, not to mention in a totalitarian country. But neither physical safety – being fed by some state or private welfare agency – nor freedom of opinion changes in the least their fundamental situation of rightlessness. The prolongation of their lives is due to charity and not to right, for no law exists which could force the nations to feed them; their freedom of movement, if they have it at all, gives them no right to residence which even the jailed criminal enjoys as a matter of course; and their freedom of opinion is a fool's freedom, for nothing they think matters anyhow. (Arendt 1976, 296)

Belonging to a political community and participating in the public life of that community is, for Arendt (1976, 297), a fundamental aspect of the human condition and human rights conceived outside of a specific and particular community cannot exist in a tangible form that is able to actually guarantee the rights it expresses. Arendt's conception of human rights arises from her conception of the human condition, which is distinguished from gods and beasts by our capacity for action and our existence in plurality, for 'no human life, not even the life of a hermit in nature's wilderness, is possible without a world which directly or indirectly testifies to the presence of other human beings' (Arendt 1958, 22). It is a 'fact that men, not Man, live on the earth and inhabit the world' (Arendt 1958, 7) and that, since Aristotle, humans have been 'defined as … commanding the power of speech and thought, … and as the "political animal" … one who lives in a community' (Arendt 1976, 297). Being a 'political animal' is not the same as being a social animal, which requires individuals to live together for procreation or more effective hunting strategies or any other labour which increases the chance of survival of the species. Politics has an added existential depth and involves the capacity to organise and create a world of human affairs, which Arendt (following the Ancient Greeks) termed the *human artifice*. It is this that distinguishes humans from other animals (Arendt 1958, 22–25). Therefore, the loss of a political community means the loss of not only specific rights, but the loss of recognition and therefore of 'some of the most essential characteristics of human life' (Arendt 1976, 297). This loss of a political community means the loss of the right to have rights.

The Human Condition as the Basis for Human Rights

In order to understand how the loss of recognition in the public sphere equates to the loss of humanity and the right to have rights, it is necessary to look in greater detail at two key aspects of Arendt's conception of the human condition; first, the human need for meaningful speech and action and, second, plurality, which consists of equality and distinction. Constructing public spaces and processes which enable meaningful speech and action within a framework of equality and distinction can then be used as an ontologically stable basis for human rights.

Meaningful Speech and Action

Arendt identifies meaningful speech and action as fundamental both to a human existence that is beyond life as a biological specimen of the species man, and also as a necessary condition for a life which is 'fully human' and enters the common world as an equal. It is through individual speech and action, recognised and judged by others, that each individual human being reveals her unique and distinct self to the world:

> In acting and speaking, men show who they are, reveal actively their unique personal identities and thus make their appearance in the human world, while their physical identities appear without any activity of their own … This disclosure of 'who' in contradistinction to 'what' somebody is – is implicit in everything somebody says and does. It can be hidden only in complete silence and perfect passivity (Arendt 1958, 179).

But a life of silence and passivity is, according to Arendt (1958, 176) 'dead to the world; it has ceased to be a human life because it is no longer lived among men.' So actively participating in public life, not just belonging to a community, is necessary for human life to be distinct from 'mere bodily existence,' and it is through meaningful engagement with others as equals that human life distinguishes itself. Ismail remarked that if he had not protested against the regimen of detention, but instead had silently and passively accepted his position, he would cease to be alive in any meaningful sense:

> Because if I didn't do those things, nothing different between me and this table. With me? I got a soul. I got a mind. I got thinking. While this table … of course, I wouldn't stay like that. (Ismail)

Sayed expressed a similar opinion when he explained why he and others took action against detention: 'That's what happens, that's the main purpose everybody do what they do. Otherwise there is no difference between the live and the dead you know. Otherwise I could be dead—nothing.'

When someone's speech and action are not recognised, their speech and actions are made meaningless, and they are treated and judged, not according to *who* he or she is (through their words and deeds), but according to their membership of a particular category of person. This refusal to recognise someone's individuality, their unique distinctiveness, is a refusal to recognise a fundamental aspect of their humanity and is profoundly dehumanising.

When Arendt speaks of the individual, it is not the pre-existing abstract autonomous individual of Enlightenment thought, upon which modern politics and modern human rights are based, but rather, she is referring to an ontologically inter-subjective and interdependent individual. As Seyla Benhabib aptly explains, 'The self for Arendt is the self of a human community that is formed through and cannot exist without interacting in the world' (cited in Parekh 2004, 52). The power of speech and action is not only a capacity for self-revelation, consisting of the disclosure of a pre-formed and complete self to a waiting world, but is simultaneously self-constituting, for it is through our interaction with other unique and distinct people, as well as through their speech and actions and their responses to our speech and actions, that we develop our own thoughts, beliefs and opinions, forming the basis for further speech and action. Humanity is fundamentally plural and plurality is both an inescapable and a desirable dimension of humanity.

Plurality: Equality and Distinction

Plurality, according to Arendt, paradoxically consists of distinction and equality, both of which have been alluded to here, but which require a little further exploration.

For Arendt, humans share certain essential characteristics, in particular the capacity for speech and action, which is the capacity to initiate, discuss, change and initiate again. Unlike the potentially homogenising force of universalist or essentialist arguments that have arisen from the project of modernity to eradicate ambivalence and to 'fix' the world in knowable and manageable categories, Arendt's 'human condition' is based on distinction, both of humans from other animals and of every human from every other human. She posits, 'we are all the same, that is, human, in such a way that nobody is ever the same as anybody else who ever lived, lives, or will live' (Arendt 1958, 8). Every human is different and distinct, though we all share the capacity to initiate, create, think, speak and act, and these capacities are core to human life. Therefore, being 'deprived of the right to utilise these capacities deprives us of something fundamental' (Parekh 2004, 46) because the self is created interdependently with other selves and yet remains distinct and unique. No two people who inhabit this earth are ever absolutely identical, and it is through the insertion of the individual self in the common or public world that each of us contributes to the human artifice, which constitutes the common world and ourselves at the same time. Therefore, failure to recognise an individual's distinction is a refusal to permit them entry to the common world and denies them a fundamental aspect of the human condition. Expulsion from the polis is a form of civic death and is dehumanising, as the expulsion or refusal of recognition reduces the individual to an interchangeable, indistinct specimen of a category or group. Therefore, distinction, but also recognition of that distinction, is essential for justice and human rights.

This discussion introduces the element of *recognition* and its importance for human life. Arendt defines this term as the recognition of an actual individual person, and not the abstract 'man' that forms the basis of modern codified human rights laws. The concept of recognition also introduces the necessary tandem element of plurality, which is *equality*. Equality does not refer to the equal distribution of material goods, nor to an abstract equality inherent in the human condition, but equality is a political decision of humans and is the basis for politics shaped by justice, rather than societal organisation based on coercion or force:

> We are not born equal; we become equal as members of a group on the strength of our decision to guarantee ourselves mutually equal rights. Our political life rests on the assumption that we can produce equality through organisation, because man can act in and change and build a common world, together with his equals and only with his equals. (Arendt 1976, 301)

Detention life was marked by inequality. Osman described that at times, there would be critical incidents in detention, such as physical confrontations between detainees and guards or protests staged by detainees, but that the lack of recognition shaped every day in a multitude of mundane events. Osman told how he would sometimes try to speak with the guards but:

> they don't talk, the guard never open personal matter. Never. They don't talk to you. For example, I'm bored, I want to practice my English. There is an officer sitting there smoking. 'How you going mate? How's your day?' Just say 'Just keep distant.' Like they been trained that we are a number. Even if they speak English, they are a number. (Osman)

He went on to say that one guard, an older man, was a 'nice guy' who explained to Osman that 'if you meet me outside, I will be different person, but that's my job. Please understand these things.' Similarly, Baha'adin described that the daily treatment in detention 'shows how they didn't respect us. Like they didn't give a damn about us, you know what I mean?' Inequality and a lack of recognition of detainees' basic humanity shaped interactions between detainees and officials and was reinforced through every aspect of detention life. The issue of food was raised by almost every person interviewed for this research. Osman described the poor quality of food as an issue of inequality. He complained to the detention manager and said, 'the way you eat in your home, bring it to us.' Most people expressed the lack of equality and rights as a lack of respect. Ibrahim, when asked what he needed to feel human, responded:

> To be respected as a human. To be treated as a human. So you can feel your humanity and dignity. It's very important. It's very simple too. That's what we were asking for and unfortunately, we didn't find it. We found the opposite thing, which is they treated us as an animal, and maybe even the dog.... because the manager of the camp has a dog, and I think the dog, he was luckier than me. Seriously. (Ibrahim)

Arendt considered that respect is an essential foundation for politics that is based on mutual equality rather than coercion or force. She described respect as a public sphere sentiment that acts as a basis for human relationships, similar to the way in which love binds relationships in the private sphere:

> Yet what love is in its own narrowly circumscribed sphere, respect is in the larger domain of human affairs. Respect, not unlike the Aristotelian *philia politikē*, is a kind of 'friendship' without intimacy and without closeness; it is a regard for the person from the distance which the space of the world puts between us, and in this regard is independent of qualities which we may admire or of achievements which we may highly esteem. Thus, the modern loss of respect, or rather the conviction that respect is due only where we admire or esteem, constitutes a clear symptom of the increasing depersonalisation of public and social life (Arendt 1958, 243).

In this light, the respect which Ibrahim and others (see, for example, Osman's quote at the opening of this chapter) said they needed in order to 'feel human' can be understood as a demonstration of their ontological equality and their belonging in the community. As we are inter-subjectively and interdependently constituted selves, a widespread lack of respect in the public sphere can easily lead to civic death, or what Farshid described as being 'the lost person, the forgotten person, you don't exist.' A refusal to be lost or forgotten, a refusal to accept their civic non-existence was a major motivation in much detainee protest action.

Human Rights as Mutual Guarantee

Arendt's understanding of equality as a human decision and a human construction marks another ontological departure from modern human rights orthodoxy. The universal human of the French *Declaration of the Rights of Man and Citizen*, the American *Bill of Rights* and the United Nations' *Universal Declaration of Human Rights* is 'born equal.' The risk of such a conception of equality, as somehow inherent in God, nature or man, is that no human action needs to be taken to ensure equality (Parekh 2004, 49). Without such human engagement and a conscious promissory decision to ensure equality and, therefore, rights, inequality, exclusion, injustice and rightlessness are sure to result. Without equality as a foundational precept, human interaction is organised not by politics, which Arendt understands as 'the right to develop an opinion and test it on an inter-subjective basis' (cited in Parekh 2004, 47) in the public sphere, but by force. Arendt points to historic events (the French Terror and the Holocaust are two powerful examples) as confirmation of the consequences of human abrogation of responsibility for equality and rights. Equality is both a necessary pre-condition for politics and a result of human political action.

It is our uniquely human capacity to guarantee one another equality and recognition of distinction that forms the only meaningful basis for realisable, enforceable human rights. According to Arendt and amply demonstrated through historical events, human rights are not inalienable. Pretending that they are founded in god, nature or 'man' is not a stable basis for rights because it denies the political reality that humans can be stripped of all rights if excluded from the guarantee. Human rights only exist when actual people decide that rights are important and make a promise to one another to guarantee 'mutually equal rights.' Shahin identified this mutual guarantee as an essential aspect of 'being human':

> It is a very tough question, you know. I don't know. That's a route and road that I am travelling along, to be fully human person. That's what I *wish* to become, so… there are very simply rights that we would like to have as whoever that we are. And I think that if I allow other people to have those rights as well, then I am human enough. There are a lot of things that I want for myself as a writer, as a existent being that I would like to have and if I allow you to have those things as well, then I think we become more human. (Shahin)

This mutual guarantee may be realised through the construction of a law, but law is not the same as the promise. Rather, the law will collapse if the promise is withdrawn. This was demonstrated in Germany through the progressive stripping of Jewish rights by the Nazis through a series of legislative changes, before marching Jews off to the gas chambers (Arendt 1976, 296). Hitler's claim that 'right is what is good for the German people' (Arendt 1976, 299) was a vulgar expression of what is demonstrably true, that is, when the will of the nation (the people) is at odds with the laws of the state, the will of the nation will always emerge triumphant. So the guarantee of human rights can, and necessarily must be laid down in law, but this is insufficient in itself. Law and politics should not be confused, nor politics reduced to bureaucratic administration of laws (Arendt 1958, 23–24). Laws are a strategy by which the guarantee of rights is enacted, but to understand laws as equating to rights is potentially dangerous because it allows us to neglect our determination to live together in plurality. The development of laws cannot reliably protect humans' rights if they are not underpinned by a collective agreement that the rights of these specific people ought to be protected. For example, Australia's introduction of the policy of 'excision,' arbitrarily removing territory from Australia's 'migration zone' through legislative amendment specifically to ensure that asylum seekers arriving in excised zones could not trigger any legal rights mechanisms, demonstrates the dominance of the nation over the state and the contingent nature of 'inalienable' human rights.

As human rights exist only as a result of human decision, expulsion from a community willing to protect one's rights means expulsion from the right to have rights, and therefore, any prolongation of life is due to chance or charity, not right. The rightless then, need to be able to either form their own political communities that are willing and able to ensure one another human rights, or gain admittance to another polity if their right to have rights is to be restored. Arendt (1976, 300) contended that simple humanity, being identified as 'nothing but human,' was an insufficient basis for claiming tangible human rights. Arendt argued that the spectacle of Europe's Jews, stripped of their national identities, demonstrated that 'the world found nothing sacred in the abstract nakedness of being human' (Arendt 1976, 299). However, for asylum seekers in Australian detention centres, 'simple humanity' was all they had. Having been stripped of all citizenship rights, they could not claim their rights as Iranian or Iraqi or Afghan citizens. They arrived in Australia in their 'naked humanness' and so needed to use this human status as a way to insert themselves into the polis, to insist that their speech and actions be meaningful. Interviewees for this research confirm much of Arendt's theory—that rendering speech and action meaningless is dehumanising, that we can only be fully human among others who recognise both our distinctiveness and equality, and that human rights rest upon human decision. However, their experiences depart from Arendt slightly, in that refugees in detention were able to use their 'naked humanity' to create a place in the world where their speech and action were meaningful. This does not entirely dispute Arendt's position, as the right to have rights has not been entirely realised for asylum seekers in Australia. It has been realised on an individual basis by most, but not all, asylum seekers who have arrived here by boat over the last fifteen years, largely by winning re-categorisation as a 'refugee' and thereby being formally admitted to the polis.

Rights of asylum seekers arriving by boat remains a highly contested issue and provokes passionate responses from a wide range of views. The majority opinion in Australia remains that asylum seekers fall outside the community and therefore outside the mutual guarantee of rights. Therefore, their rights remain very limited and, to that extent, simple humanness has been insufficient as a basis upon which to claim rights. It is possible that this has remained so because asylum seekers have been effectively dehumanised, not only in terms of their own experiences of a public political self, but also in their representations in the Australian community. Successive governments have maintained detention as a foundational policy and have maintained tight control over the information flow into and out of detention centres. Most Australians have only indirect experience of asylum seekers and rely on media representations in order to form their views (Klocker and Dunn 2003). This media representation is heavily influenced by government public relations efforts and closely reflects government positions and, further, only infrequently conveys the direct voices of individual asylum seekers (Mares 2002). As such, asylum seekers remain dehumanised in their abstraction, indistinct as individual human beings. Attempts to overcome this abstraction and explain their unique and distinct situation and the reasons for their actions (including arrival by boat and protests undertaken in detention) have been a major aim of many protests (see Chaps. 3, 4, 5, and 6 for examples).

Regaining the Right to Have Rights

Asylum seekers in detention, having been stripped of their rights through their expulsion and denationalisation, realised the importance of membership of a political community for their human rights. As such, they used their human capacities to gain entry to a new political community and to restore their rights. This was done in multiple ways simultaneously, including through:

- the formal bureaucratic procedures of the refugee application process,
- strategic engagement of the legal system (committing crimes to be brought before the courts), and
- attempting to open direct communication channels with people outside detention and to appeal to people's consciences for recognition as fellow human beings.

Detainees also formed their own alternate political communities within detention centres. Relationships, discussions and protest actions served to reassure individuals of their own capacity for agency and of their own humanity.

While they were in detention, asylum seekers were engaged in the refugee status determination process. They put forward their claims for refugee status, participated in interviews, appealed negative decisions through administrative and judicial means, and attempted to make the state's procedures for formal entry to the polis work for them. There is much to research in this process alone, it is however, beyond the scope of this work. The focus here is examining the extra-procedural efforts of detainees to be restored to a position of rights-bearing human beings.

Rights as a Criminal

The importance of agency, which is the human capacity to initiate meaningful action and speech, can be seen through people's actions beyond formal bureaucratic procedures. Asylum seekers in detention realised that as asylum seekers they had no particular status and had very limited protections through the law, but that as criminals, they could access more rights. Emad explains:

> Moreover we, let's say in the criminal justice system and the civil law system here, you have a right to see your lawyer to talk about legal aspects of your case. We didn't have the right at that time. The side that have the

> capability, the determination of giving you the right to see your solicitor is the immigration department and the ACM.[1] And I think they abused it at that time. We didn't have a frequent, regular access to the legal system in this country, and that's another frustrating thing that really pushed the refugees to demonstrate against this case. (Emad)

Issaq, who was held in a different detention centre, reached the same conclusion:

> Well yes, there is a criminal in here but there is some Criminals Right Act that someone would come and say 'well under criminal laws you shouldn't treat them like this.' In Australia criminals have rights of education, criminals have rights of phone, criminals have rights of communication, criminals... You have rights. Even though you are a terrorist, you still have rights. It doesn't matter how bad you are. That's how we got motivated. I mean, okay, we are bad, we are terrible, but we still have rights and we want that rights even if it's a right to a newspaper or a TV or communication, some forms of communications, we should have that right and we need that right. (Issaq)

By committing a crime, such as escaping from detention or damaging property, detainees attained a legally recognised status within the polis. This status of criminal meant that access to communication, legal representation and a range of minimum standards of treatment became a matter of right rather than discretion. It also opened a forum for them to speak, in which their words were accorded a more equal status with those of the government. When brought before a court, asylum seekers had the opportunity to explain their actions and to respond on a more equal footing to government explanations of detainee protest. As a person charged with a criminal offence in a court of law, the anonymous abstract asylum seeker became a specific individual with a name, a reason for their actions, and a political opinion that, even if refuted, had to be engaged with in a substantive manner (Chaps. 4 and 6 address this in more detail).

Arendt theorised that criminals, although enjoying less freedom of movement, actually have more *rights* than 'free' refugees:

---

[1] Australasian Correctional Management, known as ACM, was the private security firm contracted to run Australian immigration detention centres from 1998 to 2003.

> The fundamental deprivation of human rights is manifested first and above all in the deprivation of a place in the world which makes opinions significant and actions effective. Something much more fundamental than freedom or justice … is at stake … when one is placed in a situation where, unless he commits a crime, his treatment by others does not depend on what he does or does not do.… They are deprived, not of the right to freedom, but of the right to action; not of the right to think whatever they please, but of the right to opinion. Privileges in some cases, injustices in most, blessings and doom are meted out to them according to accident and without any relation whatsoever to what they do, did, or may do (Arendt 1958, 296).

While classified as asylum seekers and nothing else, people's treatment was dependent on charity (or lack thereof) and not right, and so was vulnerable to whim. Mohammed explained that the first time he participated in a protest was after watching 'the not well behaving of officer to the kids ... I see one officer in the kitchen throwing the apple, that didn't give the apple to kid, little Afghani girl, and she cried and they told "she didn't say me please." I was so, so cross.' Being deprived of rights meant that the company running detention centres was able to make up rules arbitrarily, and asylum seekers had no public space in which to challenge these rules. Dr Aamer Sultan understood that many of the rules he and others were forced to comply with had no basis in law. He began to challenge the guards: 'Is that law, or is that like a local law you made it?' However, any challenge from asylum seekers remained in the private sphere, due to their lack of formal status in the polis and the lack of any enforceable instituted mechanisms for asylum seekers to insert their voices into the public sphere, except by committing a crime. Farshid (whose experience in court is covered in detail in Chap. 4) discovered this when he was charged and convicted with a criminal offence. In court, he was able to speak publicly about the conditions in detention and the treatment meted out to asylum seekers. After serving three months in prison, he returned to detention 'so brave.' He felt much less intimidated by threats of legal punishment from the detention centre manager because he 'was really getting confidence in the court. You see a lot of justice in the independent court rather than the immigration court.' What Farshid termed *justice* was a place in which he was able to explain his own actions and have his words taken seriously. Committing a crime restored asylum seekers, at least partially, to a position within the polis as distinct and equal human beings. Chapter 4 discusses the greater rights that detainees achieved through committing a crime and gaining legal recognition as a 'charged person.'

Direct Communication Beyond the Bureaucracy

Asylum seekers in detention were aware that they were isolated from the community and that they were being represented to the community by the government as different, dangerous and threatening. Emad explained that,

> …it was very hard for us to change the image that the government gave about us to the external world. Just psychologically you get really frustrated when you think that oh the people that I will meet outside think that I'm a different person, you know I'm a primitive, I'm criminal, you know. It's very, very sad actually. But if you're inside the detention centre and let's say you have no access to legal system, you have no access to the media, you cannot talk to the management there, you cannot talk to the immigration department there, you don't have the ability to explain yourself. (Emad)

Establishing direct lines of communication with members of the Australian community was a high priority for asylum seekers, both in terms of a strategy towards regaining rights and in terms of creating a political space in which their words and deeds were meaningful. Speaking directly to members of the polis was a way of inserting themselves into it, regardless of any formal entry procedures.

After his release Shahin urged people he met to,

> …write letters to people in detention centres. Get in touch. There is a wall the government has created. And this wall needs to be chipped away from both ways. People from inside are doing their way, for you really the best way is to get to know them. As long as that wall is there the government can do what they want. And once it is broken or has holes in it, then it's very hard. (Shahin)

He was convinced that, with direct communication, 'people could see a human face behind the kind of stories that they had heard or they had seen on the TV. It was very different to be that close.' Shahin's comments reveal an Arendtian understanding of the political sphere: a common space in which people can come together and develop and test their opinions with one another on an equal basis and where membership is confirmed not through formal citizenship, but through recognition of one another displayed through engagement with one another's words and deeds. This draws on Ancient Greek conceptions of politics as a realm in which individual, mutually constituted human beings come together and build a common world, and not on the understanding of politics as the formal mechanisms of state such as representation, voting and administration, nor as the technocratic organisation of work which needs to be done to most efficiently meet basic survival needs or achieve some other particular end. Politics is the realm through which humans present themselves to the world *qua* human and constitutes the space for 'appearance' as equal and distinct individuals.

Formal political mechanisms of state are based on representational politics, and asylum seekers had no representative in this realm. They astutely worked towards reaching out to people outside detention as 'fellow human beings.' Mohammed explained that 'the problem was because we saw a lot of things government accuse us, abuse us and a lot, in the TV and we want to tell "we are here, we are human beings, we're not more than anything, just we are same as you."' Issaq hoped that the protests would open up a space in which he and other detainees could 'just reflect our feelings to another human being, just to see us not as a danger but as another human being who escaped from danger.' Many of the protest actions aimed at either directly, or through the media, asking 'ordinary Australians' to recognise their shared humanity, both their general sameness and distinct individual identities.

Detainees needed to find ways to speak for themselves if they were to be able to find a way into the Australian polis. Osman used to write notes and put them inside tennis balls and throw them over the fence at Port Hedland detention centre in the hope that someone would find them and read the letter inside. Most asylum seekers detained for long periods had Australian pen pals who they could write to and express themselves. Some of these letters have been collated and published in several books as collaborative efforts to increase the public reach of asylum seeker voices

(Burnside 2003; Keneally and Scott 2004). Farshid and Sayed both used to call talkback radio stations to explain riots or escapes, or simply to counter government media releases about the very good standards of treatment and facilities in detention. Asylum seeker efforts to find a way to speak publicly belie an understanding of Arendt's contention that speech must always accompany action, as without self-narration, actions lose their 'revelatory character' (Arendt 1958, 178). When hundreds of detainees broke out of Woomera detention centre in June 2000, Ibrahim and others took the opportunity to speak publicly to gathering media and to Woomera townsfolk: 'So we start to talk, we start to express what, why we have done this. We want the people to understand. We are here, we don't want to harm anyone, we just want our rights.' Protest actions were a way to prise open a space in the polis in which asylum seekers could speak and thereby participate in the human artifice and so restore some of the essential characteristics of the human condition: recognition of one's speech and action as distinct and equal human beings.

Asylum seekers protested as a way to speak for themselves and to speak to other human beings as fellow humans, rather than people acting in a bureaucratic role, such as the older guard described by Osman. Whenever they had the opportunity, asylum seekers spoke about the injustice inside detention, expressed their feelings of despair and pleaded to be recognised as human. These messages were heard by an ever-increasing number of people in the general public who recognised the detainees as fellow human beings and felt compelled to act in solidarity with them to restore their rights and status as fully human. This phenomenon challenges Arendt's belief that a global 'humanity' is an insufficient basis upon which to base rights claims. It is perhaps a precarious one, in that the general public do not have the same direct access to formalised power in the way that legislators and politicians do, but people were able to mobilise and use their power as citizens, whose speech and actions are thereby meaningful, to contribute to several changes both for individual refugees and to the system as a whole. Asylum seekers' pleas to be recognised as fellow human beings relied on a belief in human conscience and the capacity of all people to think and make moral judgements. Osman explained that, after release, he spoke with a passerby at an anti-detention rally who had made a disparaging comment about 'boat people.' Osman shared his story with the passerby and explained why asylum seekers come and how they are treated in detention. He then implored the man to 'Use your brain. Judge. You know? Who was in wrong, who was in right?'

Although Arendt rejected bare humanity as a stable or sufficient basis for achieving rights, it was the only basis available to asylum seekers in detention and, through their actions, they were able to form relationships with people outside detention and make their words and deeds meaningful.

An Alternative Polis: Mutual Recognition Among Detainees

Asylum seekers in detention, denied formal entry to the Australian polis, formed their own political communities inside the detention network. These smaller communities may not have had the capacity to ensure people's civic rights in the manner of a nation-state, but they nonetheless established a basis for protecting individual human dignity against the complete denial of the official system. Through protest, asylum seekers were able to experience their own agency and offer support and recognition to one another. Sayed explained that:

> You gain self-confidence because in the environment you are in, you are depending for everything and you abide by the rules so, you have to do like they tell you to do. They set the time for food, you don't have control on anything. When we do something like that, at least we, we, it's like a self-independence type of thing. That's what happens. That's why we protest like, because you are achieving something, even though you're not, in the short term, yes you are, but in the long run you won't, but still you will say, you will gain the self-confidence. (Sayed)

Osman expressed a similar sentiment when he said that, 'after a protest I would feel proud of myself. Cos I did something that every free man would do. You know? You are not dead body. You are human, you have got dream.'

If thinking only in terms of formal nation-states as political communities, it is easy to become alienated and disempowered. The recognition that political communities can take many shapes is crucial for maintaining one's agency, engagement and humanity. Detainees sat together and analysed their situation, their place within Australian politics, possible actions they could take, the ethics and efficacy of different actions, and how to create ways to speak directly to the Australian public. These communities extended beyond individual relationships and individual detention centres, and across language, religious and ethnic divides. Within these communities, detainees addressed each other by name and their opinions were made significant, at least at a very local level through a shared sense of solidarity and belonging. These political communities reassured detainees that they mattered:

> A lot of things for other people we done as well to show the support to other things, people that look out at you, 'you are not alone, don't kill yourself. We help you out. We try to help you as well,' yeah plenty of things … they were doing it as well for me too. (Baha'adin)

Emad saw this interconnectedness not only as situational interpersonal care, which is a matter of the private realm, but as fundamental to politics based on mutual respect and recognition, and to the human condition:

> So we all try in this world to do something better, because I can't live this life by myself without seeing you smile in this world, because I'll be frustrated at that time. You know I want to live with other humans who are happy. And I want to see them, you know, achieve their goals in this life. (Emad)

Conclusion

Detainees pleaded for recognition as fellow human beings. As Emad put it 'I'm not a perfectionist, I'm not calling for 100 percent. I need the minimum when someone treats me as a human, not like an object inside the detention centre.' Detainees sought to restore their rights by gaining formal entry to the Australian political community through both formal refugee applications as well as committing crimes. In parallel to using rights-based institutional mechanisms for restoration of the right to have rights, detainees drew on the moral and philosophical discourse of human rights, centring on the 'human.' To be stripped of rights is no distant or academic experience; it is intensely intimate and is at once both personal and political. The protests and actions of refugees in detention were aimed at 'us,' as actual people, and they were intended to trigger a sentimental, human response and so to insert the asylum seekers into the polis, in the absence of bureaucratic recognition, through human-to-human recognition. Arendt's model of human rights, as arising only from human determination, carries with it the realisation that we have the power to affect human rights and to decide who falls within the mutual guarantee. Detainee actions demonstrated an understanding of this and pushed for recognition by the Australian community beyond the legal and bureaucratic systems. Detainees may be granted a visa and with it, certain legal rights based on re-categorisation as a 'refugee,' but achieving the sort of human rights that Arendt discusses, of belonging, equality and distinction, relies on deeper political (in the Ancient Greek sense) recognition. Shahin expressed it beautifully:

> You see, Lucy, it is a massive thing to live with the title of 'refugee.' Which is something that you are bestowed on, you didn't choose it, you didn't pick it, you thought you are making a freedom of movement to get out of a problem that you are in, and now you are in another type of trouble and there is a title for you to carry on. It is very understandable that a lot of people don't want to be called by that title and as soon as you go out, that's the first thing that you get. Not many of us feel comfortable with that, but some of us feel like, I don't know, I would like to… this is something that is on me now. I would like to define it the way that I fulfil it. So yes, I'm a refugee, I'm from Iran, but I'm a human being with these passions, these emotions, this laughter and these crying moments. You know, like any other human being. And that is the way that I am that refugee. (Shahin)

References

Arendt, H. (1958). *The human condition* (2nd ed.). Chicago: University of Chicago Press.

Arendt, H. (1976). *The origins of totalitarianism*. Orlando: A Harvest Book, Harcourt Publishing.

Baldissone, R. (2009). A way out of the seventeenth-century: Human rights beyond modernities. Paper presented at *Tenth Humanities Graduate Research Conference*, Curtin Univerity, Perth, November 5–6.

Bauman, Z. (1990). Modernity and ambivalence. *Theory Culture & Society, 7*(2), 143–169.

Bauman, Z. (1991). *Modernity and ambivalence*. Cambridge: Polity Press.

Burnside, J. (Ed.) (2003). *From nothing to zero: Letters from refugees in Australia's Detention Centres*. Melbourne: Lonely Planet.

Foucault, M. (1997). *Society must be defended: Lectures at the College de France 1975–76* (D. Macey, Trans.). London: Penguin Books.

Ife, J. (2010). *Human rights from below: Achieving rights through community development*. Melbourne: Cambridge University Press.

Keneally, T., & Scott, R. (2004). *Another country*. Broadway: Halstead Press.

Klocker, N., & Dunn, K. M. (2003). Who's driving the asylum debate? Newspaper and government representations of asylum seekers. *Media International Australia, 109*, 71–92.

Mares, P. (2002). *Borderline: Australia's treatment of refugees and asylum seekers*. Sydney: University of New South Wales Press.

Parekh, S. (2004). A meaningful place in the world: Hannah Arendt on the nature of human rights. *Journal of Human Rights, 3*(1), 41–53.

Parekh, S. (2008). *Hannah Arendt and the challenge of modernity: A phenomenology of human rights*. New York: Routledge.

Rorty, R. (1999). Human rights, rationality and sentimentality. In O. Savić (Ed.), *The politics of human rights*. London: Verso.

3

Power and Resistance. Everyday Resistance to Immigration Detention

* * *

> I clearly stated that from now on I'll work hard to try to break the system.
> Aamer, detained 3 years, 6 weeks

* * *

Conceptualising Power and Resistance

One of the most significant inheritances of Foucault's body of work is a shift in the way power is conceptualised. Foucault destabilised orthodox understandings of power and convincingly mapped the ways in which power functions as a dynamic flowing through all social relations. His reconceptualisation of power radically altered understandings of power, undermining didactic models which seek to identify who 'has' power and who does not, fixing and polarising actors into 'powerful' and 'powerless.' Foucault expressed doubt about commodified understandings of power, a paradigm with roots in the Enlightenment, particularly in social

L. Fiske, *Human Rights, Refugee Protest and Immigration Detention*,
DOI 10.1057/978-1-137-58096-2_3

contract theories, and the Industrial Revolution. In this framework, power can be understood as an entity in its own right and individually held, traded, apportioned, taken or won. This power-as-commodity formulation is influential today and many theories of justice (and strategies for improving justice) are concerned with competition for power, redistribution of power, or convincing those with power to deploy it in a just manner. Foucault's body of work cuts radically through this by conceiving of power not as an entity but as a force and as coming into being when it is exercised.

Throughout his work, Foucault resisted any absolute or generalisable definition of power and, in fact, rejected the question 'What is power?', preferring instead to address questions of how power functions, what mechanisms enable power to be enacted, and what are the effects and relations of power in society (Foucault 1997, 13–16). Foucault acknowledged that power can be oppressive and repressive, but extended this by discussing it as a dynamic force pervading all social relations, enacted through language, naming, institutionalisation, knowledge production, theorising, and through all social interactions. Power here may be repressive, oppressive, constitutive or constructive, but it is, he contended, always productive. Power produces the subject and the social world. Important here is that power produces resistance (Foucault 1976, 95).

Foucault proposed that 'power must be understood as the multiplicity of force relations immanent in the sphere in which they operate and which constitute their own organisation; as the process which, through ceaseless struggle and confrontations, transforms, strengthens or reverses them' (Foucault 1976, 92). In this model, power is not to be found in one exclusive seat within one sovereign entity, but in the exchange and the struggle *between* people, ideas, institutions. 'Power is everywhere; not because it embraces everything, but because it comes from everywhere' (Foucault 1976, 93). Taking this conceptualisation of power, asylum seekers are, from the moment of arrival, and through the act of arrival, at once exercising power and engaging in a power struggle with Australia, which continues throughout the ensuing period of detention. Contra to some Agambian scholars (e.g., see Crowley-Cyr 2005; Zannettino 2008), who theorise that asylum seekers in detention camps are reduced to 'bare life' and reduced to the *Muselmann*[1]—the body in complete submission, upon which the state can exert its sovereign power unfettered—the meeting of state and asylum seeker does not actually produce a defined seat of power and a passive subject, respectively, but in fact, an unequal power relationship shaped by struggle for dominance and subjugation.[2]

The relationship established between state and detainee is marked by a cycle of struggle, power and resistance. Most writing on the topic focuses on the greater power of the state and seeks to map this power through the actions of the state to inscribe its sovereignty on the body and civic status of the asylum seeker (Maley 2003; Pugliese 2002; Tazreiter 2006). However, this addresses only one aspect of the power relationship and results in a tendency to politically eviscerate the asylum seeker further. It may equally be conceived that the originating act, the initial force that establishes the relationship, is initiated by the asylum seeker through his/her arrival. The state then responds by deploying its greater political and material force to reassert its dominance, to subjugate and control the asylum seeker. Former Australian Prime Minister John Howard's now (in)famous statement, 'We will decide who comes to this country and the circumstances under which they come,' was a *response* to asylum seekers arriving by boat (*Lateline* 2001). And so, a cycle of action and reaction, force and response is established. The exertion of sovereign power is provoked by the action (power) of the asylum seeker and it in turn creates not submission, but resistance.

Detainees are not submissive recipients of state power; they are 'never in a position of exteriority in relation to power,' and they are 'always

[1] The term *Muselmann* was used by concentration camp inmates to describe fellow inmates who had lost 'all consciousness and all personality' (Agamben 1998, 185) and who were consequently indifferent to all around them, whether pangs of hunger or cold, beatings from guards or approaches from fellow inmates. The *Muselmann* was described by Primo Levi in his account of his own experiences during World War II, *If This be a Man*. Agamben takes Levi's figure of the *Muselmann* to explore the ambiguous philosophical terrain in which 'life' and 'death', and *zoē* ('the simple fact of living common to all living beings' [Agamben 1998, 1]) and *bios* (living proper to an individual or group' [Agamben 1998, 1]) become indistinct.

[2] Some people in detention did collapse into a state which might resemble Agamben's *Muselmann* (Shayan Badraie, whose story is partially told later in this chapter, is a dramatic example of this). But when such collapses occurred, others around the person rallied and exercised their own power in many different ways on behalf of the *Muselmann*. There is an insufficiently critical acceptance of representations of detainees as 'passive victims' and the dominance of this view serves to further mask the agency of the majority of detainees who resisted throughout and beyond their detention.

"inside" power' (Foucault 1976, 95) as they are in a relationship with the state and power is present in all social relations. Power is produced by and in turn produces social relations. Once power is understood as a dynamic force created through social relations, it can no longer be spoken of as a monolithic entity to be deployed by one actor upon another, but rather, requires a new framework for thinking, new theory and new language that is a language of movement, flow and struggle. As power is a force produced through social relations, it follows that 'where there is power, there is resistance' (Foucault 1976, 95). Power relationships require power *and* resistance in order to exist:

> Their (power relationships) existence depends on a multiplicity of points of resistance… These points of resistance are present everywhere in the power network. Hence there is no single locus of great Refusal, no soul of revolt, source of all rebellions, or pure law of the revolutionary. Instead there is a plurality of resistances, each of them a special case: resistances that are possible, necessary, improbable; others that are spontaneous, savage, solitary, concerted, rampant or violent; still others that are quick to compromise, interested, or sacrificial; by definition, they can only exist in the field of power relations. But this does not mean that they are only a reaction or rebound, forming with respect to the basic domination an underside that is in the end always passive, doomed to perpetual defeat. (Foucault 1976, 95–96)

Detainees were engaged in a power struggle with the Australian state, with those who guarded them, with the bureaucrats sent to categorise and regularise them, and with their construction as a threat, a non-citizen and therefore a non-person. This struggle did not occur because they needed to seize some of the state's power for themselves, but because they were already *within* the power relationship and had to respond to its force upon them, through submission, transformation, subversion or resistance. The struggle was, and remains, multifaceted as detainees resisted the omnipotent technologies of control that constituted daily life in detention, struggled with the bureaucratic (legal) strategy of refugee status determination (another technology of the state to rationalise and regularise the asylum seeker and through that, its own sovereignty) and with cultural and semiotic processes which functioned to dehumanise them and force them into archetypal categories, principally 'prisoner' or 'patient,' both of which construct them as 'powerless,' awaiting some act of state to be re-humanised.

Resistance was not unitary, centralised or institutionalised, there was neither a 'mother-strategy' nor a central organising committee. Rather they (resistances) were 'mobile and transitory … producing cleavages … that shift about, fracturing unities and effecting regroupings, furrowing across individuals themselves, cutting them up and remoulding them, marking off irreducible regions in them, in their bodies and minds' (Foucault 1976, 96). It is more helpful to speak of 'detainee resistances' than 'Detainee Resistance.' While some actions were planned and coordinated within and across different ethnic groups and different detention centres, detainee resistances are better understood as mobile and transitory instantiations of individual and collective action and reaction 'incapable of unanimity' (Foucault 1997, 8).

This resistance may take many forms, not all of which are readily recognisable as resistance, but which nonetheless seek to subvert, disrupt or manipulate the state's power. Detainees in Australia's detention camps engaged in daily acts of resistance. Some had explicit political consciousness, such as the example of a detainee digging his own grave and constructing a headstone with an epitaph reading 'the tomb of WMA 2065,' and some did not, such as when parents attempted to smuggle food out of the dining room so that they had something to offer their child at night. Politics and power infused every aspect of detention life, and every act that departed from compliance and submission became political, whether that act sought to confront, transform or elude sovereign power. At the risk of contradiction, but following Foucault, even acts of submission could be strategic acts in the power struggle, forming a tactical collusion to gain some brief advantage, such as a cigarette lighter, an apple, or a hoped-for-debt across the divide. Even what looks like submission to a bystander may not be a *Muselmann* collapse.

Conceptualising Detainee Resistances

Resistance performed dual functions for detainees. It was a means used in pursuit of tangible outcomes and also had an existential function, providing a way to exercise and experience agency within a highly controlled environment (Carlton 2007). Most resistance actions operated simultaneously on both levels, though there are some examples where either no demand for change was made or where the expressed demand was so unlikely that the sought-after outcome was the protest itself. Drawing on primary sources (interviews with former detainees) as well as secondary resources addressing detainee resistance, the following matrix may be helpful in thinking about detainee resistance. These categories are falsely simplified and should not be read as 'truths,' but simply as vehicles for organising ideas and actions.

Tangible Functions

Much detainee resistance was outwardly aimed, that is, there was a specific external target audience and/or goal that the protest sought to achieve. This may be further broken into two categories: actions which were targeted at achieving specific material changes, such as getting a light bulb replaced in a room, getting increased access to telephones or calling for the release of all detainees. These actions were directed primarily at those with explicit power over the detention environment, comprising government officials and security guards. Other forms of resistance were aimed, not at the government or others directly involved in detention, but at the broader population, both Australian and international, seeking semiotic change in order to effect the detainees' representations and position in Australian politics. The target audience of these latter protests was the Australian community. These protests were typically made not only through the media, but also through refugee supporters outside and aimed to disrupt and unsettle government accounts of their presence in Australia and their actions in detention and to insert their own narratives alongside their own actions. Detainee resistance marked a refusal to allow official government or bureaucratic explanations of their presence and actions to go unchallenged.

My analysis is less concerned with whether these objectives were actually achieved or not, than with the attempt itself. It is through detainees' exercise of power and engagement in struggle that agency is revealed, which in turn challenges the passive victim archetypes too often ascribed to refugees and which also enlivens and problematises theoretical debates about 'human,' 'refugee,' 'power' and the modern state.

Existential Functions

Closed immigration detention centres are extraordinarily controlled environments, where communication, food, activity, movement and information is tightly regulated and monitored. Detainees have little opportunity to participate in decision-making, either at the mundane level of deciding what to eat, or in more fundamental matters such as education, work or political status. Resistance was an important way for detainees to experience their own agency, to take a decision not to eat the food on offer, or to create a disturbance and force a response from authorities such as through self-harming or breaking a piece of camp infrastructure. The aim of the protest was less about achieving a change in their environment and more about experiencing self. Farshid explained this eloquently:

> People's situation in detention was that you were the lost person, the forgotten person, you don't exist, you cannot change anything and you have no power over anything. So, self-harm in most cases wasn't a planned thing. It was in most cases out of frustration and it was good in a way that people feel they are real again, they exist, they have power over something – their body. So, blood always has a very powerful message and when people see they can get over their fear and do something, certain thing, harsh thing, they come back to that colour of existence ... I have power. I can do things. So I was calling that self-actualisation. (Farshid)

The framework of understanding resistance as externally (goal) oriented, seeking both material and semiotic change, while also serving an existential purpose, will be used alongside a Foucauldian construction of power and resistance to explore some of the multiple acts of resistance performed by detainees across the detention network.

Detainee Analyses

Whether a particular instance of resistance was externally or internally oriented, prior to any strategy came analysis. Detainee resistance was too readily explained by government representatives as arising from the inherent criminality or barbarity of the detainee and by many refugee supporters as arising from the utter despair and hopelessness of the detainees. Both explanations mask the consciousness of the actors, resting instead upon pathological or primal drivers to action, and fail to recognise the political agency of the detainees. Detainee leadership and resistance was not always organised in ways familiar and recognisable to the Western eye, as there were no formal committees, nominated group representatives or coalitions formed around fixed ideological positions. However, it would be erroneous to conflate the lack of formalised political structures and organisations with an absence of political consciousness.

Detainees spent considerable time and energy 'reading' Australian culture and politics and seeking to understand their position within the new political environment. As the asylum seeker's arrival can be seen as an exercise of power, so too was their refusal to passively accept the analysis and position given to them by the government, guards and media. This wasn't always easy to do. Farshid, who spent three years in Perth, Port Hedland and Curtin detention centres explained that with one television set for at least one hundred people 'it wasn't easy to grab news. It was difficult to convince people who were very tired and they want to watch something entertaining and to just switch to the news.' He would explain to people that 'this is really good for us to watch the news and know what's going on.' Detainees engaged critically with their environment and whatever information they could access and used this to build their own worldviews and to determine for themselves their social positioning.

Detainees' access to information was almost entirely mediated through either mass media, including newspapers and television, or contact with government officials and guards. It is important here to note that, while there are discernable commonalities of critique, these critiques were neither universal nor static. Different people held different views, the same people changed their views as they accessed more information or interpreted information differently or experienced changed subjectivities, such as the emotional changes that occurred as initial detention stretched for a longer term. One of the disciplining technologies of the state was to present asylum seekers as a dehumanised, undifferentiated, homogenous mass. But life is more complex than that and, in reality, there were ruptures, divisions and differences within the detainee groups. Nonetheless, four threads of analysis emerged consistently throughout interviews with former detainees. First, those in separation detention,[3] without access to television, newspapers or telephones, believed the camps were secret. Then, once people had access to communication, they made three more analyses, which consisted of the belief that they were being portrayed as illegal invaders and a threat to Australia, the belief that there was political capital in their suffering for the government, and the belief that their suffering was meant to be a deterrent to other prospective asylum seekers. These four analyses, along with other critiques, opportunity and emotion, formed the basis for resistance strategy.

Secret Camps

While people were held in separation detention, they were denied access to television, newspapers, telephones and all forms of contact with the outside world and with detainees who had access to communication. Separation detention typically lasted a matter of weeks, but for a significant minority of detainees, the process lasted for months. Unsurprisingly, many detainees formed the view that the detention centres were secret camps, not known about by ordinary Australians. Issaq was part of a group who had been held in separation detention for several months.

[3] Separation detention refers to the holding of a detainee in a separate compound with others who have arrived on the same boat. Separation detention is described by the Department of Immigration as a 'management tool through which the integrity of Australia's visa determination process is maintained' (HREOC 2005, section 3). The primary purpose of separation detention is to prevent communication with others who have already had immigration interviews and legal advice to prevent earlier arrivals 'coaching' new arrivals in the process and criteria that they must meet to trigger the protection visa application process (HREOC 2004, 240, 2005, section 3; JSCM 2000, 33). During this stage of detention no telephones, faxes, newspapers, television, radio or any form of communication with other detainees or with people in the Australian community is permitted (Commonwealth Ombudsman 2001, 13; HREOC 2004, 11, 240, 254, 2005, sections 3 and 4).

The group had grown tired of waiting for a resolution to their situation and began to discuss forms of protest. He described one such discussion among the detainees:

> There was politicians inside detentions and the Iranian politicians who said 'this place is a secret and when it is a secret, it's bad. They don't want public to know about it.' I mean he was politician. Because some people put their arguments in that 'if you use violence it's going to be negatives and people don't like it,' all this sort of thing. He said 'if people knew about detentions, detention wouldn't be 500k away from a city. It would have been inside a city if people were supporting it. But people are not supporting it. It's something that people don't know about. Now we just need to make sure that they know.' (Issaq)

Some detainees were concerned that the use of violence or aggression would be counter-productive, but Issaq and the fellow detainee he quoted argued (incorrectly, as he was to later discover) that the detention centres were secret and this analysis underpinned their position that violent protest was warranted. He went on to explain that by committing a criminal act, they hoped to be brought before the courts and to be able to access rights as criminals:

> Well yes, there is a criminal in here but there is some 'Criminals Right Act' that someone would come and say 'well under criminal laws you shouldn't treat them like this.' You know what I mean? We don't care. Okay, we are criminals but there is an Act. In Australia criminals have rights of education, criminals have rights of phone, criminals have rights of communication. Criminals – and he knew it, he had studied in England, in the UK in Oxford at the university and he was graduated from there. He knew all the westerns. He had a great understanding of the culture and the law and how the westerns works. I mean, in Iran a criminal doesn't have any rights. If you are in jail you don't have rights, you know what I mean? But he knew that here is not like that. You have rights. Even though you are a terrorist, you still have rights. It doesn't matter how bad you are. That's how we got motivated. I mean, okay, we are bad, we are terrible, but we still have rights and we want that rights even if it's a right to a newspaper or a TV or communication, some forms of communications, we should have that right and we need that right. (Issaq)

The detainees concurred with Hannah Arendt that the status of 'criminal' contains more protection than the status of 'refugee.' With the status of 'citizen' beyond their immediate reach, the detainees were determined to re-enter the public sphere, to no longer be held incommunicado or hidden from view, and committing a criminal act was, in their analysis, an effective vehicle for gaining some recognised status in the polis. The detainees' analysis that their presence was unknown and their status undefined underpinned decisions about strategy.

Asylum Seekers Portrayed as Criminals, Terrorists and a Threat

Once people had been moved to general detention, with at least some access to television and telephones, they were able to see how they were being portrayed in the media. All participants in this research spoke of being shocked, frustrated and angry about being portrayed as 'illegals,' criminals and threats to society. Emad spoke of his frustration over the popular portrayal of asylum seekers:

> It was very hard for us to change the image that the government gave about us to the external world. Just psychologically you get really frustrated when you think that 'oh the people that I will meet outside think that I'm a different person, you know I'm a primitive... I'm criminal,' you know. It's very, very sad actually. But if you're inside the detention centre and let's say you have no access to legal system, you have no access to the media, you cannot talk to the management there, you cannot talk to the immigration department there, you don't have the ability to explain yourself. (Emad)

Baha'adin said that he felt 'more angry and upset' when he 'was watching the news on there and I heard that Phil Ruddock[4] was saying "these people are very dangerous people and they are terrorists" ... He used us a bit of propaganda like "they are dangerous people, they are terrorists," or "they are criminals" and things like that.'

---

[4] Hon Philip Ruddock was the Minister for Immigration from 1996 to 2003.

Realising that they were already presented as violent and dangerous was a key issue in discussions between detainees about protest actions. Some, like Farshid, maintained throughout several years of detention that it was imperative that violence was never used. He cautioned fellow detainees that 'the government could take some advantages with some of the bad protest and make bad publicity for the refugees. I was fearful that it's going to make majority Australian people hate us even more.' Farshid believed that it would be too easy for the government to obtain footage of a noisy protest or one where violence was employed and use it to reinforce its position as protectors of the Australian people against a threatening invader and that he 'didn't want to help the government do what they wanted to do.' He argued that Australians 'don't justify violence in any way … regardless for the best reason in the world.… You don't get heard and you lose your credibility.' Dr Aamer Sultan held a similar view to Farshid and did not participate in any violent protests during his three years in detention, but looking back on the course of events he was less resolute in his objection. He said that he was 'very unhappy' about how 'the media had shown those aggressive criminals,' but that in hindsight,

> it was a positive thing.… At last the government did the mistake of transferring the camera into there, let the people know at least there are some people there – I mean it's just the beginning of questioning 'Who are those people. We don't know about them. We worry about them. Criminals or not, even the most dangerous people in the world, or maybe the other way around, we just want know about it.' It's just the fact that this has transferred the argument from a faceless people into actual people doing something bad or good, it doesn't matter. (Aamer)

Issaq argued that the remoteness of the camps meant that any protest action had to be newsworthy in order to get media to come. He believed that getting the media to come was more important than concerns about how their actions might be portrayed because to be invisible carried more risk than 'bad publicity':

> Peacefully doesn't answer anything because there is no journos here. We need to get journos here and how we can do it just go to a town and sit in

> there until journos gets here? Or just burn the place down and the smoke will bring journalists, you know? That became the main point just to get the journalists coming there, to make a scene, have a story for a TV or radio or newspaper to put that budget for journalists to fly in there and see us because they had to come from Adelaide and it was like 500k away. So they needed a good story. People sewing their lips in detention was a good story or people burning down the centres was a good story, even though it was relative. But it was getting into a media. … We didn't care about negative publicity. We just wanted to get people to come to detentions and sit. (Issaq)

'How to reach the media' was detainees' 'biggest question' according to Emad and everyone that I interviewed. How to get the media to come, what sort of message to portray to the media and whether the risk of reinforcing the dominant government narrative about detainees' inherent criminality and barbarity was outweighed by the need to raise awareness of their situation in detention centres was hotly contested among detainees in all detention centres.

Political Capital and Deterrence

The final two threads of analysis common across all interviews were that detainees saw that they were being used as pawns in Australia's national politics. In particular, detainees saw that there was political capital for the conservative Coalition government in their suffering and that their suffering was intended to be public and to act as a deterrent to prospective asylum seekers overseas.

Ibrahim believed that detention was 'a plan to punish these people to be honest. This plan has been well managed by someone with high authority in the hierarchy to punish these people and to make them a good example for others … people are gonna think twice before they come to here.' Osman reached a similar conclusion, saying, 'John Howard and other minister mention many time that they keep us to send a message to the smuggler, to other people, don't come to Australia,' and Mehdi stated that,

> we were the victim of Australian policy to just stop people coming illegally or something. We were the victim and they wanted to show people that we keep them… It's not a matter of 'what's your story or what…?' it's just

> 'keep that person.' That's it. They needed to keep some people… for a long time to say that 'We are strong against these people.' (Mehdi)

This analysis is important because once people had determined that their fate rested not on an individual assessment of each person's claims, but on national political interests, detainees lost faith in the official systems and began to consider alternate actions to resolve their situation.

Emad also saw that prolonged detention was not, as the government stated, non-punitive administrative detention, but a punishment for arriving unlawfully and a means of deterring those who might yet come. He added that the theatre of detention gave material proof of the government's strength and resolve to protect Australia's borders and that this was a deliberate strategy to retain government:

> Their intention was to give a real strong lesson to the outer world not to come to Australia, okay, by restraining us as a group. It's just a misfortunate incident, bad timing for us. Someone wants to give a lesson to the whole world through us. They wanted to say, 'If you come to Australia that will be your destiny. You will be treated like this.' *So, we are subjected to a political, not legal, pressure – a political pressure that the government, at that time, needed to get votes from the ordinary Australian people* [emphasis added]. And that's what I think happened. In reality one of the main aspects for John Howard election – and he won the election at that time – is that he used immigration as a pressure point, as an element in his campaign to defeat Labor. So we were the source of this election campaign… Unfortunately they didn't look at us as humans in need for their help. They looked at us as a human that they can use in their election to win and to prevail. And I think that's completely wrong. (Emad)

Emad was highly critical of this political strategy, labelling it Machiavellian because the government's focus was on retaining power, regardless of the human cost. 'This way of thinking was really belonging to 300 or 400 years ago of political thinking… Whenever it's good for them, for the votes, they take it. They remind me of the old monarchs in France—Louis XIV and XV and XVI—where just the power was all what they think of, you know.' Emad insightfully identified several key issues in Australian politics at that time. As a lawyer with an interest in human rights, Emad recognised that the Coalition's focus on retaining power overrode two centuries or more of developments in political thinking and systems, that individual rights were secondary to maintaining a strong state. He also identified the difference between legal 'pressure' and political 'pressure,' and that the lack of hard law enforcement mechanisms in international law made asylum seekers' legal rights subservient to national political agendas. This analysis implies that Emad should have turned to political rather than legal strategies to insist on the rights of detainees, but he did not. Throughout his eight months of detention, Emad consistently discouraged fellow detainees from protest, as he was determined that 'the law will rule in the end … from the head of the states to the normal people.' Not long after his release, a group of detainees broke out of Curtin IDC and protested outside the fence. The protest received extensive media coverage and soon after, greater numbers of people began getting visas and were released from detention. Emad believes the escape caused the acceleration in processing:

> I think it was a big scandal to Philip Ruddock government in front of the international media, and the international reputation of Australia was the main element to think about. Seeing refugees who are being, let's say more than one year in the detention centre without their application being processed, and suddenly they broke out, they left, they jumped over the fence and the media started to cover this in the news. I think that's what pressured the government to release bigger groups. Otherwise I don't think they would release them … It shouldn't be this way. (Emad)

A common critique among detainees was that the government was determined to stop asylum seekers from coming and to retain power. The government viewed asylum seekers not as individual human beings with rights, but as criminals who had offended against Australia's sovereignty. Government ministers felt no ethical or moral discomfort in using detainees as a means to their own political ends.[5] Reaching this realisation was key in shaping detainees' compliance with detention and

[5] Some government backbenchers were an exception to this but there was no discomfort publicly expressed by government Ministers.

refugee status determination systems and underpinned discussions about resistance and strategy.

Strategy

While there was a high degree of agreement between detainees about analysis, there were far more divisions and disagreements about strategy. Several people interviewed were opposed in principle to the use of violence, as outlined by Farshid above. Others, such as Issaq, remained convinced that spectacle (which often involved violence) was a necessary ill to make their voices heard. Still others, such as Osman, argued neither for nor against violence, but simply saw it as an inevitable part of the dynamic between officials and detainees. 'You push me, I push you. That's the way everywhere it works, you know.'

Strategy sits between analysis and objective. It is designed to achieve particular ends and is shaped by each person's or group's analysis of the situation and their ethics and belief systems. I have divided the aims of resistance into two categories: externally oriented and internally oriented. Externally oriented actions were aimed either at exerting pressure on officials with direct power over detention and detainees to achieve a particular material change, or at the broader Australian and international community to achieve semiotic change of detainee representation and understanding of their circumstances.

Through their resistance, detainees showed inventiveness, ingenuity, creativity, courage and determination. They employed a broad range of strategies including work strikes, sit-ins, letter writing campaigns, smuggling information and items in and out of detention centres, launching legal actions, lodging official complaints, hunger strikes, self-harm, unauthorised communication, both between detention centres and different compounds, particularly with those in separation detention, formed alliances with activists outside detention, staged rooftop protests, damaged detention infrastructure (such as smashing light bulbs, stealing a guard's walkie-talkie), rioted, escaped, spoke to visiting politicians and other officials, engaged in civil disobedience, art work, theatre and calling in to talk-back radio shows to name just a few measures. One interviewee even applied for a job as detention centre manager:

> They were having a problem to get a detention manager. Always tried change this one, that one, you know, acting all the time. I said OK, why not? I have a lot of experience, I been here four years, I know all the rules. I write my credentials and send it to them. (Sayed)

Damaging detention centre property was widely believed to be an effective strategy for achieving an immediate and specific individual change, such as getting access to a dentist or obtaining a paracetamol tablet. Sayed explained that, 'if you ask for the request—you don't get it, but if you shout and do something, break something up, you get all these things done.' Salah reported a similar belief: 'I mean after two or three years we found out, after all these experiences and stuff people they're breaking things and eventually they got visa. Or they hang themselves, they cut themselves, they get visa. What's happening? What's going on?' Osman thought that, 'the ACM organisation wanted that things to happen, cos if you smash one lamp, they charge the government treble.' All agreed it was a more effective strategy of getting simple needs met than through the official system of request forms.

Most actions, though, were not targeted at government officials or ACM guards, but instead aimed to achieve semiotic change, to insist on a political voice for detainees and a place in the polis. As identified by Foucault (1976), resistance by marginalised and subjugated voices is mobile, transitory and fractured. The relative consensus discernible in detainee analyses is not present in strategy. I will make no attempt to unify what was never unified and will instead outline a few different examples of strategies used by detainees to change their own and others' detention.

Farshid and Shahin

Farshid and Shahin met in Curtin IDC in 2001. Farshid had already been detained for more than a year in Perth and Port Hedland detention centres, as well as in a WA prison following a conviction for leading a breakout from Port Hedland in June 2000 (see Chap. 4 for more detail on this action). Shahin had spent eleven months in separation detention and met Farshid when he was transferred to the main compound. He described the meeting thus:

> Oh that's the first time to meet Farshid and Farshid's wealth of knowledge. Oh, Farshid! He knew everything and everyone... Perhaps that's why we have stayed such close friends after all these years because I think we could read something together that was beyond those four walls. I don't want to discredit anybody else in that. There were other people who did a magnificent job as well, but… I think myself and Farshid just hooked up at the best time… and it was a magnificent partnership. (Shahin)

The two men shared a similar worldview, a commitment to nonviolence and a firm belief that the struggle was political and semiotic. They shared a need to convince the Australian people that asylum seekers were no threat and to win support in order to force a change in government policy. During his time in several places of detention, Farshid had developed a good network of contacts and allies outside detention. He was informed one night that a commercial television news crew would be visiting Curtin IDC the following morning and that this would be the first time the media had been permitted into the remote detention centre. Farshid was determined to seize this opportunity to get a message out to the Australian people, although he was also concerned about the risk of footage being presented as confirmation of the violence and threat of asylum seekers.

Farshid was acutely aware that the 'Australian government tried to create an environment where the Australian people knew these people are so violent and to be fearful of them. A protest to me wasn't a violent act, it was the available peaceful option that raise awareness or just raise the voice of justice.' Farshid thought carefully about who to involve and,

> called for a meeting with the people that I knew were going to understand the sensitivity of the situation… And trying to find the right person to come up with ideas so I was really pleased with Shahin. He's an artistic person, he came up with brilliant ideas. It was fantastic to work together, to get something meaningful done…. We didn't sleep that night, we just work. (Farshid)

Farshid, Shahin and a few other detainees sat up all night discussing this opportunity and planning their action. They decided that movement and chanting could too easily be construed as a security risk and the media visit would be immediately terminated, or that any footage of adults chanting and marching could be reported as threatening or violent behaviour. Shahin explained that,

> we could see the way that Philip Ruddock was portraying us, so that was a small opportunity for us to show this is the way that we are... (we were) sitting down and thinking 'How can we send that message out? What we really would like here?' It was giving a true face to what we were, but in a very small window of opportunity. (Shahin)

The plan was to stage a series of silent protest actions in different sections of the detention centre so that wherever the media were taken, they would see powerful symbolic messages. They needed more people than their small group to effect the action. Farshid said that they were 'selective first to convince people that can convince other people' to join in this carefully choreographed and highly disciplined protest.

Two main actions were planned for the following day. A fellow detainee who 'look like Jesus… he was with long hair and green eyes' (Farshid) was draped in a blanket with 'Sharing, Caring, Brotherhood' written on it and posed by a fence as if crucified on the cross. He was under strict instruction not to move. Anticipating that the Centre Manager would quickly move the camera crew on to the education room, the detainees planned another protest there. The men invited some children to join the planning group and asked them what message they would like to give the outside world. The men then sat up all night painting A4 size posters with slogans and drawings such as 'we hate cage' (with a picture of a bear in a cage), 'we like to go to school' and 'we want to play.' Twenty-five children were recruited to hold these posters and to pull them out when the camera crew came by. Adults near the education room were given strips of material from torn up bed sheets to tie around their mouths and to stand perfectly still and silent. The bands were to show 'that they can't speak, it doesn't go anywhere… If we talk it shows us a violent people so we just sit back and not move. If we move, it consider that you are just, that they show us a violent people so we are just standing' (Farshid).

The media visit unfolded almost exactly as Shahin, Farshid and their co-collaborators had expected. The Centre Manager took the journalists into the main compound, directly to where Shahin and 'Jesus' were waiting. Shahin recounted the moment with more than a little delight: 'We knew that this is going to happen, he didn't know. It was amazing. It was amazing to see it. It was amazing to see the Centre Manager take a second look "what the hell was that?!"' The Centre Manager quickly moved the media towards the education room where Farshid, the children and several adults were waiting. As soon as the journalists arrived, the children pulled out their posters, the adults wrapped their 'gags' around their mouths and all stood perfectly still. Those detainees not included in the action saw the cameras and the show being staged and began chanting 'Freedom, freedom.' The Centre Manager ordered the media to stop filming, 'but you know how they report. He just hold down the camera but he was holding it towards the refugees. So it was a very short footage' (Farshid). The footage was shown on commercial television nation-wide, and Farshid and Shahin, though disappointed that the careful choreography of their protest had been interrupted by the other detainees shouting, were satisfied with their actions. 'It didn't go well in the end, but at least some of the message got across. It was enough for us in there, to show some sort of civilised protest' (Farshid).

Farshid and Shahin believed that government policies towards asylum seekers and 'border protection' were both supported and driven by a majority view within the Australian population that asylum seekers are dangerous people who need to be locked up, and that they needed to change this dominant belief if longer term change to detention and asylum policy was to be achieved. They were particularly careful to reject modes of protest which could be used to reinforce the image of asylum seekers as dangerous. Consequently, much of their resistance was designed 'to make people think twice and think "is it fair to do all of this to these people? Maybe they are reasonable people and they can be dealt with in a different way"' (Farshid).

Also discernible within Shahin's account in particular are elements of existential satisfaction, a transformation of the power relationship between detainees and officials, if only momentarily. Ordinarily, in detention, the guards and officials have greater knowledge and power, but Shahin remembers the feeling of knowing what was going to happen and the Centre Manager's ignorance and the pleasure of seeing the shock on the manager's face. Farshid identified getting the footage of the children and their posters on the news as a major achievement of the protest. Shahin was supervising the 'Jesus on the cross' protest, but didn't mention whether any footage of this made it to the news. For Shahin, there was at least equal satisfaction, or pleasure, in the brief exercise of power and capacity to know 'more' than the manager as there would have been in any tangible 'outcome.'

Although Farshid and Shahin have now been released from detention for nearly ten years, both have continued their resistance to detention and efforts to shift public opinion about asylum seekers and detainees. Shahin is a writer, director and actor by profession. Soon after his release he wrote a one-man play *Refugitive* and staged more than 280 performances in cities and country towns around Australia. *Refugitive* tells the story of an anonymous detainee on hunger strike. After his release, Shahin 'had heaps of stories in my brain. I made a list, there were some things I wanted to talk about. I thought "What is the *main* story I want to tell?"' He had also been asked by people after his release why detainees hunger strike and self-harm. He felt compelled to answer, to explain the actions of detainees:

> The story was the story of a person who's a hunger striker. No nationality, no name, nothing. Somebody who has been in a detention centre. And because everybody knew that I have been through that system they would think that maybe it's exactly my story but it wasn't. It's a collective story because I had lived next to all those people. And I would always say, this would happen because you have no other choice. You can't make any decisions in your life. Just to show that you are alive you could make a decision to stop receiving anything in your body. That would show you that you're alive, because you could make a decision, in a place that you can't make any decision. (Shahin)

After most performances, Shahin would return to the stage and invite the audience to ask questions and make comments. 'You see, there is a lot in this for me to gain, that there was a huge victory after this, because not only have they sat through this performance, but now they are also hungry for more information. They want to know more.' Shahin was particularly keen to hear from people who held negative views about detainees. He said that audiences would often boo someone who made a negative comment, but he would quickly respond saying 'No, no, no. I'm more happy to have you here than the rest of these people. That's a very valid question because I know there are millions of you outside these doors.' Shahin was willing to sit and talk, sometimes for hours, after a show in an effort to explain what was happening in detention centres and to shift public opinion about asylum seekers. At the end of these discussions, he was inevitably asked, 'What can we do?'

Shahin told his audience that there were four things they should do:

> The first thing I would ask them I'd say is perhaps a very hard thing, but let's talk about it at your dinner table. Maybe sometimes you get in fight with your husband, daughter, son or whatever, but let's just raise it. Tell them this story of you came to this performance, you saw this and you heard this stuff. Let's just discuss it in our little communities.
>
> Then I would ask them to write to your local member. If there is something that you heard tonight that you think is against policy, against what you believe in as an Australian just write to your local members, talk about it, ask them for answers.
>
> And then go above, go to your federal members and ask them, make them to talk about it in the parliament. If you really believe in what you saw in this performance is unjust. Let's just discuss it now further.
>
> Definitely you have a power. Every letter that you write to your local or federal member would be one hundred opinions so they will really react to it.
>
> Fourth thing I would ask them is to write letters to people in detention centres. Get in touch. There is a wall that this government has created. And this wall needs to be chipped away from both ways. People from inside are doing their way, for you really the best way is to get to know them. As long as that wall is there the government can do what they want. And once it is broken or has holes in it, then it's very hard.
>
> These are the four things. (Shahin)

Shahin was a prolific writer while in detention, writing to various external bodies such as the United Nations, Australia's Human Rights and Equal Opportunity Commission, Amnesty International and assisting fellow detainees in writing appeals to the Australian Federal Court. He also used his theatre and performance skills to carefully choreograph messages and images from inside detention, explaining that 'I'm not saying that I was, that we were the good people, we were the ones who believe in that side of things. Because we were able to express ourselves ... I was able to be in that front, and fight the war in that front.' He saw the media visit recounted earlier as a 'very small window of opportunity' to insert his voice into the public sphere. He continued his activism after release, again using his writing and performance skills to try to shift public opinion, which he saw as underpinning government policy. He now had greater and unmediated access to Australians and his strategies expanded accordingly: 'But of course I had a better window after release and that was why I did *Refugitive*.'

Farshid has also continued his activism over the last decade. Soon after his release, he attended a large refugee conference in Sydney. Over four days, he was delighted to hear so many people discussing refugees and detention and how to shift public opinion and government policy. 'I was amazed at what I was hearing, but I thought something was missing here. There is no refugees talking, there's no real voice of refugees.' Farshid decided that he should speak:

> So at the closing I went down and I said that I really need to say thanks to people. I got there and I had a few points that I wanted to make. It was great. I found the courage to talk in front of 600 people for the first time in my life. I need to talk here. (Farshid)

The conference participants were as happy to hear from Farshid as he was to speak and 'from that point so many people asked me to go and talk to their group so I was very pleased that people were welcoming the voice of refugees.' He is an articulate and gentle man, and he soon became well known. He has spoken multiple times to television, radio and print journalists, assisted writers and researchers documenting detention policies and events and is acknowledged in several books and publications. He explains that speaking out is,

> the extension of my protest - that I needed to continue because I was still feeling powerless to just change anything except telling the stories and just education properly what was the real story behind what they heard from the media about what was going on inside at that time with the news. (Farshid)

Farshid had held political opinions in his native Iran and had attended some low-key student political meetings there, but didn't feel safe enough to become actively involved in politics in that environment; 'I wouldn't dare to go out and talk in public for those things that I believed because it wasn't the environment where I could do that.' But after release from detention in Australia and meeting other activists, he managed to,

> …grow that sort of bravery to go to the public. It was a different environment here. I was appreciating that I am in a democratic country within a people that they want to know what is the truth and they want to act according to justice. The level of consciousness was amazing and I couldn't believe that I am amongst so many conscious people that they have no benefit to be involved here. That they just act upon their consciousness. I was thinking that probably this is the heaven that I was looking for. I'm among conscious people and it was a really great appreciation for me. (Farshid)

Farshid continues to speak out at every opportunity.

Dr Aamer Sultan

Doctor Aamer Sultan was detained in Villawood detention centre from 19 May 1999 to 2 July 2002 (three years and six weeks). He is a medical doctor from Iraq, specialising in surgery but also with some experience in psychiatry. He became a high-profile detainee, speaking out and writing about the harms and injustices of detention.

Aamer spent his first year in detention improving his English language skills, doing basic translations for fellow detainees and watching and learning the systems of detention and refugee status determination. He obtained English grammar books and studied to improve his language skills. As one of the few people who could read and write in English, fellow detainees soon began asking him to translate documents relating to their cases. 'I found myself in the position, like doing extensive work of translating and explaining the system as best I can … So given the fact I was free 24/7, I would sit with someone for eight hours … try to work out their case and how to put it in a way to concise it and to sell it to a barrister or lawyer outside by phone only to take it for free, pro bono.'

As he assisted more people from many different backgrounds, including Arabic-speaking people, Afghans, Iranians, North Koreans, Southeast Asians and Cambodians, Aamer saw patterns emerging and began to question the paradigm of the refugee determination process:

> Well that's the question I'm asking. What's the political ideology underpinning that bureaucracy? What is the target of this political? What was behind it? What was it aiming for? It looks to me that this bureaucracy complication of things was aiming of denying those people a visa, simple. (Aamer)

At the start, Aamer said, he was 'just reacting to immediate necessity. There were one hundred, two hundred people around me who just needed to be safe and out.' It was only later that he developed a position which was fundamentally opposed to detention itself. Aamer's early work in detention was to assist individuals to navigate the system and get out of detention. As he saw patterns emerging, he asked for meetings with Department of Immigration officials to 'try to work with them to change things, but this is going nowhere because the Minister for Immigration made it so clear it was coming from him.' Aamer began to recognise that detention policy was guided more by politics than law. He believed that ACM and the Minister for Immigration would create their own rules, regardless of any legal rights detainees had. He gave the example of cameras being banned from detention centres;

> There is no camera allowed in the detention centre and no camera allowed around detention centre for 500 metres. There is no law in Australia that can prove that, but it is a local law to prevent people to know what's happening. When many officer would came and ask me 'Do you have a camera in your place?' I'm not answering that question. 'Is that law or is that like a local law you made it?' (Aamer)

Aamer said that 'after almost a year I start to take a big step towards activism outside ... I clearly stated that from now on I'll work hard to try to break the system.' Aamer's analysis shifted from an initial trust in the official systems to achieve justice for individuals, during which time his strategy was to engage in individual advocacy and education about the refugee status determination process, to believing that the system itself was corrupted by border protection politics. He changed his strategy accordingly to target the system itself. Aamer said that when he realised 'they are doing it deliberately,' he 'didn't feel any despair,' but instead told himself 'Oh well, it's time to make it right.'

Aamer stated that the 'local' making of laws left much of detention life in a 'grey zone,' a grey zone which enabled the arbitrary exercise of power by officials, but which also gave him room to move. 'That was my field of play, I can play there.' Aamer thought carefully about his skills and positioning, as well as his reading of Australian politics around asylum seeking and detention, and decided on his approach. 'I would divide into three main streams I was working on activism wise':

- Legal strategy
- Medical and mental health strategy
- Media strategy

Legal Strategy

Although he had now pledged that he would 'work to break the system,' Aamer continued to work with individuals in detention to try to understand their claims and to find them a good pro bono lawyer. He recognised that the system would not be changed quickly and in the meantime, individuals had to work within the system. As well as individual case work, Aamer also hoped the 'lawyers will be able to change things' and passed on information to lawyers lobbying for law reform.

Medical Strategy

During his first year in detention, Aamer started to notice patterns of mental ill-health among longer term detainees. Initially, his response to this observation was to prioritise who to help with their case first:

> I started to realise the mental health problems and then I realised the sooner I get someone out the better because eventually they are not getting

> any better, it will get worse. So with time I started to prioritise whom I shall work for urgently and support first is the people who need to get out sooner. (Aamer)

At the same time, Aamer soon started asking more systematic questions. He wondered if the people he saw had any pre-existing mental health issues before detention or if the symptoms he saw were caused by detention. He decided, within a few months of arrival, to 'run a core study,' tracking people's mental health status from 'day one over a long period of time and document everything … and see whether if they are trailing into serious mental health issues.' Aamer noted that Australia's detention policy meant that 'unfortunately many of them stay that many years, which made the research possible.' He described Villawood as a 'paradise for mental health researchers … in a negative way … It's way out of the percentage of unhealthy people, probably anywhere I've seen.'

Aamer was aware of the cultural status of doctors and medical professionals and recognised that, although he was a detainee without formal legal status, he had cultural status as a doctor. He also holds a very high opinion of the commitment of doctors to the Hippocratic Oath and their medical ethics. He believed that if he could document what he saw happening in detention and get the news out to the international medical community, 'all the medical professionals would not let that happen … Really I held my hope very high with that horse to win.' Aamer explained that in 1995, Saddam Hussein 'introduced this decree of shaming soldiers who deserted the army by putting a burning sign, a permanent scar on their head... and cut part of their ear.' Saddam Hussein ordered doctors to conduct these operations. 'I still remember that despite his dictatorship and his perfect system as a superpower … countless surgeons resigning and few consultant frankly refused to do it. They disappeared. We never see them again.' After two months, Hussein had to repeal the decree as no doctors would conduct the surgery in spite of threats and disappearances. Seeing the resolve of doctors in a more extreme situation gave Aamer 'a big hope that well, it comes to kind of like doctor-patient relationship. You can still rely on that. So I was really hoping on the medical … in Australia and internationally.'

Aamer asked a detention visitor to find out if any previous studies had been conducted on mental health and detention. Through this he obtained articles written by Derrick Silove, Zachary Steel and Kevin O'Sullivan. He made contact with each of them and discovered that O'Sullivan had previously worked as a psychologist at Villawood detention centre. He discussed his research idea with him. Throughout his time in detention, Aamer kept meticulous notes about his fellow detainees' length of time in detention, their mental health, the detention environment and events happening to the individuals, such as refusals of claims, and conducted semi-structured interviews with thirty-three long-term detainees. Through their research, Aamer and O'Sullivan identified a four-stage process of decline in people detained in excess of nine months. They wrote up this study, naming what they observed 'Immigration Detention Stress Syndrome,' and it was published in the *Medical Journal of Australia* in 2001 while Aamer was still in detention (Sultan and O'Sullivan 2001). The article received extensive media coverage as well as reaching the medical community (CNN 2001; Hassan 2001; Manne 2001; Nowak 2001), and prompted the Minister for Immigration to publish a letter refuting the work in the following edition of the journal (Ruddock 2002). Aamer received a High Commendation in the Human Rights and Equal Opportunity Commission's Human Rights Awards in December 2001. The article continues to be regularly cited by medical and other researchers (Kenny et al. 2004; Robbins et al. 2005; Robjant et al. 2009;).

Media Strategy

Aamer recognised the absence of detainee voices in the media coverage of detention and resolved to 'try to be the voice from inside ... It's a very special position to be in to see things inside and then it's hard to be discredited, even by the government, for someone who is talking from inside because you already know better than the government.' Aamer was determined to use his position as a doctor inside detention to speak out against it:

> Here I can see the same attitude coming from many people, different ages, they do respect doctors to some extent and that was to my great benefit.

> We were having this debate with the government, so even with the Minister was coming and telling that Dr Sultan's statement was full of factual errors, but he just admit he was lying, he was telling me that I was lying. Still, it would be seen by most people well – I mean how could you imagine or people will not accept a fact that a doctor is telling lies easy. (Aamer)

He recognised that his voice would be harder to discredit than the voices of other detainees. He would use his status as a doctor to give a credible account of the treatment of detainees and the harms caused by detention.

Aamer had already spoken with journalists on several occasions when he met Jacquie Everitt, a journalist and lawyer who was then studying a Master's degree in International Law. She was researching 'something about international law about asylum seekers and children.' Aamer introduced her to the Badraie family, which consisted of six-year-old Shayan, his one-year-old sister Shabnam, father Saeed, and step mother Zahra.[6] The family had been in detention for one year and four months at the time (O'Neill 2008, 256). Shayan was severely traumatised by detention, particularly from witnessing self-harm, and violence between guards and detainees in Woomera. Shayan had been present during riots in Woomera, when tear gas and water cannons were used (for more on this see Chap. 6). He gradually became more traumatised, suffering from insomnia, bed wetting and nightmares. By the time Jacquie met him in July 2001, he had stopped eating, drinking and speaking and the family had been transferred from Woomera to Villawood due to his deteriorating health. Each time his condition reached a life-threatening stage, he was transferred to hospital for treatment. Each time he improved, he was returned to detention. All the medical staff who had treated Shayan, both in detention and in hospital, believed that his condition was a direct result of detention and that recovery was not possible while he was still there. All of them recommended that the family be released from detention (O'Neill 2008, 72).

[6] The Badraie family's real names are used here as their story is well documented in the public sphere.

Jacquie describes her first meeting with Shayan:

> The child's dark, half-open eyes stare sideways, unmoving and unblinking. It is the first time I have met him and this lifelessness shocks terribly... his skin has the waxy colourless look of death, and I wonder how long there is left (Everitt 2008, vii).

With medical opinion being ignored by the Minister, who has the power to release someone from detention on a bridging visa, Jacquie and Aamer resolved to bring Shayan's plight to public attention.

Jacquie wrote a feature article, 'Suffer the Children,' about Shayan and other children in detention, which was published in the *Sydney Morning Herald* on 1 August 2001 (Everitt 2001). This prompted Debbie Whitmont, a journalist with ABC's *Four Corners*, to contact Jacquie. Aamer, Jacquie and Debbie decided to get a camera to Aamer and film both Shayan and life in detention. Jacquie smuggled the camera into Villawood through the metal detector by wearing layers of silver necklaces and bracelets, coupled with charm and bravado, to get past the guards without a search. Aamer's admiration for her courage is clear:

> So Jacquie Everitt, the mother of seven kids and the international lawyer, she broke all the rules by being such a character, becoming such a naughty kind of girl by wearing all this silver ornaments and big winter coat to hide the camera under her arm so when the metal detector beeped she said 'Oh, it must be my jewellery …' (Aamer)

Aamer then filmed an interview with Saeed with Shayan's limp body across his lap. Aamer also spoke to the camera, explaining what life was like in detention. Aamer kept the camera for three days, smuggling tapes out through detainees held in the low security stage three compound, 'every day to make sure because there was a possibility the camera would be captured.' The footage went to air on national television on 13 August 2001 (Whitmont 2001) and caused a nationwide outcry. In many respects, this could be seen as an important turning point in community opinion about detention. It was the first time that footage had been filmed inside a detention centre without the government having editorial control. It showed a different side of the story and detainee voices were heard unmediated for the first time.

Aamer believed that speaking through the media to 'Australian people' was necessary. He stated 'that the government really wants this policy for a hidden agenda... Is it possible that they deliberately do that hard line to win the votes? If it's true, then it's a very dirty game.' He believed that 'most Australians are quite good hearted and well intentioned people' and that the government was telling them lies about 'dangerous boat people.' He described watching a television show in which a doctor became politicised about asylum seekers after treating some hunger strikers and realised that direct contact and personal stories were necessary to shift public opinion and government policy. He described it as 'a battle you have to win, not for one thing, for re-establishing your faith in something.' Aamer continued his three-pronged approach to resistance throughout his time in detention.

Post-Detention Activism

Aamer was granted a protection visa in July 2002. He took a couple of months 'off' to rest and recover from his three years in detention but then realised,

> the responsibility is still there, the feeling that it's unfinished work in a way. The cause or the argument was still, the issue that triggered all that. The sense of injustice was still there. Detention was still there. Kids were still in detention. The nation was still in the dreamy period and people in detention. (Aamer)

Aamer joined up with *Medicines Sans Frontieres* and visited six major Australian cities, setting up a shipping container in the mall and sitting inside it and talking to anyone that came along. He also went on a bicycle ride from Broken Hill in Western New South Wales to Geelong in Southern Victoria,[7] travelling through country towns meeting 'ordi-

[7] A distance of approximately 900 kilometres.

nary Australians' and getting to know his new country (Stephens 2002). Aamer met with activists and politicians and continued to advocate for an end to mandatory detention. He devised several strategies for talking to people about detention and boatpeople. 'So I get around and talk about it in 100,000 ways I would say. It depends on whom you're talking with.' When talking to politicians, Aamer would draw on the *Refugees Convention* and Australia's legal obligations; when talking to medical professionals, he talked about his study with Kevin O'Sullivan and the psychiatric harms caused by detention; when talking to church people he spoke of ethics and being true to your word; and when talking to others, he tried to explain why boatpeople 'come through the window' instead of the door.

Aamer still speaks to journalists, researchers, friends and anyone who is interested. He even considered writing a book about his experiences, but has decided against it: 'I believe that someone who writes a book needs to have skills of writing a book. I may end up causing damage to the cause by my lousy writing.'

Conclusion

The resistances of other detainees are documented in the following chapters. Detainees subverted, confronted, rebutted and eluded the power enacted upon them by the state in many ways: through refusal and riot, hunger strike and lip sewing, letter writing and cultivating contacts with journalists. Detainee resistances were multifaceted, opportunistic, courageous, creative and astute. Different readings of power, politics and law, coupled with different personalities, ethics, emotions, skills and opportunities to produce a ceaseless struggle. There was, as Foucault (1976, 96) theorised, 'no single locus of great Refusal,' but multiple, shifting, transitory resistances, temporary alliances, solidarity and lasting friendships, carefully planned actions and spontaneous eruptions. Power flowed through detention centres as the primary physical sites for sovereign exercise of power and asylum seeker agency and strategy, shaping relations between detainees, guards, government officials, health workers, visitors and all who had contact with the centres and the policy.

The following chapters will look at some specific strategies of resistance: escape, hunger strike and self-harm and riot.

References

Agamben, G. (1998). *Homo Sacer. Sovereign power and bare life*. Stanford: Stanford University Press.

Australian Broadcasting Corporation (ABC). (2001). Liberals accused of trying to rewrite history. *Lateline*, November 21. Transcript. Retrieved January 3, 2009, from http://wwwabc.net.au/lateline/ (home page).

Cable News Network (CNN). (2001). No day pass for detained doctor, December 9. Retrieved August 29, 2011, from http://articles.cnn.com/2001-12-09/world/aust.refugee.detention_1_asylum-seekers-philip-ruddock-detention-centers?_s=PM:asiapcf

Carlton, B. (2007). *Imprisoning resistance. Life and death in an Australian Supermax*. Sydney: Institute of Criminology Press.

Commonwealth Ombudsman (2001). *Report of an own motion investigation into the Department of Immigration and Multicultural Affairs' immigration detention centres*. Canberra: Commonwealth Ombudsman.

Crowley-Cyr, L. (2005). Contractualism, exclusion and 'madness' in Australia's 'outsourced wastelands'. *Macquarie Law Journal, 5*, 81–102.

Everitt, J. (2001). Suffer the children. *Sydney Morning Herald*, August 1. Retrieved November 12, 2010, from http://smh.com.au (homepage).

Everitt, J. (2008). *The bitter shore*. Sydney: Pan Macmillan.

Foucault, M. (1976). *The history of sexuality, Volume 1* (R. Hurley, Trans.). London: Penguin Books.

Foucault, M. (1997). *Society must be defended. Lectures at the College de France 1975–76* (D. Macey, Trans.). London: Penguin Books.

Hassan, T. (2001). Asylum seeker honoured. *AM*, ABC Radio, December 10, 2011. Transcript. Retrieved August 25, 2011, from http://www.abc.net.au/am/stories/s436257.htm

Human Rights and Equal Opportunity Commission (HREOC) (2004). *A last resort? National Inquiry into Children in Immigration Detention*. Sydney: Human Rights and Equal Opportunities Commission.

Human Rights and Equal Opportunity Commission (HREOC) (2005). *Report of an inquiry into complaints by immigration detainees concerning their detention at the Curtin Immigration Reception and Processing Centre: HREOC*

Report No. 28. Sydney: Human Rights and Equal Opportunities Commission.

Joint Standing Committee on Migration (JSCM) (2000). *Not the Hilton. Immigration detention centres: Inspection report*. Canberra: Commonwealth of Australia.

Kenny, M. A., Silove, D., & Steel, Z. (2004). Legal and ethical implications of medically enforced feeding of detained asylum seekers on hunger strike. *eMedical Journal of Australia, 180*(5), 237–240.

Maley, W. (2003). Asylum-seekers in Australia's international relations. *Australian Journal of International Affairs, 57*(1), 187–202.

Manne, R. (2001). Punishing toll of detention centres. *The Press*, December 11. Retrieved August 29, 2011, from http://business.highbeam.com/62849/article-1P2-17459784/punishing-toll-detention-centres

Nowak, R. (2001). Detention destroys asylum seekers' mental health. *New Scientist*, December 19. Retrieved August 29, 2011, from http://www.newscientist.com/article/dn1707-detention-destroys-asylum-seekers-mental-health.html

O'Neill, M. (2008). Blind Conscience. Sydney: University of New South Wales Press.

Pugliese, J. (2002). Penal asylum: Refugees, ethics, hospitality. *Borderlands, 1*(1). Retrieved December 21, 2014, from http://www.borderlands.net.au/vol1no1_2002/pugliese.html

Robbins, I., MacKeith, J., Davison, S., Kopelman, M., Meux, C., Ratnam, S., et al. (2005). Psychiatric problems of detainees under the Anti-Terrorism Crime and Security Act 2001. *The Psychiatrist, 29*, 407–409.

Robjant, K., Hassan, R., & Katona, C. (2009). Mental health implications of detaining asylum seekers: Systematic review. *British Journal of Psychiatry, 194*, 306–312.

Rogalla, B. (2003). Modern-day torture: Government sponsored neglect of asylum seeker children under the Australian mandatory immigration detention regime. *Journal of South Pacific Law, 7*(1). see: http://www.paclii.org/journals/fJSPL/vol07no1/11.shtml

Ruddock, P. (2002). Asylum seekers and health care. *Medical Journal of Australia, 176*(2), 85.

Stephens, T. (2002). Freed asylum seeker looks for Australia's soul. *Sydney Morning Herald*, October 9. Retrieved August 26, 2011, from http://www.smh.com.au/articles/2002/10/08/1034061205727.html

Sultan, A., & O'Sullivan, K. (2001). Psychological disturbances in asylum seekers held in long term detention: A participant–observer account. *Medical Journal of Australia, 175*(11), 593–596.

Tazreiter, C. (2006). Security and the use of state violence. Justifications and limits in the treatment of asylum seekers. In J. Madeira & I. Gozaydin (Eds.), *Evil, law and the state*. Oxford: Inter-Disciplinary Press.

Whitmont, D. (2001). The inside story. *Four Corners*, ABC Television, August 13. Transcript. Retrieved February 16, 2012, from http://www.abc.net.au/4corners/stories/s344246.htm

Zannettino, L. (2008). En/countering the camp: Bare life, bio-politics and diaspora in Australian refugee communities. Presented at *Diasporas: Exploring critical issues. Inter-disciplinary. Net First Global Conference*. University of Oxford, Oxford, July 5–7.

4

Escape

* * *

> It was so difficult to live in detention; there was so much panic and people fighting because of the limitation with everything. There was no room for living. Resources were limited. People were frustrated because there was no result and no decision. No one was getting through. People were getting frustrated with the whole situation and at the time we were thinking of so many things. I was thinking of escaping the detention centre and going to Canberra with a few people that I thought we can make this happen. We try to find a connection outside who can help us and go and chain ourselves to Parliament.
>
> Farshid, detained 3 years.

* * *

Between 1999 and 2008, there were 373 escapes from Australian immigration detention centres (O'Neill 2008, 103).[1] Section 197A of the

[1] Not all of these escapes were by asylum seekers. It is difficult to obtain an accurate breakdown of numbers of escapes in each facility and by each category of detainee (asylum seeker, visa overstayer, criminal deportee). 'Snapshot' figures available through the Australian National Audit Office (ANAO 2004, 141) report 48 escapes from Villawood IDC in 2002. Department of Immigration (DIMIA 2003) figures for 30 December 2002 report that Villawood then held 513 detainees, only

L. Fiske, *Human Rights, Refugee Protest and Immigration Detention*,
DOI 10.1057/978-1-137-58096-2_4

Migration Act 1958 (Commonwealth of Australia) makes it an offence to escape from immigration detention, although it does not define 'escape.' Various state and commonwealth laws define escape as absconding from custody, which includes prisons and the custody of a police or prisons officer (Butt and Hamer 2011, 213). 'Escape' implies that a person leaves lawful custody and continues to evade the law and, while some of the incidents of escape from immigration detention centres do fit this model, many more are better understood as acts of civil disobedience. In these instances, people breached a perimeter fence of a detention centre, but made no effort to evade capture and instead staged sit-ins or other forms of protest in the vicinity of the detention centre and submitted to the legal consequences of their actions. Escape as civil disobedience was aimed primarily at staging a protest which would be covered by the media and thereby give detainees an opportunity to insert their voices into the public debate on detention of asylum seekers. Escape also had another, probably unintended, consequence in establishing a legal status for detainees. Once charged with escaping custody, detainees became prisoners and so, as Arendt (1976) points out, were restored to a recognised legal status within the polis. This chapter explores escapes to evade detention and the omnipotent power of the state and escapes as civil disobedience.

Escape as Civil Disobedience

Throughout 2000, pressure on the capacity of Australia's detention centres steadily increased. New detention centres had been opened in Derby and Woomera in September and November 1999 to accommodate the rising numbers of asylum seekers coming by boat. However, the processing of refugee claims was sufficiently slow that there was a pervasive belief among detainees that claims were intentionally not being processed in order to punish asylum seekers for arriving unlawfully and also to act as a deterrent against further arrivals. Farshid explained that,

> Everything was getting tighter and tighter for us. For nearly seven months not more than a few people left the detention centre. We are getting more

14 of whom were unauthorised boat arrivals. These figures indicate that it is probable that most escapes from Villawood that year were by detainees other than asylum seekers.

> and more people coming in and not many people get processed. Probably they try to send their signal as much as possible to Indonesia that this is not a good place. (Farshid)

Detainees lost hope with established processes and began to think about what they could do to draw attention to their plight. At the same time, Australia was preparing to host the 2000 Olympics and the Olympic torch was making its goodwill tour around the country. Detainees recognised the irony of the situation and saw this as a unique opportunity to stage a protest:

> We were thinking all the time about how we can protest and create an awareness for the Australian people that we are not demanding as they are told... We can make a protest; that is the best time. We are all looking at the torch and looking at Australia. Getting all this publication. It is going to be very embarrassing – when the torch of the Olympics is taking the spirit of brotherhood and multi-nationalism and fairness, whatever good things with it and Australia is treating some people in that way. (Farshid)

Farshid and a few fellow detainees in Port Hedland began discussing different protests. They decided they wanted to organise a large-scale protest that included all nationalities and that was staged at all the large detention centres:

> With a group of people that were thinking, trying to plan together, we decided to grab people from different groups. Different boats had different nations, someone trusted – had some sort of big brother, some sort of leader, someone that they believe more and if we could convince that person we could convince a whole group. So for some time I was talking to different people from different groups, and I was trying to convince them that this is good for all of us and then we found a connection with a relative of someone outside that knew someone in Woomera and also Curtin detention centre, and I thought that if we can do this all together that would be great. (Farshid)

The plan was that detainees from Port Hedland, Woomera and Curtin detention centres would break out and stage a short march near each detention centre before sitting down in protest overnight and then returning to detention the following day. The action was planned for

9 June 2000, to coincide with the launch of the Australian leg of the Olympic torch relay at Uluru that day (Zinn 2000).

Woomera Detention Centre

Ibrahim was not involved in the core planning group in Woomera, but was approached by the leaders a few days before the breakout and asked to assist on the day. He readily agreed.

> They planned already. They'd done everything, but they want some support from the other people. Especially the close ones to them because they didn't want to reveal anything about the plan until the time come. And when the time come, I was one of them, but I don't know anything. They came to me and said 'You have to swear. We gonna tell you this. It's the time now.' 'OK. I'm with you.' I didn't even hesitate for one minute. Nu-uh 'I'm with you.' Straight. (Ibrahim)

Ibrahim did not mention the Olympic torch relay in his account of the action. For him, his motivation was primarily about acting in solidarity with the organisers and to feel a sense of his own power in breaking the fence. 'To break the fence is a major thing. It's a major thing, you can't imagine. And forget about what happens after that. It's the fence. That's the thing—the fence!' Detainees in Woomera had been preparing for weeks. They smuggled some pliers from the workshop, '[swore] with each other on something just to make it a strong bond between each other' and allocated tasks to different people. At approximately 2:00 a.m., three detainees used the smuggled pliers to cut a hole in the fence

Ibrahim's job was to cover the edges of the hole with a blanket and hold it back while detainees slipped through. Once out, a group of approximately 300 people began the walk to Woomera town centre (Lohr 2000). They were joined by two more groups of approximately 100 detainees each over the next few hours. The detainees gathered in the central mall around the public telephones. Some chanted, 'We want freedom!' and similar slogans, while others sat and rested after the three-kilometre walk. Ibrahim recalls his surprise at the Woomera residents' arrival: 'People surprised, seems to me they know nothing about the camp, people in Woomera.'

The detainees were soon surrounded by ACM guards and were prevented from moving around the town. On the second day of the protest, food and water was given to the children, but adults were instructed that if they wanted to eat, they could do so back in detention (Lohr 2000; Oakley 2000). The Department of Immigration instructed local shopkeepers to close their businesses, thus ensuring that detainees could not buy food or water. Ibrahim described it as a 'siege,' aimed not only at preventing access to food and water, but also at keeping detainees from speaking directly to local residents or the media:

> Well, the people in the town can't [help us] because the siege was really strong, so no-one could get close to us. Because they told them we are dangerous, we are criminals. So who wants to help a criminal? And people listening to the authorities. That's OK. We understand this, but what the company have done to us is really horrible to prevent you to drink water. The water just a few metres from me. And the third day people start to fall over and ambulance start to get them. So every few minutes there's someone falling on the floor because no food and nothing for three days and it was really horrible. (Ibrahim)

The mass breakout, as anticipated by organisers, attracted significant media attention and nominated detainee spokespersons told the media of long delays in processing their applications, their complete isolation from the outside world, mistreatment by the guards in detention and poor food and facilities at the centre (Coleman 2000; Debelle and Clennell 2000a, b). Detainees requested that the Minister for Immigration come to speak with them and that their cases be processed quickly:

> We need someone from the government to come down to ask us why we have done this. We are not violent people. We don't want to give the image for the people in Australia that we are violent people or that we are criminals or whatever… We done something wrong maybe, but we have not another choice. You know what I mean? So we try to explain this for the people. OK get someone to talk to us and we will go back peacefully to the camp. We don't want to harm anyone. We need someone to talk to him [Minister Ruddock], to know what's gonna happen about our cases, our future. We gonna stay here forever in this camp or what?! (Ibrahim)

After two nights, a number of detainees were hospitalised due to lack of food and water:

> So on the third day it was really crisis. Because some people tried to break the siege to drink some water, and they start to fight with them. And the guys were very weak, you can imagine what happened. They just allowed the kids to drink some water, and a little bit a small amount for the women. I can't believe it, seriously, I can't. Even when I remember that, seriously, that this was going on in Australia. Is this Australia? You can't do it like this. (Ibrahim)

Departmental negotiators promised detainees that their cases would be processed and that the Minister would come to meet with them, but only if they agreed to return to detention. There was some dispute among the protesters about what to do.

> Some people said 'Come on, that's enough guys, let's just go back. There's nothing gonna happen, we gonna lose it.' And some they said 'No, we get out of the camp, we not going back. We need to get out of Australia now, not just out of the camp. We don't want Australia anymore.' So it was some differences between people want to go back, people want to stay and to fight, to keep fighting, but… to fight who? (Ibrahim)

Eventually, all the protesters agreed to return to detention. Buses were organised to take people back, but a group of detainees, including Ibrahim, in a final act of defiance, refused to go on the bus:

> But when they ask us to go back to the camp, we decide to go back walking. We came to Woomera walking, we not going to ride in the bus. Because they brought some buses for us to take everyone back and we said to them whoever wants to go on the bus, that's alright, but we going walking on our feet. We came to here walking, and we going back walking. (Ibrahim)

Curtin Detention Centre

While the Woomera breakout lasted for three days, the breakouts in Port Hedland and Curtin only lasted a matter of hours. Curtin detention centre is located on a military base approximately forty kilometres south-east of

Derby, Western Australia and is surrounded by seemingly endless miles of desert. Detainees there managed to break a hole in the fence, and about 150 people left the detention centre and began walking along the only road. The police quickly established a roadblock and intercepted the escaped detainees (Gray 2000). Most escapees were returned to Curtin detention centre, but twenty-four people were arrested and charged with escape.

Emad was released from Curtin just before the escape. He was aware of the plans and attempted to dissuade his fellow detainees from escaping. His dogged belief in 'the rule of law' precluded him from joining in any protest which broke a law. Although he disagreed with the escape, Emad was highly critical of the police response:

> Now, some of the guys succeeded in crossing the razor wire, and the police used the dogs against them. And they were able to catch every one of them and return them to the detention centre. Now the use of force, by even the police at that time, wasn't necessary, because you imagine in a small town like the one we… you know we're living in, it's so easy for police force, for the management to track everyone. Where you'll go? You know he's a foreigner. He don't know the country, he don't have money. They took all the money, they took the mobile phones, they took all our stuff – even the paperwork, the papers we have, the IDs, everything [upon arrival in detention]. So we don't have anything actually. So the use of force, you know just give you the impression that you're dealing with someone who have no understanding at all for human rights, and just you know they're treating you like a criminal, like a normal let's say convict. And this is not right, because we are covered by an international treaty. And this right was admitted 50 years ago – more than 50 years ago – after the World War II, you know to save the people who are in need for protection not to be mistreated again. So that's what happened unfortunately. (Emad)

He was also convinced that the escape triggered the subsequent processing of refugee claims:

> then surprisingly after June 2000, after the guys broke the razor wires and the media covered the whole incident there, the management decided to release most of the groups. I mean it shouldn't be this way … I think it was a big scandal to Philip Ruddock government in front of the international media, and the international reputation of Australia was the main element

> to think about. Seeing refugees who are being, let's say more than one year in the detention centre without their application being processed, and suddenly they broke out, they left… they jumped over the fence and the media started to cover this in the news. I think that's what pressured the government to release bigger groups. Otherwise I don't think they would release them. (Emad)

The Minister for Immigration and departmental officials maintained that protests did not accelerate the processing of refugee claims, but Emad's perception is not entirely unsupported. On 9 June 2000, Minister Ruddock appeared on the *7.30 Report* and confirmed that no one detained in Woomera had, at that time, received a decision about their refugee claim (ABC 2000a). The Department of Immigration does not publish statistics on how many people are released from each centre every month, and so Emad's claim cannot be positively demonstrated. However, the first visas for people detained at Woomera were issued in July 2000, one month after the mass breakout (Woomera Lawyers Group 2005; ABC 2000b).

Port Hedland Detention Centre

Detainees from Port Hedland also broke out as planned. The plan was to break the fence and a group of about 100 detainees would march to South Hedland (a satellite town about twenty kilometres away) and stage a twenty-four hour sit-in before returning to detention. Detainees had prepared slogans to chant, including, 'We want fairness and protection' and 'Protection not detention!' They had appointed spokespeople to talk to the media. As with the Curtin staged protest described by Farshid and Shahin in chapter 3, Farshid and his collaborators were determined that the detainees remain highly disciplined and present a peaceful image of themselves during the breakout. The main message they wanted to convey was 'that we are legitimate refugees, we want fairness and protection, we escaped from terrorist governments' (Farshid).

Mohammed was also involved in the breakout. He explained that the physical and psychological pressure in detention had been steadily building as the centre became increasingly overcrowded and no visas were being issued:

> Because suddenly government stopped every door, they closed the detention door and keep every man there. Suddenly detention become more than 800 detainees. Each room for six mattress got six people, five people, live together and they talk and they told they're going to be – that time it was the huge, huge protests started because the people try to figure out what they came to do and how to – because a lot of children and families there, that was the broke of the fence, all this stuff happening because huge people, the population there. (Mohammed)

The Port Hedland detention centre is located within the town of Port Hedland. Having seen the Woomera breakout the night before, the local police were prepared for a similar event at Port Hedland. Farshid explained that as soon as they broke the fence, they were confronted by a significant police presence:

> The day that we broke out they were so prepared. They had more than enough people, equivalent to anyone outside they had one or one and a half persons. So we were so surrounded. We couldn't get more than one kilometre out of detention and after I realised that people are getting beaten so severely. There was a guy I told you, an old guy, he was very brave but he was going according to the plan when the police grab him to take him to the police car. He was telling him 'I'm going myself, I'm not resisting' and the guy was holding his hair from back and bang his face to the corner of the car and there was blood, and I was thinking, 'God, that's bad.' I just raised my hand and I just ask everyone to be quiet and talked to the head of the business that this was planned and we wanted to have a peaceful protest and we are going back. We want to make a promise to go back. It wasn't a plan to escape, it was just a protest. People try to make this protest to the South Hedland city and then go back the next day. It wasn't a plan to escape, it was just a protest. (Farshid)

Fearing further violence, the escapees returned to detention. Seventeen people, including Farshid and Mohammed, were arrested and charged with escape from immigration detention. The charged men from both Curtin and Port Hedland were taken to Roebourne Prison, about

330 kilometres south of Port Hedland and held in the cells there. In several media interviews, the Minister spoke of the breakouts as criminal rather than legitimate protest actions, and he warned that any subsequent criminal convictions would have an adverse effect on visa grants for those directly involved (Gray 2000). Ministerial and Departmental statements were in keeping with government efforts to criminalise asylum seekers (see Chap. 6). However, the tactic had consequences that the government would neither have anticipated nor desired.

Criminal Charges

Detainees charged with escape from Curtin and Port Hedland detention centres met in Roebourne Prison and were able to talk about the different centres and form direct relationships, rather than relying on relayed messages and long distance phone calls. Having discussed plans for the breakout, they now discussed strategies for responding to the charges. They were also restored from the liminal non-status of 'asylum seeker' to a recognised legal status as a 'charged person.'

Farshid explained that most of the people facing charges wanted to follow legal advice to plead not guilty and to contest the charges, but that he thought it better to plead guilty:

> I wanted everyone to plead guilty. I can't talk but it seems that people had every right to be so afraid because it seems that the government was furious with what happened with the first protest in Australia. They needed to show some harsh reaction because they didn't want it to happen again. It could be a big sacrifice from those people. Anyway, we started something and there was no place to regret it. I had to plead guilty so I was only going to plead guilty and even the lawyer was thinking 'Does he know what he is doing?' Yes he does. We talk about this before. I couldn't really do anything with the charge because the charge was escape in the first place and the definition of escape was leaving legal custody even if the police officer asks you to stay it is escape so there is no way I could argue that one. I wanted to explain the situation and why. Mitigation after that. And for that reason I plead guilty. (Farshid)

Despite his fears about receiving a strongly punitive sentence intended to deter future breakouts, Farshid wanted to use his appearance in court to explain conditions in detention, including the overcrowding, slow processing and mistreatment by guards. He was shocked though, when the Public Prosecutor sought to lay additional charges against him, alleging he had weapons and intended to commit violent offences during the breakout.

> It was shocking and I was really afraid that so many things I was charged that I was making arson or had a knife or razor—I mean I'm a serial killer generally, not a protester. So it was a dangerous situation. (Farshid)

Fortunately for Farshid, the judge disallowed the charges due to lack of evidence. Farshid had taken time in prison to think about what he wanted to say and had 'prepared five pages for my lawyer to present to court, up to twelve or thirteen minutes, and I asked the court if I could read my statement.' The prosecution objected and accused Farshid of wasting time, but again the judge found in Farshid's favour saying, 'I want to hear him. Something is going on here and I don't know whether it is good or bad.' Farshid read his statement to the court and outlined the conditions in detention, why the detainees had escaped, how the breakout had been carefully planned to be a nonviolent protest, and how the detainees had abandoned the protest as soon as people were hurt. Farshid was also permitted to present character witnesses during the sentencing proceedings. The prosecution sought a two-year prison sentence in maximum security (the maximum sentence permitted under law at that time), but the judge pointed to Farshid's good standing in the detention centre, his work in translating and interpreting for others, his advocacy on behalf of fellow asylum seekers, and the fact that he had been escorted outside detention on several occasions with minimal security and without incident. The judge stated that he believed Farshid to be of good character and that maximum security imprisonment was not justified. He sentenced Farshid to three months in prison, saying that he accepted the breakout was a protest, and that Farshid seemed to be 'the most peaceful guy in the camp' (Farshid, paraphrasing the magistrate).

Ironically, efforts to further criminalise Farshid and use him and the others as an example of what prospective protester-detainees could expect served only to strengthen Farshid's confidence in justice beyond the walls of the detention centres:

> It was a life-changing experience. After that I was so brave. In the next detention centre every time they tell me they are going to send you to prison, the detention manager at Curtin said 'We are going to send you to prison' and I said, 'On what charges?' 'Child abuse.' And I said 'I would really like to see that in the court.' I was really getting confidence in the court. You find lots of justice in the independent court rather than the immigration court, so I was very grateful for that experience. (Farshid)

Ibrahim, who was not charged but was warned by fellow detainees and detention centre staff that the breakout would slow visa processing further, believes that it was because of the breakout that visa processing accelerated. Ibrahim was among the earliest groups of people to be released from Woomera in September 2000. In Curtin, Emad also believed that the breakout was a direct trigger for the resumption of processing. He said that 'the most powerful manner they followed I think, is the breaking out of the detention centre,' adding, 'it shouldn't be this way.'

Rather than producing a more compliant detainee population, the government's strategy of charging protesters with criminal offences actually functioned to embolden the detainees. Detainees began to see both that their protests exerted political pressure on the government, leading to faster processing and that Australian courts were sympathetic to detainees' reasons for protesting. Speaking in court provided a rare and valuable opportunity to air detainee voices in a formal setting that was open to the media, exposing the conditions of detention to public scrutiny, and where detainee grievances were acknowledged and often legitimised by judicial comments.

In 2001, the federal government amended the *Migration Act* to increase the maximum penalty for escape from two to five years of imprisonment. The amendment also provided that attempted escape was to be treated as an actual escape and would therefore attract the same penalty. In the *Explanatory Memorandum* accompanying the Bill, the government explained that these changes were 'prompted by instances of inappropriate behaviour by immigration detainees' (Parliament of Australia 2001, para 2). The mass breakouts from Woomera, Curtin and Port Hedland detention centres in June 2000 were specifically cited as reasons for 'the Government seek[ing] to strengthen its capacity ... to control inappropriate behaviour by immigration detainees' (Parliament of Australia 2001, paras 3 and 4).

No mention was made of the relatively lenient sentences issued to Farshid and his co-offenders. Nonetheless, the amendments were clearly a response to the breakouts and affirmed the government's position that 'escape' was to be treated as a serious criminal offence, carrying a lengthy prison term to reflect its gravity in the government's eyes. It is difficult not to read the amendments as a message to the judiciary of the government's position, which afterwards needed to be addressed when sentencing people convicted of escape.

Judicial Responses

It was not long before the judiciary needed to apply the new sentences on escaped detainees under the amended *Migration Act*. In March 2002, community activists organised a convergence of refugee supporters to meet at Woomera detention centre over the Easter long weekend. Protesters were able to reach the perimeter fence of the detention centre and, using bolt cutters and other tools brought with them, assisted detainees in making holes in the fence. Fifty detainees escaped. Most were recaptured within a few hours, and almost all were back in custody within a few days.

Three months later, on 27 June 2002, a smaller group of activists again assisted detainees to make a hole in the perimeter fence of Woomera detention centre, through which thirty-five detainees escaped. As with the earlier escape, most were captured within hours. Tariq was part of this escape and remained living in the community for three years before handing himself in to the Department of Immigration. His story of the escape is told later in this chapter. At least eleven recaptured detainees were arrested and charged with escape. Their cases were heard in the South Australian Magistrates Court, which took a lenient approach to sentencing. For the most part, magistrates imposed good behaviour bonds and did not record convictions against the detainees. The federal government appealed many of the sentences in the South Australian Supreme Court, arguing that the magistrates failed to give proper consideration to the legislature's policy intentions, as made clear through the 2001 amendments and *Explanatory Memorandum* outlined above.

Australian law allows only very narrow grounds for defending a charge of escaping legal custody. One of these is the defence of 'necessity' which may be available in conditions such as when the detainee's life is in immediate danger from a fire or other imminent threat and where escape is the only way to ensure survival (Grewcock 2010, 7). In the USA, the jurisprudence allows a defence against a charge of escape arising from 'intolerable' conditions of detention (Grewcock 2010, 5), a defence that Australian courts have not recognised.

Mahran Behrooz, a former immigration detainee, sought to test this in relation to immigration detention. Behrooz escaped from Woomera on 18 November 2001. He was arrested within a few hours and was charged with escape under the *Migration Act 1958* (Nicholson 2004). Behrooz sought to have the charge dismissed on the grounds that conditions in detention were such that detention went beyond 'administrative detention,' as lawfully permitted under the *Migration Act*, and were, in fact, punitive and therefore not lawful. If detention itself was not lawful, then no charge of escape could be laid (*Behrooz v Secretary, Department of Immigration and Multicultural Affairs* [2004] HCA 36, para 4).

In aid of his defence, he sought to introduce evidence about the conditions in Woomera and served summons on the Department of Immigration and ACM, requiring several documents to be provided to the court. ACM and the Department refused to hand over the documents and argued that as 'intolerable conditions' was not a recognised defence under Australian law, the documents that would provide evidence of the conditions in Woomera were therefore not relevant to the proceedings. Successive South Australian courts found in favour of the Department and ACM, and Behrooz appealed the decisions to the High Court of Australia.

Six justices of the High Court found in favour of the Department and ACM, with only Justice Kirby dissenting. The majority stated that 'the conditions under which he was being held do not form part of the statutory concept of "immigration detention"' (*Behrooz v Secretary, DIMIA* [2004] HCA 36, para 7) and therefore, detention at Woomera remained lawful. The majority justices said that civil protections are available to non-citizens in immigration detention and that 'if those who manage a detention centre fail to comply with their duty of care, they may be liable in tort. But the assault, or the negligence, does not alter the nature of the detention. It remains detention for the statutory purpose identified' (*Behrooz v Secretary, DIMIA* [2004] HCA 36, para 22). The remedies available to Mr Behrooz and other detainees were limited to lodging a complaint with relevant authorities or to launch civil action against the Department or ACM, but that even harsh or inhumane conditions of detention did not warrant 'an exercise of self-help' (*Behrooz v Secretary, DIMIA* [2004] HCA 36, para 10). The justices also addressed the jurisprudence from the USA permitting 'self-help' to evade intolerable conditions and noted that US cases rested upon 'the reach of the constitutional guarantees found in express terms not seen in Australia' (*Behrooz v Secretary, DIMIA* [2004] HCA 36, para 57). It followed, then, that if the conditions of detention are irrelevant to the lawfulness of detention, they cannot be relied on as a defence to the charge of escape (Crock et al. 2006, 180; Nicholson 2004).

Justice Kirby, in his dissenting judgement, noted the 'considerable body of disturbing evidence, assembled for the appellant's case, from which inferences might be drawn that the conditions of supposed "detention" in which he was kept were inhuman and intolerable' (*Behrooz v Secretary, DIMIA* [2004] HCA 36, para 96). Kirby J. concluded that, in his view, the Australian Constitution and international law enabled an interpretation of the *Migration Act* which indeed set parameters on the conditions of detention, and that Mr Behrooz had an argument that ought to be tested in law. In a strongly worded dissent, Kirby J. labelled the proposition that Mr Behrooz and other detainees should rely exclusively on a civil remedy in tort as 'absurd,' noting the physical (the fact of detention), legal (real risk of deportation before such an action could be heard), geographic, cultural, linguistic and financial barriers to detainees accessing necessary legal resources to launch such an action (*Behrooz v Secretary, DIMIA* [2004] HCA

36, paras 135–137). Kirby J. further commented that the High Court 'should not give a legal answer that future generations will condemn and that we ourselves will be ashamed of' (*Behrooz v Secretary, DIMIA* [2004] HCA, para 139).

Notwithstanding Kirby's strong dissent, the Behrooz case meant that intolerable conditions of detention were not available as a defence to criminal charges of escape in Australia. While no longer able to plead 'not guilty' on the grounds of inhumane conditions, the High Court's judgement did not, however, prevent detainees from raising the conditions of detention as factors of mitigation in sentencing proceedings.

Returning to the eleven or more detainees charged with escape following the March and June 2002 Woomera breakouts, the importance of the Behrooz case for detainees responding to escape charges can be seen. Following the Behrooz High Court decision, escaped detainees had no legal defence against the charge itself available to them, and faced up to five years in prison. A conviction also presented subsequent difficulties in meeting the character requirements for an Australian visa, should they eventually be found to be refugees. The potential consequences were very serious for individuals, and the Commonwealth intended to make a show of strength as a deterrent against possible future escapes (Parliament of Australia 2001, para 4).

Detainees charged with escape following the 2002 escapes from Woomera entered pleas of 'guilty' in the South Australian Magistrates Court and then brought information regarding the conditions of detention into proceedings as mitigating factors in sentencing. The court, in response, developed a practice of invoking a 'merciful approach to sentencing' (e.g., see *Bridle v Gomravi* [2005] SASC 295, 42) and imposed a range of lenient sentences on people convicted of escaping immigration detention. The sentences imposed ranged from 'no conviction recorded' and a twelve-month good behaviour bond of $100 (*Shillabeer v Hussain* [2005] SASC 198) to a three month prison sentence followed by a three-year good behaviour bond of $500 (*Bridle v Gomravi* [2005] SASC 295). One escapee was released with no conviction recorded and no conditions imposed upon his release (*Boonstoppel v Hamidi* [2005] SASC 248).

In sentencing comments, the magistrate(s)[2] referred to material put before the court regarding the conditions of detention and the impact on each charged detainee. In hearing an appeal on sentencing, Gray J. of the South Australian Supreme Court cited the magistrate's comments on the regular practice of addressing detainees by their ID numbers in immigration detention and the 'concern' which this caused Mr Kakar, observing that 'it is a very unusual thing in our society to refer to people by numbers. We are a community which prides itself on our individuality and the promotion of identity' (*Police v Kakar; Elder v Kakar* [2005] SASC 222, para 12). Gray J. allowed the appeal, imposed a three-year good behaviour bond and released Mr Kakar on his own recognisance (back into immigration detention).

In sentencing Sajid Hussain to a twelve-month good behaviour bond with no conviction recorded, the Magistrate said, 'I am very mindful of the material that is before me that relates to conditions at Woomera.' He/she then drew attention to Justice Kirby's comments in the Behrooz case, drawing particular attention to paragraph 96 (quoted above in this chapter), in which Kirby J. discussed publicly available information regarding the mistreatment of detainees in Woomera. The Magistrate also referred to a report by the United Nations High Commissioner for Human Rights, Justice Bhagwati, which was highly critical of conditions in Woomera and other detention centres (*Shillabeer v Hussain* [2005] SASC 198; *Boonstoppel v Hamidi* [2005] SASC 248).

In unconditionally discharging Abdul Amir Hamidi due to the seriousness of his mental ill-health, the Magistrate accepted that detention in Woomera was a major causal factor in his mental ill-health. The link between detention at Woomera IRPC and mental ill-health was noted in each of these cases and relied upon by the magistrate(s) to reach a conclusion that the men's 'personal antecedents allow a merciful approach to be taken when sentencing' (*Police v Kakar; Elder v Kakar* [2005] SASC 222, para 43). The legal reasoning of the Magistrate was that, 'while Mr Hussain's suffering does not excuse his behaviour, it does provide an

[2] Only transcripts from cases which were appealed are publicly available. In each case the original sentencing magistrate is not named and so it is not known how many different magistrates heard the cases.

explanation for his conduct and suggests that his criminal culpability is materially diminished' (*Shillabeer v Hussain* [2005] SASC 198, para 42). Despite the federal government's efforts (through the *Behrooz* High Court case) to exclude detention conditions from judicial review, detainees were still able to explain what life was like in detention in an official public forum. In response, the South Australian Magistrates Court appeared to be sympathetic to detainees' arguments that conditions in Woomera were indeed 'intolerable.'

The federal government repeatedly appealed against the sentences imposed by the Magistrates Court, arguing that in each case, the magistrate failed to adequately take into account the policy purpose of the legislative scheme of the *Migration Act*: to ensure the regulation and control of entry into Australia, and that maintaining order within detention centres was a key function of that policy and purpose. The Commonwealth further argued that the intention of the legislature to maintain control in detention centres was made clear by its increasing the penalty for escape to a maximum five years imprisonment in 2001. The accompanying *Explanatory Memorandum* stated that the increased penalty is intended to reflect the gravity of the offence of escape and 'that sentences imposed in relation to this offending ought to deter others from engaging in such conduct' (*Morrison v Behrooz* 2005 [SASC] 142, para 30). However, the South Australian Supreme Court upheld most sentences, determining that a 'merciful approach' was warranted because of the stresses inherent in immigration detention.[3]

Rights as a Criminal

Federal government attempts to further criminalise detainees and to extend the already extensive reach of its power over detainees, through

[3] The only changes to sentences were as follows: the sentence for Hamidi (discharged with no conditions) was amended to be discharged under the care of the Public Advocate. Justice Gray stated that 'Mr Hamidi's mental health problems require treatment and supervision.' Hadi Gomravi was initially sentenced to a 12 month good behaviour bond after being caught by Department of Immigration officials in Sydney eleven months after his escape from Woomera in March 2002. The SA Supreme Court imposed a three month prison sentence and a three year good behaviour bond instead.

both legislative amendments and criminal prosecution, failed. Detainees charged with escape, although compelled to plead guilty, found a political voice and experienced the status of a rights-bearing person recognised before the law.

Hannah Arendt (1976) theorised that criminals have more rights than asylum seekers and stateless people. She contended that what we speak of as 'human rights' are in fact 'national rights,' rights which exist only in so far as one is a member of a political community willing to guarantee those rights. Expulsion from a polity entails being stripped of one's rights and results in vulnerability to the goodwill (or otherwise) of a community of which one is not a member. 'His treatment by others does not depend on what he does or does not do... Privileges in some cases, injustices in most, blessings and doom are meted out to them... without any relation whatsoever to what they do, did, or may do' (Arendt 1976, 296). It was precisely this stripping of rights and subjection to arbitrary treatment which triggered the more dramatic protests in immigration detention centres, such as riots and escape (see Chap. 6 for more detail on arbitrary injustice). Ironically, Arendt contends, the most immediate way in which a rightless person can attain a status recognised by law, and thus be brought within the polity, is to commit a crime. Through being charged with a crime, an asylum seeker comes before the law as a charged person and therefore has access to a range of rights, such as the right to speak in a forum in which his or her speech is guaranteed by law and supported by effective enforcement mechanisms. 'When a rightless person commits a crime he is put in a better situation than other rightless people because he is at least being recognised by the law as a criminal' (Parekh 2004, 46).

As articulated so clearly by Farshid, asylum seekers in detention had no effective or accessible recourse to legal rights regarding their conditions of detention or their treatment in detention, but when brought to a court as a charged person, they were restored to the status of a rights-bearing person recognised by the law. In that forum, detainees' voices became meaningful and were given greater credibility and legitimacy when judges recognised their actions as protest or as a reasonable reaction to intolerable conditions. Formal recognition was a profound restoration beyond merely legal status, and restoring a person's experience of themselves as 'someone who matters.'

When detainees were sentenced to imprisonment, many found the regimen of prison preferable to immigration detention. Ismail reached the end of his sentence and asked the prison authorities '"Can I stay another month?" But unless you do something, no. 'Cos I find it's much better than detention centre. When I went there I start to go to English class 'cos before that I couldn't talk English at all, in prison I start to go ... in class and I learned that and I want to stay more. And I want to do more things, not like in detention centre.' Sayed was sentenced to three months prison for escaping from Port Hedland detention centre. He too found that time 'much easier to spend' because 'you know why you're there,' 'when your time finishes,' and the rules are consistent and predictable.

Mohammed received a three-month prison sentence for his role in the June 2000 Port Hedland breakout and served his time in Roebourne Prison. Roebourne Prison was identified as a 'failing prison' by the Western Australian Inspector of Custodial Services in 2002. The Inspector described the prison as,

> a hard prison for prisoners to be held in and staff to work in. The Inspector has been well aware, since his first visit to the prison in September 2000, that the prison's service delivery standards were inadequate; that prisoner conditions were poor, and as a consequence the prison was squarely in the category of a failing prison. Note was taken of the overbearing security arrangements in the prison, the squalid conditions of much of the cell accommodation, the poor hygiene standards and conditions in the prison kitchen, the inadequacies of ventilation and cooling systems in several parts of the prison and the shortage of purposeful activity for prisoners in the form of work or educational opportunities. (WAICS 2002, 6–7)

Mohammed, who was in Roebourne Prison at the time of the Inspector's visit in September 2000, had a very different opinion. 'Three months Roebourne. That was the best ever place I'd been. Yeah that was much better than any, any detention I've been in, Villawood, everywhere. But the Roebourne, it was—I give it five stars.'

The right to speech that matters and to be heard extended beyond the semantic or psychological implications as described by Farshid, to include material differences to the conditions that a person can be held in. In response to Behrooz's request to produce documents relating to the conditions in Woomera detention centre, the federal government did not argue that conditions are not inhumane or degrading, only that the conditions of detention do not affect the lawfulness of that detention. While detained as an unlawful non-citizen, a person had extremely limited rights enforceable in law. When detained as a convicted criminal, a person had more rights and more effective protections of those rights.

Escape as Escape

As mentioned in the opening paragraphs of this chapter, not all escapes were acts of civil disobedience intended to protest treatment in detention. Some escapes were simply attempts to get away from intolerable conditions. Hadi Gomravi, who escaped from Woomera in March 2002, remained at large until his recapture by Department of Immigration officials in February 2003 (*Bridle v Gomravi* [2005] SASC 295). Upon his recapture, he was taken back into detention and charged with escape. He was sentenced to a twelve-month good behaviour bond, which was increased to a three-month prison term and a three-year good behaviour bond upon appeal. Tariq escaped from Woomera detention centre on the second occasion that outside protesters assisted detainees to escape in June 2002. He remained living physically 'free' but unlawfully until he surrendered himself to the Department of Immigration in 2005. It is interesting to note that a number of the detainees who escaped with Tariq on 27 June 2002 were prosecuted. By the time Tariq handed himself in to authorities on 21 June 2005, the federal government appeared to have lost its appetite for prosecuting escapees. Tariq discerned a change in the political environment, and it was this, alongside the ongoing stress of a life without legal status, which prompted him to turn himself in. Tariq was not prosecuted and, ultimately, was granted a Temporary Protection Visa and released from detention lawfully.

Tariq's Story

Tariq arrived in Australia in August 2001 and was detained in Woomera IRPC until his escape on 27 June 2002. He spent three years 'couch surfing' in Melbourne before presenting himself to the Department of Immigration and being re-detained. He spent a further five and a half months in detention before he was granted a Temporary Protection Visa and released into the community.

Tariq explained that several people escaped in March 2002 when pro-refugee activists organised a mass action at Woomera. The activists managed to reach the detention centre's perimeter fence and together with the detainees, they made a large hole in the fence and detainees leapt out. The activists hid escaped detainees in cars and attempted to drive people away from the area and into the relative safety and anonymity of Australia's larger cities. Very few made it and most escapees were back in detention within a day (for a more detailed account, see O'Neill 2008, 96–103). However, Tariq did not escape at this time because he was scared both of the activists ('they were crazy looking people') and of,

> what immigration would do, of what would happen. But a few months later I heard about a man in Curtin, they injected him and deported him. We heard about all this, about who was being deported and we were scared – who's next? I was scared that the next one would be me. Am I the next one? I started freaking out. (Tariq)

Tariq did not plan his escape three months later. He was returning to his room after handing a paper to the Department of Immigration office when he heard a commotion and car horns beeping. He went over to see what was happening and saw, 'activists, they were funny looking, hippies with dreadlocks …' According to Tariq, the activists, 'went crazy and broke the fence.' Still in his pyjamas and without his cigarettes, Tariq took his chance and slipped through the hole in the fence and ran towards the activists' cars:

> There were five cars, four of them were full of refugees, a van with lots of refugees in the back. I went to the last car, there was lots of fruit and

> vegetables in the back, no room for me. I ran round to the right side of the car – in Iran the driver sits on the left and the passenger on the right, but of course, it's different here and there was a hippy woman driving, maybe 50 years old. I couldn't speak English, but she told me to get in. There was another hippy couple in the front seat, so I jumped in, I sit on her legs and we start driving. (Tariq)

Tariq and his rescuers evaded a roadblock by driving into the desert, with Tariq bouncing on his rescuer's lap throughout:

> We drove about one kilometre. You could see Woomera – little lights in the distance. She stopped the car and told me to get out, she said she'd be back at sunrise. I thought she meant sunset and I was scared I would die – it was very cold and I only had my pyjamas. (Tariq)

As sunset came, Tariq became fearful of dingoes, snakes and other dangerous creatures in the bush. The temperature was also plummeting and, believing himself to have been abandoned, he decided to go back to detention. He found the road and tried to wave down a car, and although a couple of cars passed, no one stopped. Tariq settled in for a cold and sleepless night in a water drain running under the road. Early in the morning, he emerged from the drain and before long, the activists returned and picked him up. They drove into the desert and set up camp, smoking marijuana, drinking and waiting for police searches to end and roadblocks to be removed. He remembers this time camping in the desert fondly:

> I met this girl, we stay the night together and … Well, probably you don't need this for your research, but it was the funniest bit! The fun part of the story. She slept with me five nights and on the morning she told me she is born the same day as me. The day, same month, same year – pretty freaky huh? (Tariq)

Of the thirty-five escapees, twenty-five were caught immediately, but ten (two Iranians and eight Afghans) camped in the desert 'and had a little celebration. We drank vodka—I think it was off, it was terrible vodka, but we had a little party to celebrate' (Tariq). After a week in the desert, the activists took the escapees to Sydney, Melbourne and Adelaide. Tariq went to Melbourne and was supported through a network of activists. Life as an 'illegal' was extremely difficult, and he had to constantly move, sleeping in spare rooms or on couches.

> I didn't know anyone in Melbourne. I met some people and stay with them a few weeks. They found another for me for a few weeks, a week, ten days, eight months, two weeks.... until three years. I get panic attacks since then. Heart problems, stomach problems, I have to drink soy milk. For three years I couldn't be in touch with my family. To call Iran you have to go out at night, I couldn't go out at night in case the cops catch you. You must always buy a ticket for the tram. You have to be VERY careful. It was SO stressful. No Centrelink (social security), no Medicare card if you get sick... But somehow there's a network. (Tariq)

Tariq had a series of casual cash jobs, washing dishes or painting houses, and was always vulnerable to exploitation. Tiring of a life in the shadows, he 'decided I had to do something about it, it was so stressful. And now things were changing. Petro Giorgio[4] was talking, there was more pressure on the government, more eyes on detention. So I thought maybe now, it's the time to give myself up and apply for a visa.'

Tariq went to the Refugee Immigration Legal Centre (RILC) and spoke with a lawyer. Together they went to the Department of Immigration, who were 'actually a little bit impressed that I had given myself up, not many people do that. I thought I had a chance now. Petro Giorgio was pushing.' Tariq was taken into detention in Maribyrnong (in Melbourne) before being transferred to Baxter, which he described as 'terrible.' Although his three years living unlawfully had been stressful, he does not

[4] Petro Giorgio was a Liberal Party backbencher (retired in 2010) who led a small group of fellow government MPs in challenging the government's position on asylum seekers. He began speaking publically against the government position, drafted a Private Members Bill to improve the rights of asylum seekers in detention, threatened to cross the floor and vote against the government on a 2006 bill and managed to negotiate with the Prime Minister for significant improvements, particularly getting children out of detention centres and getting a new class of bridging visa introduced to get long term detainees out. Giorgio's public criticism of the government's position became a key focal point for changing community attitudes (For more on Giorgio and fellow backbencher dissidents, see Fleay 2010, 121–126).

regret his escape. When he went to Baxter, he met a friend who was in Woomera when he first arrived:

> He was a fit and healthy young man, excellent soccer player, agile, energetic. When I went back after three years outside 'Reza' was still there, but a completely changed man. He was depressed, he didn't move much, and very slow. He didn't talk much, didn't make eye contact. I still see him now and he still suffers. He still doesn't look at anyone, he's very quiet. Damaged. (Tariq)

Tariq talked at length about the damage detention does and wondered how the people who spent long periods of time were doing now. He worries about the children who were detained, and one little girl in particular sticks out in his mind. She was in Woomera during the Easter convergence in 2002 and had tear gas sprayed directly at her. Tariq remembers her screams of pain and said she cried for two days. She was just eighteen months old and 'I think of her often and wonder how she is, if she still suffers.'

Tariq was found to be a refugee and was released from detention on 5 December 2005.

Conclusion

During the height of overcrowding, protests and political posturing about border protection, the federal government sought to use a range of methods to further criminalise and demonise asylum seekers in detention. Government ministers made many public comments about the protests in detention, casting escapes not as protest, but as further evidence that 'these people' were not law-abiding and would not be a welcome addition to Australian society. The government also amended the legislation to increase the powers of the Department of Immigration staff and subcontractors (at that time ACM) to search detainees and their property and to 'manage inappropriate behaviours' in detention centres. The *Explanatory Memorandum* and the first and second reading speeches accompanying these changes provided further opportunity for the government to portray asylum seekers not as conscious individuals protesting against intolerable treatment, but as an inherently criminal and difficult group. The third strategy of the government was to prosecute offenders through the criminal justice system for offences committed in detention. This final strategy was not particularly effective and, in fact, provided a stage for detainees to explain their own actions and draw attention to their protest in a formal setting.

As well as seeking to insert themselves in the polis in order to make their speech and actions meaningful through the criminal justice system, detainees also used their bodies to make visible the hidden injustices of detention and to create a space in which their voices would be heard by 'ordinary Australians.' The following chapter looks at embodied protests, particularly through hunger strike, lip sewing and self-harm.

Bibliography

Arendt, H. (1976). *The origins of totalitarianism*. Orlando: Harcourt Publishing.

Australian Broadcasting Corporation (ABC). (2000a). Ruddock on illegal immigrants' break-out. *7.30 Report*, ABC Television, June 9. Transcript. Retrieved October 7, 2011, from http://www.abc.net.au/7.30/stories/s139044.htm

Australian Broadcasting Corporation (ABC). (2000b). Peolicy leaves asylum seekers out in the cold. *7.30 Report*, ABC Television, July 17. Transcript. Retrieved October 7, 2011, from http://www.abc.net.au/7.30/stories/s153036.htm

Australian National Audit Office (ANAO) (2004). *The Auditor-General Audit Report No. 54 2003–04. Performance Audit. Management of the Detention Centre Contracts—Part A. Department of Immigration and Multicultural and Indigenous Affairs*. Canberra: Commonwealth of Australia.

Butt, P., & Hamer, D. (2011). *LexisNexis concise Australian legal dictionary* (4th ed.). Chatswood: LexisNexis Butterworths.

Coleman, M. (2000). Woomera escapees describe detention centre life. *PM*, ABC Radio National, June 8. Retrieved October 7, 2011, from http://www.abc.net.au/pm/stories/s138661.htm

Crock, M., Saul, B., & Dastyari, A. (2006). *Future Seekers II. Refugees and irregular migration in Australia*. Annandale: Federation Press.

Debelle, P., & Clennell, A. (2000a). Woomera under siege after 500 escape camp. *Australian Associated Press*, June 9. Retrieved September 24, 2011, from http://www.nahrain.com/d/news/00/06/aust009.pdf

Debelle, P., & Clennell, A. (2000b). 250 more refugees escape camps. *Australian Associated Press*, June 10. Retrieved September 24, 2011, from http://www.nahrain.com/d/news/00/06/aust009.pdf

Department of Immigration and Multicultural Affairs (DIMIA). (2003). Mass escape foiled at Villawood. *Media Release*, January 1. Retrieved October 3, 2011, from http://www.immi.gov.au (homepage).

Fleay, C. (2010). *Australia and human rights: Situating the Howard government.* Newcastle-Upon-Tyne: Cambridge Scholars Publishing.

Gray, D. (2000). WA illegals in copycat breakouts. *The Age*, June 10. Retrieved October 7, 2011, from http://www.watelevision.com.au (homepage).

Grewcock, M. (2010). The great escape: Refugees, detention and resistance. *University of New South Wales Faculty of Law Research Series, Paper 8*. Retrieved September 21, 2011, from http://law.bepress.com/unswwps/flrps10/art8

Lohr, R. (2000). Desperate refugees break out of Australian detention centres. *World Socialist Website*, June 13. Retrieved September 23, 2011, from http://www.wsws.org/articles/2000/jun2000/ref-j13.shtml

Nicholson, J. (2004). Does the Australian constitution allow harsh and inhumane detention? The decision in Behrooz. *Research Note No. 19, 2004–05*, Laws and Bills Digest Section, Australian Parliamentary Library, November 16. Retrieved September 26, 2011, from http://www.aph.gov.au/library/ (home page).

Oakley, V. (2000). Immigrants back in custody. *Australian Associated Press*, June 10. Retrieved September 24, 2011, from http://www.nahrain.com/d/news/00/06/aust009.pdf

O'Neill, M. (2008). *Blind conscience*. Sydney: University of New South Wales Press.

Parekh, S. (2004). A meaningful place in the world: Hannah Arendt on the nature of human rights. *Journal of Human Rights, 3*(1), 41–53.

Parliament of the Commonwealth of Australia (2001). *Migration Legislation Amendment (Immigration Detainees) Bill 2001. Explanatory memorandum.* Canberra: House of Representatives.

Western Australian Inspector of Custodial Services (WAICS). (2002). *Report of an announced inspection of Roebourne regional prison April 2002: Report No. 14*. Perth: Office of the Inspector of Custodial Services. Retrieved February 21, 2012, from www.custodialinspector.wa.gov.au

Woomera Lawyers Group. (2005). Submission to the Senate Legal and Constitutional Committee. *Inquiry into the administration and operation of the Migration Act 1958*, August 8. Retrieved October 7, 2011, from http://www.aph.gov.au (home page).

Zinn, C. (2000). Olympic torch lights up Australia. *The Guardian*, June 9. Retrieved June 23, 2011, from http://www.guardian.co.uk/world/2000/jun/09/2

Court Cases

Behrooz v Secretary, Department of Immigration and Multicultural and Indigenous Affairs. (2004). HCA 36; 219 CLR 486; 208 ALR 271; 78 ALJR 1056 (August 6, 2004).
Boonstoppel v Hamidi. (2005). SASC 248 (July 1, 2005).
Bridle v Gomravi. (2005). SASC 295 (August 9, 2005).
Morrison v Behrooz. (2005). SASC 142 (April 15, 2005).
Police v Kakar; Elder v Kakar. (2005). SASC 222 (June 17, 2005).
Shillabeer v Hussain. (2005). SASC 198 (June 2, 2005).

5

Hunger Strike, Lip Sewing and Self-harm

* * *

> My hunger strike was about twenty-one days ... I lost nearly twenty-five kilo when I was on that. The reason I break it, I couldn't move nothing. I was just lying there and I didn't know what's going on around me. Suddenly I saw they put their syringe through my nose, through my thing and it was really hurting in my nose. It was really hurtful. They broke my fast. I was kind of like fainted. I didn't know what was going on and all I was doing, just sleeping. I just wanted to die. I didn't want to see how I'm going to die, I just wanted to sleep, sleep, sleep and go under the blanket ... After fourteen days or fifteen days I was very, like kind of conscious, you know. I didn't know what's going on. It was terrible. They forced me ... they hold my hands and they put the syringe in my nose by force because I was nearly. . . I wanted to die really bad. So I was close to it.
>
> Baha'adin, detained 5 years.

* * *

Hunger strike, even of relatively short duration, can have serious effects on the body. In the first three days, the hunger striker will experience severe hunger pangs and stomach cramps. Muscle functioning

L. Fiske, *Human Rights, Refugee Protest and Immigration Detention*,
DOI 10.1057/978-1-137-58096-2_5

weakens and the immune system becomes impaired, increasing the risk of secondary infections and disease. After about one week, the striker will experience dramatic weight loss and every system in the body is adversely affected. From week two the striker's vital organs begin to atrophy: first the liver, intestines, kidneys and then the heart. The striker's pulse will slow, blood pressure falls and he/she experiences dizziness, lethargy, fatigue, faintness and headaches. The striker's concentration is significantly impaired and he/she becomes apathetic and bedridden. The 'ocular phase' occurs between days thirty-five and forty-two, in which progressive paralysis of oculo-motor muscles occurs, causing uncontrollable, involuntary rapid oscillation of the eyeballs and visual impairment. The striker becomes progressively less able to swallow water and suffers compulsive vomiting despite having an empty stomach. This phase lasts approximately one week, and once it passes, the striker is left physically weakened, sleeps extensively, loses awareness of their surroundings and often becomes incoherent. Death occurs anytime from day forty onwards (Kenny et al. 2004; World Medical Association 1991; ICTY 2009; Kenny and Fiske 2013). Recovery from a hunger strike is also dangerous. Re-feeding following a strike of twenty-one days or more carries dangers of oedema (excess water accumulating in tissues, including the lungs), encephalopathy and cardiac failure, among other serious medical consequences. Hospitalisation to enable close medical supervision of re-feeding is recommended for the first several days post-hunger strike (Peel 1997).

Hunger Strike and Self-harm in Australian Detention Centres

People detained in Australian immigration detention centres have used hunger strikes as a method of protest since detention was introduced in the early 1990s. In 1992, when mandatory detention was introduced, two detained asylum seekers from Cambodia went on a hunger strike. As their conditions deteriorated, each was taken to hospital for rehydration. Both refused to give consent for medical treatment. The government applied to the court to have the two women declared 'prisoners,' thereby giving it power to enforce medical treatment against the will of the strikers. Before the case could be determined, the government introduced Regulations 182C and 182D to the *Migration Regulations*. These regulations gave the Minister of Immigration and the Secretary of the Department power to authorise non-consensual medical treatment, where there is a serious risk to the detainees' health, and for the use of 'reasonable force' (such as physical restraint or chemical sedation) to enable the treatment to be effected (*Minister for Immigration, Local Government and Ethnic Affairs v Gek Bouy Mok* [1992] Powell J., 4982). This power was redrafted in 1994 and is now contained in Regulation 5.35 of the *Migration Regulations*. In its 1998 *Inquiry into Immigration Detention*, the Human Rights and Equal Opportunity Commission (HREOC 1998, 102) reported that Regulation 5.35 had not been used. Despite several written requests for information from August 2010 onwards and several follow-up telephone calls, the Department of Immigration has not confirmed how many times Regulation 5.35 has been invoked in response to detainees on hunger strike. In July 2002, the Minister for Immigration confirmed in an ABC *Radio National* interview that he had used Regulation 5.35 to force feed hunger striking detainees, saying that, 'I think the state has a responsibility to ensure in those circumstances, that they survive, and that's what we've sought to do' (ABC 2002). *The Guardian* reported in 2014 that Regulation 5.35 had been used to force feed hunger strikers ten times between 2005 and 2012 (Farrell 2014).

The use of hunger strikes by immigration detainees increased between 2000 and 2003 as the number of people incarcerated and length of detention increased. Hunger strikes are again being frequently reported since the re-introduction of the 'Pacific Solution' in 2012, with the attendant prolonged periods of detention in poor conditions with little or no progress of refugee claims (Laughland 2014; Hall 2013). It is difficult to establish a clear picture of the incidence of hunger strike as information on hunger strikes is not separately collected or published by the Department of Immigration. Some inquiries into immigration detention have revealed that in the six-month period between January and June 2002, 'there were 760 major incidents involving 3030 detainees across all detention centres' (HREOC 2004, 299). These incidents included 248 incidents of self-harm as well as two mass hunger strikes involving several hundreds of detainees (HREOC 2004, 299–310). The United Nations Working Group on Arbitrary Detention, citing the Department of Immigration, noted 264 incidents of self-harm in the eight-month period between 1 March and 30 October 2001 (UNWGAD 2002, 12). Hunger striking in Australian detention centres was possibly most frequent and widespread in 2002. Hundreds of detainees across all detention centres were involved in a series of hunger strikes throughout the year. Some strikes lasted only days, while others extended beyond two weeks, the point at which strikers face a high risk of serious medical consequences. While most strikers were persuaded to end their fasts through negotiation, some fasts were broken only with force feeding, against the will of the strikers. Particularly significant mass hunger strikes were undertaken in January and June 2002 at Woomera detention centre.

The Story of One Hunger Strike: Woomera Detention Centre, January 2002

Following a government announcement to 'freeze' the processing of refugee claims from Afghans, detainees at Woomera detention centre launched a hunger strike in January 2002. Detainees reported that 370 people participated in the strike, although the Department of Immigration maintained that 'only' 259 people were involved (Barker 2002). Most strikers were Afghans directly affected by the policy announcement, but Iranians, Iraqis and detainees of other nationalities also joined the hunger strike in solidarity with the Afghans. Men, women and children participated in the strike, with up to seventy detainees also sewing their lips shut both to 'prove' they were not eating and to symbolise their voicelessness and silencing by the Australian government.

The hunger strike lasted for sixteen days, with strikers dragging mattresses outside and lying in the sunlight for the duration of the strike. The federal government called in members of its hand-picked Immigration Detention Advisory Group (IDAG) to meet with the hunger strikers and attempt to restore the 'normal' functioning of the detention centre. Daytime temperatures at Woomera in January consistently reach higher than forty degrees Celsius and not infrequently exceed fifty degrees Celsius. At night, the temperature plunges to near freezing. Paris Aristotle, a member of IDAG and Director of the Victorian Foundation for Survivors of Torture, described the scene: 'In the blazing sun ... detainees lying or writhing under blankets ... a constant stream of stretchers move back and forth to the camp's medical centre as people collapse ... It was the most terrifying thing I had ever seen. I'll never forget it' (cited in O'Neill 2008, 91).

The protesters were initially calling for the processing of claims to be restarted, but the demands broadened to protest the appalling conditions at Woomera detention centre. The government remained firm in its position, refusing to be 'manipulated' by such 'barbaric' behaviour, accusing the hunger strikers of forcibly sewing shut the lips of their children and of secretly eating (Klocker and Dunn 2003). After spending several days at Woomera meeting with detainees and listening to their concerns, IDAG members Air Marshall Ray Funnell, former head of the Royal Australian Air Force, and Paris Aristotle flew to Canberra to meet with then Immigration Minister Philip Ruddock and brief him on the Woomera hunger strike. They reported to the Minister that the hunger strikers had legitimate grievances and were intent on their strike. They advised him to close Woomera detention centre, as the environment and culture there was irreparably 'toxic' and that a detainee fatality was a significant possibility (O'Neill 2008, 93).

As negotiations dragged on with no resolution in sight, several detainees began to talk of a mass suicide attempt (Barker 2002). The government deflected the threat as further manipulative behaviour and warned that the government would not be blackmailed. Mahzar Ali, a spokesperson for the hunger strikers, feared that many people might be seriously injured or die in their attempts to force the government to listen. He implored his fellow detainees not to commit suicide, promising that he would 'do something' (O'Neill 2008, 94). On Australia Day, 26 January 2002, Mahzar Ali climbed up one of the fences and threw himself onto the razor wire. He suffered deep lacerations to his arms, legs, torso, neck and face. Somehow he survived the incident. His actions were seen as 'heroic' by fellow detainees:

> On the twelfth day of our hunger strike our brave leader Mazhar Ali climbs to the top of the fence and throws himself on the razor wire in an effort for us to be taken seriously. It gives a boost to people's courage (Changazi 2010).

A graphic photograph was leaked by someone working at Woomera detention centre at the time which showed a close-up image of deep lacerations on Mazhar Ali's right arm. The photograph had a caption superimposed on it, reading, 'good effort WMA 365 jump into razor wire.' This caption reveals the derision of Mazhar Ali's guardians and shows the degree to which the system of detention had so dehumanised all who were caught up in it, whether as guards or guarded, that someone would throw himself onto razor wire and that the response of those charged with ensuring his safety was not only to graphically document his injuries, likely a contractual obligation with the Department of Immigration, but to add a derisive comment to the photograph.

On 30 January 2002, the government agreed that it would resume the processing of Afghan asylum claims and would consider all information put before them by claimants. The protesters collectively agreed to call off the hunger strike. There were no fatalities and no one was force fed during this strike, though many people were medically rehydrated. 'Normality' was restored to the operations of Woomera. However, it wasn't long before further individual and collective acts of self-harm, suicide attempts and hunger strikes were enacted in Port Hedland, Curtin, Villawood, Maribyrnong and Woomera detention centres in protest against the continued denial and violation of detainees' human rights.

Reading Refugee Protest

The Australian government narrated detainee hunger strikes, self-harm, suicide attempts and lip sewing, in particular, as manipulative actions that were 'alien to our culture' and as efforts to hold us 'hostage to our decency' (Fonseca 2002; Pugliese 2002; Wolfram Cox and Minahan 2004). Refugee advocates and supporters called upon Australians, and the government in particular, to recognise the pain and despair in detainee actions and to respond with compassion. The high incidence of self-harm and suicide was a product of an epidemic of mental health problems that was exacerbated, if not caused, by prolonged and indefinite detention in an 'environment so toxic that you can't treat anything meaningfully' (Jureidini, cited in Briskman et al. 2008, 139). Largely missing in the public discussion about the high rate of bodily protests in immigration detention centres was the voice of the participants themselves. Detainees did manage to smuggle out some notes or make telephone calls to media and supporters outside detention, but their voices were largely drowned out by more powerful voices with greater access to public forums. Also missing was a critique of *why* people would harm themselves in an effort to escape harm. Images of people who had voluntarily sewn their lips and whose bodies lay limp on a mattress in the full desert sun were confrontational and difficult to understand. The government and refugee supporters offered simple answers to complex and multi-layered acts. The government message can be summarised as, 'They are so unlike us, their morals and mores so alien to ours, they couldn't possibly live among us and, so our jails and guards are needed to protect Australia from such unintelligible, unknowable threats,' while refugee supporter messages tended more towards, 'they are just like us, they suffer, are depressed and need our care and compassion.'

A Brief History of Hunger Strikes

Hunger strike has a long history and has been used by prisoners, protesters and disempowered groups around the world. It is rarely a first action in protest against a perceived wrong, and is generally embarked upon only when all other courses of action have been exhausted. While not all hunger strikes are enacted in prisons and detention centres, there is a strong link between imprisonment and hunger strike (Ellmann 1993). One of the most famous hunger strikes was undertaken in 1981 in Ireland by Irish Republican Army (IRA) prisoners in Long Kesh Prison. The men were protesting against the revocation of prisoner of war status and their reclassification as 'common criminals.' While some material benefits (such as not needing to wear a prison uniform or engage in prison labour and having greater access to visitors and communication with the outside world) attended the different status of prisoner of war, the political significance, for both the British government and the IRA, was of far greater importance (Howard 2006, 69). The IRA considered themselves republican freedom fighters, fighting against a foreign oppressor. The

British government considered the IRA terrorists and thugs committing criminal acts. By revoking prisoner-of-war status, the British government hoped to erode the legitimacy of the IRA and to evacuate their actions of political meaning.

The political status of IRA prisoners was revoked in March 1976, compelling them to wear prison uniforms and participate in prison work programs. IRA prisoners refused to comply, and the five-year long 'blanket protest' began. Stripped of their own clothes and refusing to wear prison garb, 400 men draped themselves in blankets from their cells. After two years, this escalated to become the 'dirty protest' in which the men refused to enter the prison bathrooms, a protest both against the lengthy delays between a request to go to the bathroom and its grant and against the invasive body searches conducted there. Excrement built up in their cells and the protesters remained unwashed. The British government, led by Margaret Thatcher, remained unmoved. On 1 March 1981, a hunger strike began which lasted 217 days and killed ten men (Howard 2006, 71). Prisoners volunteered to strike and a central group of leaders decided who would participate and when each strike was to begin. The first to refuse food was Bobby Sands, who was also the first to die. Deaths from the hunger strike were carefully timed to ensure a steady stream of coffins emerging from the prison (Andriolo 2006, 105). The British government may have been able to 'manage' a single death, perhaps being able to 'spin' the death as a suicide and evidence of an individual's personal despair, which was notable because of its exceptionality (Pugliese 2002). However, coffins emerged day after day, exemplifying the problems hidden from view by the prison walls and calling into question the legitimacy of the state (Ellmann 1993, 92). Allen Feldman explained that, 'the act of hunger striking purified and decriminalised the striker, but the queue of corpses emerging from behind prison walls would shake the moral legitimacy of the British state' (cited in Andriolo 2006, 104).

While on strike, Bobby Sands stood for, and was elected to, the seat of Fermanagh and South Tyrone. Sands' victory in the British elections proved that the IRA was not, as the British government asserted, a radical minority group of criminals that lacked popular support. The hunger strike not only rallied the men within the prison around a common cause (recognition as legitimate actors in the eyes of their enemy), but also provided a focal point for those outside the prison to articulate their support for the Republican cause. The strike transcended the walls of the prison (Andriolo 2006, 104).

After ten deaths, and with dozens more prisoners at different stages of hunger strike and all determined in their resolve to fast until death if need be, the British government was eventually forced to back down and the hunger strike was called off on 3 October 1981. The IRA had won a significant victory, not least consisting of the realisation of the depth and breadth of support for the IRA. Afterwards, all exchanges between the government and the IRA took place in a vastly altered power relationship.

With regard to the IRA hunger strikers, Ellmann (1993, 17) argues that, 'it was not by starving but by making a spectacle of their starvation that the prisoners brought shame on their oppressors and captured the sympathies of their co-religionists.' While there are some parallels between the IRA hunger strikers and Australia's immigration detainees, particularly in their desire to assert their place as legitimate political actors, there were a number of key differences. Detainees in Australia did not share sufficient common identity traits with the community outside detention (such as language, nationality or religion) and they had been effectively dehumanised in the public arena. This meant that their hunger strikes, as much as they may have garnered support from some, were limited in their capacity to transcend prison walls and build a broad base of solidarity which would bring shame on their oppressors. Their actions could too easily be presented as further proof of their barbarity and otherness. Furthermore, detainees did not get to narrate their own actions. Government control of access to the detention centres and the detainees' lack of pre-existing links and organisations within Australia meant that they were effectively isolated and their actions were too often viewed alongside the government-supplied narrative. As hunger strike relies substantially on triggering other people's conscience, articulating the reasons of a hunger strike is essential if the strike is to realise its full force. A hunger strike must also have a 'statement that supplements the wordless testimony of the famished flesh. To hold the body up for ransom, to make mortality into a bargaining chip, hunger strikers must declare the reasons for their abstinence' (Ellmann 1993, 17). Without this self-narration, the political act can too easily be subsumed by individual pathologising explanations.

Emotion and Political Action

Public discourse around hunger strike, and lip sewing in particular, has tended to be dichotomised in Australia. The government narrative focussed on detainee hunger strike and lip sewing as evidence of 'their' moral bankruptcy, deviousness and difference from 'us.' Refugee supporter narratives tended to explain hunger strike and lip sewing as proof of 'their' despair, pain and suffering, calling on 'us' to respond with care and compassion. Missing from these competing views was a recognition of detainee protest as informed political action, arising from a critique of the injustices enacted by government policies to 'boat people.' Both accounts, criminal or mentally disturbed, rely on pathology and politically eviscerate the actions of detainees. To read hunger strike and lip sewing as only political, however, would deny the intimate, emotional experience of injustice. Detainees *were* distressed, depressed, feeling hopeless, powerless and despondent. These feelings informed and drove their actions protesting detention, but so too did political analysis. The emotional impact and experience of detention co-existed with, and informed, detainees' political critique, and the two cannot be disentangled.

Detainees spoke again and again of the frustration and despair they felt in detention. The words 'frustrated,' 'frustration' and 'frustrating' appear and reappear throughout the transcripts of interviews for this research. Frustration occurred because written requests for soap, to see a doctor, access to a telephone, information about the progression of claims were simply ignored time and time again. Frustration occurred because of the sameness of every day: the unchanging landscape of razor wire, routine and 'chicken and rice, rice and chicken. Everyday chicken!' (Osman). Frustration was felt because nothing that detainees said or did mattered or made any difference at all.

As explored in Chapter 2, Arendt (1976, 296) articulates that 'human' rights outside a political community that is willing to recognise them are meaningless. She eloquently states that a 'refugee's freedom of speech is a fool's freedom for nothing she says matters anyway.' And so it was that detainees were free to speak in detention but their voices were rendered silent and irrelevant by their exclusion from the polis. Their words of protest, expressed through requests, letters, phone calls and painted banners fell into a void and were largely unheard and not responded to. Faced with the reality of Arendt's astute observation made so many years before, detainees escalated their actions to insist upon their voices and actions being heard.

With no formal political community, detainees had been stripped of their status as political subjects and reduced to objects of Australia's national politics. They were existing in a state that Arendt described as biological specimens of the species 'human.' Reduced to this corporeal state, yet rejecting this reduction, and having learned that 'words do not grip unless one gives them hands to do so, unless one embodies them' (Andriolo 2006, 102), detainees used their bodies to reinsert themselves into the polis. Conversely, Arendt warned, action must always be accompanied by the narration of the actor if it is to be political communication and, thereby, participation in the human artifice:

> Action and speech are so closely related because the primordial and specifically human act must at the same time contain the answer to the question asked of every newcomer: 'Who are you?'... Without the accompaniment of speech, at any rate, action would not only lose its revelatory character, but, and by the same token, it would lose its subject, as it were; not acting men but performing robots would achieve what, humanly speaking, would remain incomprehensible. Speechless action would no longer be action because there would no longer be an actor, and the actor, the doer of deeds, is possible if he is at the same time the speaker of words. The action he begins is humanly disclosed by the word, and though his deed can be perceived in its brute physical appearance without verbal accompaniment, it becomes relevant only through the spoken word in which he identifies himself as the actor, announcing what he does, has done, and intends to do. (Arendt 1958, 178)

Detainees understood the need to narrate their own actions, to explain what they were doing and why. But quiet speech, speech without physical action, had failed and so people in detention began to use their bodies to make their voices heard. The risk, of course, was that their narratives would become separated from their actions, enabling the government to present their actions as 'barbaric' and 'unknown to our culture.' Nonetheless, detainee hunger strikes and some acts of self-harm were primarily communicative acts insisting on a response from both the Australian population and the government.

Detainee hunger strike and self-harm must be understood in multiple ways:

- As profoundly political acts, arising from both strategic analysis *and* intimate despair.
- As both individual and collective action. Hunger strike and self-harm are perhaps the most personal and individual acts one can take, and yet are often undertaken within (and often for) a collective.
- As the use by detainees of their bodies to make visible both their depoliticisation and their rejection of the reduction to a corporeal state. Regardless of the outcome of the strike, whether the immediate goals of the protest were achieved or not, detainees' sought to exercise control over their own bodies; to re-establish sovereignty of self against the omnipotence of the sovereign state which detained them.
- As communicative, using bodies and performance where words alone had failed.

I will now turn to each of these analyses in turn.

The Politics of Personal Despair

In *Discipline and Punish*, Foucault (1977, 28–29), drawing on the work of Kantorowitz, proposes that, in the same way that 'The King's Body' needs to be understood as being at once 'a transitory element that is born and dies' and an ongoing representation of the kingdom, a 'physical yet intangible' icon maintained through ritual and ceremony, so too the condemned man must be understood as both an individual and a representative of state power. This analysis can be applied effectively to detained asylum seekers. The nexus of personal despair and political action is made visible using this analysis.

The asylum seeker is at once an individual, unique in his or her specificity and temporal in status, and anonymous and enduring in their function as a site for the performance of state power. The asylum seeker's presence enables ceremonies (detention and its accompanying rhetoric) in support of the kingdom (nation-state) to be performed and, thus, maintain the 'physical yet intangible' icons of state. The asylum seeker occupies a duality of being; an extra-legal non-citizen stripped of rights, and an essential body in the performance and maintenance of state power and national identity. It is in this duality of specificity and anonymity that we can effectively read detained asylum seeker hunger-striking and self-harming as being at once intimately personal acts of despair and public political acts; a cry of pain *and* political action.

Most of the former detainees interviewed for this work explained hunger strike and self-harm using both psychological and political frameworks. Emad did not refuse food himself, but participated in a hunger strike in 1999 as a spokesperson and mediator between the hunger strikers and the government. He described the mood in detention in the lead-up to the hunger strike:

> The immigration didn't listen. The refugees, they lost any hope of leaving... We have kids in the detention centre, and we have a lot of women, and they have a lot of problems. The psychological pressure was really high at that time, living in what they call it, a donga[1], with tens of people. You can't sleep at night; you have security guards from the Australian Correction Management knock on the door every half an hour to count the refugees or to check on them. It is a very disturbing environment for them. No talking to their families and they're overseas, no talking to anyone, the feeling of isolation, the feeling that no-one knows anything about us makes them do what they done. (Emad)

He also explained that the strike was a reaction to a specific political development. Temporary Protection Visas had just been introduced.

> So once the guys there knew about the new system that was a reason for hunger strike, demonstrations, a lot of actions... So partly because of the legislation, the other part is because of the ACM behaviour in the detention centre. The guards there needed to be more aware of the human rights system. (Emad)

[1] A donga is a temporary removable building. Dongas were used extensively in the larger detention centres.

There can be little, if any, doubt that morale in detention centres was extremely low, that people felt angry, frustrated, depressed and despairing about their current situation, with a sense of hopelessness for their future. All participants in this study, when asked about hunger strike, self-harm and suicide, responded with explanations that blended their emotional state with complaints about both politics on a local level, most particularly regarding their immediate treatment in detention by both guards and Department of Immigration staff, and broader national and international politics. Salah explained that he and several other detainees conducted a ten-day hunger strike in Curtin detention centre. He was part of a group of detainees who had been 'screened out' and not permitted to lodge protection visa applications. For a period of ten months, they had been held in separation detention, with no communication with asylum seekers in the main compound, lawyers, friends or family and no access to newspapers or television. The government was unable to return people to their countries of origin and there was no end in sight to their predicament. The group of detainees were all single men except for one family. The family had a young child who had by then spent seven months in separation detention with no contact with other children and no access to school or play opportunities. The group had been requesting for several months that the family be transferred to the main compound where there were other children and slightly better facilities, but without success. Eventually, the group decided that their requests using official processes were futile and,

> we got a hunger strike because of that family, because straight up, they got one kid, a little girl, and it's really hard. We stayed like I think ten days on hunger strike… Yeah, after ten days they took that family and put them to another (compound)… We said 'okay' and we broke down the hunger strike. (Salah)

Salah and his fellow detainees' protest was most immediately directed at the local level enactment of asylum seeker policy, and specifically about one young girl who could not play with other children.

Issaq spent almost five years in immigration detention before being found to be a refugee and granted a visa. During this time, he participated in many protests, including hunger strikes and lip sewing. He also committed several acts of self-harm in detention. Issaq had been detained in Port Hedland, Woomera and Villawood detention centres. When he had been in detention for twenty-seven months he heard that detainees in Port Hedland and Woomera had sewn their lips. He was in Villawood at the time, but knew how isolated the other centres were,

> We heard that in Woomera and Port Hedland they sewed their lips as a sign of protest. But I knew that in there that it wouldn't get across because they don't have visitors, they don't have the freedom that we have here. We had visitors, activists coming in and see us. In there no one could get in and see them in person. They were handing out the notes and writing something in notes. It's different from personal experience. It was me and another two teenagers where we thought 'let's sew our lips and that will get some attentions.' (Issaq)

Issaq displayed an acute political awareness in his decision to sew his lips. He understood that narration of the event was essential 'if they intend[ed] to make their self-starvation readable as protest' (Ellmann 1993, 19), and so he was very deliberate in his decision about how to reveal his sewn lips to the wider world. He decided that Dr Michael Dudley, a psychiatrist, would be the best person to narrate his actions. He explained that he could have called a journalist himself, as he had direct phone numbers for several journalists at major news outlets, but,

> the first thing I did was before telling anyone or any officers or anything, I just handed a tissue in front of my mouth. I came in and the first person who saw my lips are sewn was Dr Michael Dudley because I knew that he will go out and reflect it positively. He's a psychiatrist ... he's not just a journalist going around and saying 'people sewed their lips because they are desperate.' I mean, journalists saying that, it means something. But when a psychiatrist saying that, it means a lot. It means different from people who are just saying it... So that was the first thing we did, telling him. He went out, he expressed it and that caught bigger attentions. The way he expressed it to journalists, like 'well, there is a seventeen years old boy inside detention who sewed his lips off a hunger strike. He sewed his lips in protest of what we are doing ...' which magnified the publicity by a hundred as just a normal journalist or person just sitting in a seat. (Issaq)

At that point, Issaq was a teenager with limited education; nonetheless, he understood the effect of cultural authority. He understood that his fate was tied up with the fates of unknown others detained in Woomera and Port Hedland, and that they were at once unique individuals and anonymous representations of the universal asylum seeker. He understood too that their actions would be more effective if undertaken collectively and that these actions could be further enhanced through strategic use of allies with more power than they had. Issaq wanted his actions to be understood as protest, arising from pain and despair, but not an indication of individual pathology, rather as a 'normal' human response to unjust policies. Issaq recognised that his lip sewing might appear to be an instance of psychological self-harming to others, and so he chose a psychiatrist to explain the difference to a general public who had not met him personally and who likely saw him only as an anonymous asylum seeker.

Detainees were always acting with the duality of being specific individuals and also the universal asylum seeker. Their actions, whether undertaken individually, as most acts of self-harm and suicide attempts were, or collectively, as most hunger strikes were, were tied to the status of 'detained asylum seeker,' itself an intimate, personal state of being and a highly politicised status shaping Australia's national politics at that time.

Individual and Collective Action

Although the incidence of hunger strike, lip sewing, self-harm and suicide attempts were alarmingly high in detention centres, not all asylum seekers participated in these actions. Several participants reported that while some actions were spontaneous, more commonly there would be lengthy discussion before a big protest. These meetings rarely reached full consensus either within the detainee population as a whole or within each subgroup detained (detainees often loosely organised themselves in nationality or ethnicity based groups within detention). Emad, Aamer and Farshid were all opposed to hunger strike for different reasons. Emad, a lawyer, explained;

> I opposed the idea of hunger strike … I didn't think of it as a practical solution … The other people thought hunger strike as the only thing that they

> know. Me personally, I thought of communicating with the management at that time – sending groups to them, asking for appointments, let's say to see them and talk to them. But unfortunately most of my requests were ignored at that time. Actually they didn't listen even to the most moderate let's say, way of thinking on the refugees' side. (Emad)

Emad went on to explain that he had escaped a lawless regime and wanted desperately for the official systems in Australia to work. Although the conditions in detention were terrible, he wanted to engage with his gaolers and negotiate a resolution. In his view, hunger strike undermined the rule of law, and it was with dismay that he saw the strikes and other protests achieve more than previous strategies of negotiation and lodgement of request forms had.

Aamer's objection was different again. By the time he became involved in a group meeting about hunger strike, he had already learned that the official systems didn't work. But as a doctor, he believed that one needed to be as alert and clear-thinking as possible to survive detention. He explained that,

> I disagree with it. Principally, eventually, I know a hunger strike how it damages the body… Hunger strike will not help mental health at all. If anything it causes much way worse. So mentally it doesn't help and physically it does damage parts of the body irreversibly. (Aamer)

Farshid's objection was different again. Early on in his three years of detention, he watched an older detainee undertake a hunger strike. Farshid arrived in the detention centre sixteen days into the man's twenty-plus-day strike. 'I watched him for a few days and realised no one cared. It seems no one gives a damn.' This seems to have been a formative moment for Farshid, who explained that in principle, he supported hunger strike as a method of protest:

> I still believe in hunger strike as the most peaceful way of protesting against injustice – where you can't do anything else most probably peaceful would be the hunger strike. I mean, there's no other that can beat that one. (Farshid)

However, Farshid went on to say that he thought in that particular time and context that hunger strike was ineffective:

> I thought it was over-used. It seems that it was a good way of being heard but because it was over-used… Probably because of good connections that I did have outside I was getting more of a reflection of what's going on and what's working and what's not working. (Farshid)

Some hunger strikes were undertaken by individuals acting alone and wanting specific changes to a particular situation. For example, Sayed went on hunger strike twice during his nearly six years in detention. On one occasion, he had been transferred to a prison to alleviate accommodation pressure at the Perth detention centre.[2] He felt affronted by this and believed he was being 'wrongly imprisoned.' He went on a hunger strike until he was returned to the detention centre. On an earlier occasion, Sayed had gone on a hunger strike lasting around ten days. His application had been refused by the Department of Immigration, and, not understanding he had the right of appeal to the Refugee Review Tribunal (RRT), he went on a strike against his prospective removal from Australia.

More often, however, hunger strikes were undertaken collectively and in solidarity with others. Issaq's account above explains that his lip sewing was done to draw attention to the strike of others not known to him personally, while Salah's strike was to help a child and had no direct benefit for him or his fellow strikers. Tariq, Mohammed, Osman, Aamer and Baha'adin all spoke of meetings where hunger strike was discussed:

> We had a meeting and decided we should do this. We talked about how we can bring this message outside… We made decisions as a group, not as individual. So the group made that decision. We talked about what to do, what not to do. We were all together. (Tariq)

While having a high degree of consensus, with some dissent as outlined above, there was also room for individual determination as to what form of participation to have. Emad did not refuse food or water but

[2] The United Nations Working Group on Arbitrary Detention reported that some immigration detainees were transferred to prisons 'because of a lack of space in the centres' and found that this practice amounted to arbitrary detention and constituted a breach of the International Convention on Civil and Political Rights (UNWGAD 2002, 14).

considered that he participated because he was a mediator between the strikers and the Department. Osman explained that some people would refuse food but take water and tea, while others would refuse both food and fluids. He also explained that,

> everyone is responsible for himself. Everyone and then it's up to other people who wants to join us. Like many people didn't come, didn't join us for hunger strike, but they would come to look after us. Helping us… Like if we need water, they bring water. If I collapse will bring the officer to come in, all this stuff. All involved, in any way, you know? (Osman)

Paradoxically, the dehumanisation and de-individuation of the detention regime elevated the status of 'detainee' to a political identity. Identifying as 'detainee' enabled relationships and solidarity bonds to form across differences which would previously have precluded such collaboration. At least at certain moments, Hazaras acted alongside Pashtuns, Iraqi Sunnis and Shias aligned with Iranians, and Issaq, from Iran, and his fellow lip sewers, an Iraqi and an Afghan, went on strike in solidarity with detainees in Port Hedland and Woomera, knowing nothing of their national, ethnic or religious identities. This is not to say that differences between individuals and groups ceased to exist or that there were no tensions within detainee populations, but the status of *detainee* acted as a mobilising identity and formed the basis for several group actions. Osman reported that he would act for, 'anyone! Anyone who are detainee. It doesn't matter if you are Iraqi, Afghan, No No. We *are* detainee. We are detainee.' This was echoed by Baha'adin, who said he joined one hunger strike because, 'everyone was pretty much protesting. I said "alright you guys going to protest? I'm going to be with you as well and it doesn't matter how far you go, I'm going to be with you."'

The sense of collectivity and solidarity spanned beyond being current immigration detainees and included an identification with others who had used hunger strike as a form of protest against injustices of the past. Several former detainees, when interviewed for this research, cited Gandhi and Bobby Sands in explaining their hunger strikes. This implies that detainees felt a solidarity that transcended spatial and temporal limits and extended to include identification as defenders of justice or survivors of injustice. It further indicates an awareness of the importance of locating their actions within a broader historical framework and through this, give greater strength to their resolve, rightness to their actions and legitimacy to their struggle in the public arena (Hall 2008, 170).

Embodying and Rejecting a Corporeal State

Foucault explains that historically, the power of the sovereign was rooted in the sovereign's right to determine life and death. Punishment was organised around the body of the criminal and sentences involved public floggings, imprisonment with hard labour, execution, or in some cases, public torture and execution. Foucault theorises that public physical punishment ('punishment-as-spectacle' [Foucault 1977, 9]) as a display of the sovereign's might and right carried significant risks as it also raised unsettling questions about the moral superiority of the sovereign who ordered such violence over the condemned who bore it:

> … although it was always ready to invert the shame inflicted on the victim into pity or glory, it often turned the legal violence of the executioner into shame (Foucault 1977, 9).

Consequently, over the seventeenth and eighteenth centuries, state punishment shifted its focus away from the body of the transgressor and towards the soul. In an effort to evade the shame of the executioner, modern state punishment sought to avoid making a spectacle of the state's violence and infliction of pain on the body of the condemned. 'Rehabilitation' and the soul of the prisoner became the new targets. 'From being an art of unbearable sensations punishment has become an economy of suspended rights' (Foucault 1977, 11).

Modern punishment, rather than triggering discomfort and raising questions among citizen bystanders, as public executions or flogging do, is now designed to demonstrate the power of the state over life while simultaneously hiding the violence of the state. This obfuscation of state violence functions to separate power and violence in rhetoric and performance while protecting the monopoly of violence that the state holds from critical public scrutiny. Transgressors are identified, judged and subsequent punishment is meted out through a complex web of institutions and rules that self-represent as reasonable, proportionate, and justified as necessary for the good of the whole. Punishments are presented as a consequence of the transgressor's own actions, thereby divorcing the state from any moral questioning. At the same time, punishment is aimed primarily at the soul of the transgressor and is 'for his own good.' In this way, modern policing, justice and penal systems are able to define their moral superiority and, through their own actions, produce and reproduce a paradigm of knowledge which reinforces and reinscribes its own moral superiority (Foucault 1977). Modern prisons function as both a public display of state power and provide walls behind which the state can hide its violence. In the public paradigm, narrated by the state, the prison is a site of rehabilitation and necessary curtailment of the rights of the few in order to protect the rights of the many. Deaths in custody unsettle this and are to be avoided as much as possible. Dr Aamer Sultan explained that detention centres were carefully managed to prevent suicide and the attendant scrutiny and possible moral discomfort such an event might provoke through the use of isolation cells, stripped of hanging points and under twenty-four-hour surveillance, but that nothing was done to make people feel less suicidal. 'That's the worst thing you can do to someone who is suicidal [put them in isolation], but physically they are preventing it which is probably why the incidence of suicide in detention centre is low. So they physically prevent it … without trying to actually solve the problem' (Aamer). Any testimony from offenders about the violence inside prisons is easily discredited by the state as the most powerful voice in the power-knowledge paradigm (Foucault 1997).

This dynamic nexus between institutions, power and knowledge, which frames public life, infuses immigration detention and refugee protest. The state has been able to criminalise asylum seekers and, with that, deploy centuries of inherited 'knowledge' about crime and punishment against asylum seekers. And so asylum seekers' detention has been turned into a consequence of their own (criminal) actions and any protest against that detention is further evidence of their criminality and moral inferiority. The appropriate state response then is to tighten security and policing of Australia's shores. The citizen bystander is content that they have a full picture and need not ask questions of why people are detained, the conditions of detention or what other readings there might be of detainee protest. Detainees rioting, breaching perimeter fences or setting fire to buildings are easily accounted for within this framework.

Running parallel to the penal operations of immigration detention and of the rhetoric surrounding the arrival of boat people, the government also repeatedly denied that detention was punitive (Brennan 2007), asserting time and again that immigration detention was administrative detention and the minimum practice necessary to protect Australian people against the potential arrival of criminals, terrorists or other undefined threats (Mason 2004, 235; UNWGAD 2002). The government claimed that detainees' rights were limited only to the extent necessary to achieve the greater good of protecting Australians. In this way, the government was able to use detention as a performance of state power and suppress any discomfort caused by displaying state violence in its exercise of power and control.

Government control in immigration detention centres was omnipotent. The purpose-built detention centres in Baxter and on Christmas Island eerily reflect Bentham's panopticon. Cameras are everywhere, enabling guards to observe detainees in every action. Visitors must pass through a metal detector and all bags are scanned by an x-ray machine. All movement in and out of the centres is logged. Perimeter fences are electrified, and motion sensors and security camera monitor a 'sterile-zone' between the internal and external perimeter fences. A control room looms above the centre in a tall tower that enables full view of the site. Work opportunities within centres are extremely limited, recreation programs are sparse, meals are set and delivered on schedule, and detainees are allocated a detention identity number and are regularly checked by guards. Mobile phones are prohibited and all communications into and out of the detention centres are controlled. Request forms must be lodged for any needs falling outside the daily routine of the centre. Detainees' futures depend on the outcome of their visa applications, which are determined by Department of Immigration officials. The life of the detained asylum seeker is subsumed in a web of bureaucracy and governance.

Australia's immigration detention centres exemplify Foucault's 'economy of suspended rights.' Through detention, the state exercises its penal power in a way that leaves no traces on the body, for its target is the soul of the transgressor. State violence is made invisible through the physical isolation of detention centres, the carefully controlled access to detention centres and through the semiotic and rhetorical distancing of detainees from the Australian public. As Maud Ellmann (1993, 85) eloquently points out, 'pain without marks is like speech without writing, doomed to pass into oblivion.' Detainees' acts of self-harm, hunger strike and lip sewing were an effort to embody the violence of the state, to make visible the effects of the state's hidden violence and, in so doing, to refuse to pass into oblivion but rather to 'trick the conscience of [their] viewers, forcing them to recognise that they are implicated in the spectacle that they behold' (Ellmann 1993, 17). Detainee hunger strikes strove to raise questions about the moral legitimacy of immigration detention and, by implication, of the government itself and Australian society. Ramatullah, a spokesperson for detainees on hunger strike in Woomera in July 2002, told outside supporters that the hunger strike was to 'show the cruelty of persecution on us. If we die, it will make conspicuous our innocence and the guilt will be on the government' (McKay 2002).

Detainees recognised that they had very limited power, their words were not being heard and so they used the only power they had, their bodies, to challenge detention. The challenge operated simultaneously on two levels. As well as being aimed at the Australian government and population, it was also a way for asylum seekers to experience a sense of self and some control in their lives. Issaq explained that sitting doing nothing created a vacuum and that self-harming was sure to provoke a reaction, through which he gained some sense of his presence in the world:

> I wanted to have something to look forward, then slash my wrists and see what's going to happen. You know what I mean? Just something out of ordinary. I mean I know that I'm sitting here and watching that tree, nothing going to happen. I won't get a visa, I won't get out of here and everyday going to be the same. But I want to change it. The only power I have to just slash my wrists and see what's going to happen after it. Will it cause attention or not? Will it, you know? You'll hope for a change. To use all what you have to change – I mean, not to get out of detention, but change what's happening now. I mean, I'm sitting here, by doing nothing, nothing would

> change. But by slashing my wrists there are going to be some action at least. At least five officers are going to come out of the door, nurse is going to come and all these things. Something going to happen out of ordinary and in terms of self-harm that was the thing I was looking for. All the power that you have. That's all the power, not just a little of it. That's all you have. (Issaq)

Issaq's self-harming was an effort to make his actions meaningful. His discussion of self-harm displays an understanding of Foucault's critique of how sovereign power has shifted from the power over death to the power over life and the risks of a death in detention to the moral legitimacy of the government. If he self-harmed, the authorities *must* react. Paradoxically, his apparently destructive self-harming actions brought him closer to a place in the world in which his actions were meaningful.

Farshid didn't resort to self-harm during his three years in detention, but he was a trusted confidante of many fellow detainees and talked with many people who were self-harming. His explanation is similar to Issaq's, but with less concern for provoking an external reaction as an internal one. He said self-harm,

> … was out of real psychological frustration and self-actualisation. People's situation in detention was that you were the lost person, the forgotten person, you don't exist, you cannot change anything and you have no power over anything. So, self-harm in most cases wasn't a planned thing. It was in most cases out of frustration and it was good in a way that people feel they are real again, they exist, they have power over something – their body. So, blood always has a very powerful message and when people see they can get over their fear and do something, certain thing, harsh thing, they come back to that colour of existence – I have power, I can do things. So, I was calling that self-actualisation out of frustration in that situation. (Farshid)

The omnipotent power and control of the detention environment reached into every aspect of detainees' lives. Their daily routines were micromanaged to such an extent that people lost a sense of self. Shahin explained that hunger strike was a way for detainees to experience their own agency and will, regardless of whether any specific goals of the protest were achieved or not:

> This would happen because you have no choice. You can't make any decisions in your life. Just to show you are alive you could make a decision to stop receiving anything in your body. That would show that you were alive, because you could make a decision, in a place that you can't make any decision. (Shahin)

Sayed conducted two hunger strikes in detention and said that when he protested he regained self-confidence and a sense of himself:

> I think you gain self-confidence because in the environment you are in, you are depending for everything and you abide by the rules so, you have to do like they tell you to do. They set the time for food, you don't have control on anything. When we do something like that, at least we, we, it's like a self-independence type of thing. That's what happens. That's why we protest like, because you are achieving something, even though you're not … but still you … will gain the self-confidence. Because you're so dependent. You don't have the ability to make decisions or … because you lose ability to make decisions … That's what happens, that's the main purpose everybody do what they do. Otherwise there is no difference between the live and dead you know. Otherwise I could be dead – nothing. (Sayed)

Detainees' bodies became a site for the exercise of state sovereignty, but they were also sites for detainees to reclaim sovereignty of self. Lacking power over their external environment, detainees sought to exercise power over their own bodies and through this to exert some influence on their environment and regain a sense of self. However, this sovereignty of self was limited because the government, through Regulation 5.35, retained the power to administer medical treatment against the will of the detainee. Whereas Bobby Sands could defiantly claim that 'it is not those who can inflict the most, but those who can suffer the most who will conquer' (cited in Andriolo 2006, 105), the capacity to fast until death was denied to detainees and so their capacity to perform the violence of state policies through self-suffering, already limited by their physical and semiotic isolation, was further circumscribed by the state's ultimate power to use physical and chemical force to administer medical treatment. Sylvia Pankhurst, an early suffragette, described her experience of being force fed to break her hunger strike as 'an oral rape that violates the essence of the self' (cited in Ellmann 1993, 33). Pankhurst's description of being force fed, of the physical pain and violation involved, differs little from descriptions by detainees who tell of being taken by armed guards in the middle of the night and being physically restrained while tubes were forced inside them. A debate continues in the international medical and human rights field as to whether force feeding can be justified, given that it violates many international human rights and common law principles (Kenny and Fiske 2013; Kenny 2002; Nicholl et al. 2006). Ellmann (1993, 34) captures the multi-layered effects of force feeding when she writes, 'what has been forced into her is not only the food but the ideology and even the identity of her oppressors. Under this torture, starvation rather than ingestion has become the last remaining recipe for authenticity.'

Force feeding of hunger strikers is problematic. In addition to the physical pain of the procedure and the medical risks to the striker, force feeding raises ethical questions about the power of the state, individual autonomy and the responsibility of the state to a person in its care, particularly when that person is a refused asylum seeker to whom the state has formally determined it has no obligations (Kenny 2002). The World Medical Association *Declaration on Hunger Strikes* (the Malta Declaration) states that 'forcible feeding is never ethically acceptable. Even if intended to benefit, feeding accompanied by threats, coercion, force or use of physical restraints is a form of inhuman and degrading treatment' (WMA 1991).

Communicative Acts

Hunger strike and self-harm must also be read as communicative acts that are designed to reach out to the consciences of the oppressor or the citizen bystander. A hunger striker needs an audience and the desired outcome is for a response from those with the power to end their suffering. Death is a risk, but not the goal.

Woven throughout detainee accounts is an awareness of how their protest might be received by the Australian government, the Australian people, the media and the world. Mohammed talked of the need to find a 'legitimate' or 'acceptable' form of protest. He supported hunger strikes primarily because,

> … you're not hurting anybody. You're hurting only yourself. You're not damaging anything, you're not breaking anything, you're not breaking any law. This is the one everybody knows and everybody accepting, like the Bobby Sands as you remember… (Mohammed)

Detainees wanted others to know that they were being locked up in remote detention centres, that they were suffering and to respond to them. Respondents identified ACM, Department of Immigration staff, the Australian government, the media, the Australian public, the United Nations and the world community as targets for their message.

Most respondents said that hunger strike was a way to reach Australian citizens and ask them to question the government's policies and to question what was happening in detention centres. The hunger strikers saw that the government was restricting the flow of information out of detention centres and that they were being held in secret. Baha'adin explained that the guards would sometimes come and take hunger strikers and hold them in isolation, 'because they didn't want us to show to the people what we were doing and they wanted to keep everything secret. This kind of thing was shocking for Australian people I think.' Osman echoed Baha'adin's thoughts:

> And when we say the hunger strike, that's the most peaceful action. It's anyone can believe in peaceful, will do the hunger strike. Many famous people, like Gandhi and eight Irish … they did the hunger strike because they believe in peaceful, ok? I have got something, but I can't, nobody listen to me, I do this action and the people will say 'oh, why he's doing this?' So my attention, or my problem will be heard. (Osman)

In her extensive work, *The Hunger Artists: Starving, Writing and Imprisonment*, Maud Ellmann repeatedly draws links between food and words, in that humans need sustenance of both body and soul. She quotes Wole Soyinka, who went on a hunger strike while imprisoned: '"Why do I fast?" he writes. "I ask for books, writing material … I also ask for an end to my inhuman isolation … To feed my body but deny my mind is deliberate dehumanisation,"' (Ellmann 1993, 106). In this research, Shahin spoke similarly. Although he did not fast himself, he attempted to explain why detainees did. He explained that when all other forms of communication had elicited no response, people would use their bodies:

> I was never involved in hunger strikes… Because perhaps I was able to express what I wanted to say through language. What I did with *Refugitive*[3] when I got out of detention was answering the questions about people who would self-harm, who would go on hunger strike… (Shahin)

Hunger strike relies on the interconnectedness of human beings and on human conscience for its power. It speaks to the oppressor (the detaining state) and onlookers (the nation), implicating them in the dialogue through their gaze, and requests a response. Issaq was sure that sewing lips forced people to question what was happening in detention centres:

> John Howard was saying 'they are criminals' and media were backing it up. But after that we saw how it changed and people started to – I mean journalists, lawyers, everyone just get together, those who saw something in there, you know. I mean, they sew their lips. 'Why do they sew their lips?' Not just 'seen sewing lips' but going for the reasons of why. Just asking a question… That's what was good about all these protests, you know, just reflecting our feelings to another human being, just to see us not as a danger but as another human being who escape from danger. You know what I mean? (Issaq)

Andriolo (2006, 110), writing about protest suicides, including hunger strikes, describes such actions as 'acts of hopeful despair,' and argues that 'we ought to pay attention to protest suicides,' as, 'those who take notice … also register themselves as conscious participants in humanity.' The government's rhetoric around asylum seekers in Australia denied any similarities between 'those sort of people' and 'us' and refused to acknowledge the existence of any possible points of connection across the overemphasised cultural and religious divides. However, what remained was

---

[3] *Refugitive* is a play that Shahin wrote and performed after his release from detention to explain hunger strike and self-harm by detainees. For further detail, see Chap.3.

a biological similarity, as we are all still made of flesh and blood, and it was on the basis of the physical body that detainees attempted to build a dialogue and communicate with their unwilling hosts.

Hunger strike and self-harm in detention, as communicative acts, ask the question of *who* is responsible for the detainees' suffering (Anderson 2004). Ellmann notes that the verb 'to starve' contains an ambiguity at its root, for it means both 'to cause starvation [and] to suffer it' (Ellmann 1993, 92). Detainees, through lip sewing, hunger strike and self-harming sought to provoke a response in the general public, to create discomfort which might then lead to bystanders asking questions. Aamer, who opposed hunger striking, nonetheless told the story of how a doctor who attended to two hunger strikers who were transferred to hospital for treatment subsequently began to question immigration detention. According to Aamer,

> when he met them he realised there is something extremely wrong happening in these detention centres. So he got engaged, he found himself impulsion to be engaged. He had to engage with immigration and try to work out why this is happening. (Aamer)

The communicative aspects of self-harm and hunger strike were limited by the government's ability to narrate the action, but the government could not entirely control the message sent nor the interpretation of the audience. Despite government efforts to narrate detainee hunger strike and self-harm as 'barbarism' and 'blackmail,' these actions forced open a small space in the polis in which detainees were able to insert their voices.

Mivan explained that there were lengthy discussions and competing views in detention. Many detainees thought that lip sewing and self-harm would be an affront to Australian people and that the strategy would backfire and help the government's portrayal of asylum seekers as people to be frightened of, whereas others disagreed. Mivan believed that such physical protests would reach a sympathetic audience:

> But at least you can find somebody who has a good heart, they can say something. People they were sewing their lips and throwing themselves onto the razor wires and stuff, they were messages. Messages from the

> people in the detention centre. For example those messages made this Petro Georgio[4] or other backbenchers or something to push the government 'What are you doing? What are you doing with these people?' (Mivan)

Issaq maintained that detainees had to 'make a noise, let someone hear it' and that even if 'ninety percent of them don't care … one of them will come to the door and say "what's going on in here?" and that's all we needed, and you tell them why.' Hunger strike and lip sewing was a way to 'make some noise,' provoke the question 'why?' and create a public space in which detainees could speak.

Conclusion

Hunger strike, lip sewing and self-harm were strategies used by detainees to escape the omnipotence of detention. They served multiple purposes. Bodily protests reached out to the consciences of people outside of detention, bypassing the bureaucratic relationships which surrounded them. These strategies had great symbolic power. Detainees and the treatment meted out to them inside detention were largely hidden from public view, but by sewing lips or cutting themselves, detainees were able to make visible the injustice of the state. Indeed, these protests were effective. Refugee supporters mobilised and grew in number as the frequency and intensity of detainee protest grew. Lip sewing in particular had a significant impact on the public debate, polarising opinions and making 'neutral' positions harder to hold. By using their bodies to challenge the cruelty of detention, detainees were able to force open a space in the

---

[4] Petro Giorgio was a Liberal Party backbencher (retired in 2010) who led a small group of fellow government MPs in challenging the government's position on asylum seekers. He began speaking publically against the government position, drafted a Private Members Bill to improve the rights of asylum seekers in detention, threatened to cross the floor and vote against the government on a 2006 bill and managed to negotiate with the Prime Minister for significant improvements, particularly getting children out of detention centres and getting a new class of bridging visa introduced to get long term detainees out. Giorgio's public criticism of the government's position became a key focal point for changing community attitudes (For more on Giorgio and fellow backbencher dissidents, see Fleay [2010, 121–126]).

public debate, insist that their actions had meaning, and insert, although still in a mediated fashion, their voices into the polis.

The hunger strikes also gained some concessions from the government. Processing of Afghan refugee claims were resumed as a direct consequence of the mass hunger strike in Woomera in January 2002. Further, repeated hunger strikes, riots and breakouts from Woomera were likely to have influenced the government's decision to close that centre in April 2003. Importantly, hunger strikes and self-harm enabled people detained to experience themselves as agents in their own lives, to experience the speech and action that Arendt places at the core of the human condition.

The hunger strike is a slow and patient protest. It enables the expression of a range of critiques and feelings, but sometimes the anger, indignation and immediacy of injustice leads to a different kind of protest. The following chapter looks at riots in detention centres.

Bibliography

Anderson, P. (2004). To lie down to death for days. *Cultural Studies, 18*(6), 816–846.

Andriolo, K. (2006). The twice killed: Imagining protest suicide. *American Anthropologist, 108*(1), 100–113.

Arendt, H. (1958). *The human condition*. Chicago: University of Chicago Press.

Arendt, H. (1976). *The origins of totalitarianism*. Orlando: Harcourt.

Australian Broadcasting Corporation (ABC). (2002). Force-feeding and the law. *The Law Report*, ABC Radio National, July 16. Transcript. Retrieved January 10, 2012, from http://www.abc.net.au/radionational/programs/lawreport/force-feeding-and-the-law/3521916

Barker, A. (2002). Afghan youths threaten suicide at the Woomera detention centre. *7.30 Report*, Australian Broadcasting Corporation, January 28. Retrieved December 7, 2011, from http://www.abc.net.au/7.30/content/2002/s468052.htm

Brennan, F. (2007). Lawyers' role in a democracy. *Eureka Street*, November 29. Retrieved August 19, 2010, from http://www.eurekastreet.com.au/article.aspx?aeid=3892

Briskman, L., Latham, S., & Goddard, C. (2008). *Human rights overboard. Seeking asylum in Australia*. Melbourne: Scribe Publications.

Changazi, R. (2010). From persecution to resistance: Rahmatullah's story. *Socialist Alternative* website, April 23. Retrieved June 10, 2010, from http://www.sa.org.au (home page).

Department of Immigration, Local Government and Ethnic Affairs v Gek Bouy Mok. (1992). NSWSC Equity Division 4982 (Powell J., 30 September, unreported).

Ellmann, M. (1993). *The hunger artists. Starving, writing and imprisonment*. London: Virago Press.

Farrell, P. (2014). Immigration approved treatment for detainees without their consent. *The Guardian*, March 3. Retrieved April 26, 2014, from http://www.theguardian.com (home page).

Fleay, C. (2010). *Australia and human rights: Situating the Howard government*. Newcastle-Upon-Tyne: Cambridge Scholars Publishing.

Fonseca, M. (2002). Lip-sewing chicken dinner advertisement. *PM*, ABC Radio National, July 29. Transcript. Retrieved December 7, 2011, from http://www.abc.net.au/pm/stories/s635561.htm

Foucault, M. (1977). *Discipline and punish. The birth of the prison*. New York: Vintage.

Foucault, M. (1997). *Society must be defended. Lectures at the College de France 1975–76* (D. Macey, Trans.). London: Penguin Books.

Hall, B. (2013). Hunger strikes won't work: Gillard. *Sydney Morning Herald*, February 25. Retrieved May 2, 2014, from http://www.smh.com.au (home page).

Hall, K. F. (2008). "Use words. Not your body:" The hunger that has no name. *Women & Performance: A Journal of Feminist Theory, 18*(2), 169–180.

Hazou, R. (2008). *Refugitive* and the theatre of dys-appearance. *Research in Drama Education: The Journal of Applied Theatre and Performance, 13*(2), 181–186.

Howard, P. (2006). The Long Kesh hunger strikers: 25 years later. *Social Justice, 33*(4), 69–91.

Human Rights and Equal Opportunities Commission (HREOC) (1998). *Those who've come across the seas. Detention of unauthorised arrivals*. Sydney: Human Rights and Equal Opportunities Commission.

Human Rights and Equal Opportunities Commission (HREOC) (2004). *A last resort? National Inquiry into Children in Immigration Detention*. Sydney: Human Rights and Equal Opportunities Commission.

International Criminal Tribunal for the Former Yugoslavia. (2009). *Voluntary protest fasts: Information for detainees.* Retrieved April 27, 2014, from http://www.icty.orgf (home page).

Kenny, M. A. (2002). Force-feeding asylum seekers. *Alternative Law Journal, 27*(30), 107–111.

Kenny, M. A., & Fiske, L. (2013). Regulation 5.35: Coerced treatment of detained asylum seekers on hunger strike. Legal, ethical and human rights implications. In S. Juss (Ed.), *The Ashgate research companion to migration theory & policy* (pp. 423–442). Williston: Ashgate Publishing.

Kenny, M. A., Silove, D., & Steel, Z. (2004). Legal and ethical implications of medically enforced feeding of detained asylum seekers on hunger strike. *eMedical Journal of Australia, 180*(5), 237–240.

Klocker, N., & Dunn, K. (2003). Who's driving the asylum debate? Newspaper and government representations of asylum seekers. *Media International Australia, 109*, 71–92.

Laughland, O. (2014). Asylum seekers on Christmas Island start hunger strike over Manus death. *The Guardian*, February 26. Retrieved May 2, 2014, from http://www.theguardian.com (home page).

Mason, V. (2004). Strangers within in the 'lucky country': Arab-Australians after September 11. *Comparative Studies of South Asia, Africa and the Middle East, 24*(1), 233–243.

McKay, D. (2002). 6.30pm hunger strike update. June 26. Retrieved December 7, 2011, from http://groups.yahoo.com/group/Ausnews/message/3118

Nicholl, D., Atkinson, H., Kalk, J., Hopkins, W., Elias, E., Siddiqui, A., et al. (2006). Force feeding and restraint of Guantanamo hunger strikers. *The Lancet, 367*, 811.

O'Neill, M. (2008). *Blind conscience.* Sydney: University of New South Wales Press.

Peel, M. (1997). Hunger strikes. Understanding the underlying physiology will help doctors provide proper advice. *British Medical Journal, 315*(7112), 829.

Pugliese, J. (2002). Penal asylum: Refugees, ethics, hospitality. *Borderlands, 1*(1).

United Nations Working Group on Arbitrary Detention (UNWGAD). (2002). Civil and political rights, including the question of torture and detention report of the Working Group on Arbitrary Detention: Visit to Australia. *United Nations Commission on Human Rights, 59th Session*, October 24. Document E/CN.4/2003/8/Add.2.

Wolfram Cox, J., & Minahan, J. (2004). Unravelling Woomera: Lip sewing, morphology and dystopia. *Journal of Organizational Change Management, 17*(3), 292–301.

World Medical Association (WMA). (1991). *Declaration on Hunger Strikers (Declaration of Malta): Adopted by the 43rd World Medical Assembly Malta, November 1991 and editorially revised at the 44th World Medical Assembly Marbella Spain, September 1992*. Retrieved December 16, 2010, from http://www.legislationonline.org/documents/action/popup/id/8591

6

Riot

* * *

I tried to work with them to try to change things but otherwise this is going nowhere because the Minister for Immigration made it so clear that was coming from him or whoever with him and it was heading towards, what do you call it? Full war. It was like a complete war against detainees. It was like he considered detainees as his enemies and he was launching this war on media in every possible sense. In a way dealing with him – and he's got his own personal agenda – you can't really, there's no point. It's just like a rabbit try to negotiate with a lion the conditions of not eating him. It will eat eventually. I mean they lose, so there's no point to try.

Aamer, detained 3 years, 6 weeks.

* * *

The first riot in an Australian detention centre took place in July 1999 in Port Hedland. Australia's Human Rights Commission reported that, in 2001, there were fourteen separate riots in Woomera, Curtin and Port Hedland detention centres, up from one riot in 2000 and more than double the number that occurred in 2002 (HREOC 2004, 300–301).

L. Fiske, *Human Rights, Refugee Protest and Immigration Detention*,
DOI 10.1057/978-1-137-58096-2_6

This chapter examines detainee testimonies of riots alongside sociological, criminological and anthropological theories of riot. First, a riot in Woomera detention centre in August 2000 is reconstructed using interview transcripts, witness statements tendered to the Australian Human Rights Commission and People's Inquiry into Detention, media reports and other material available in the public domain. This incident is illustrative of the dynamics involved in riot episodes and the complex interplay between participants, authorities, emotion and reason. Academic literature and reports from government inquiries into riots are then used to analyse why riots happen and to contextualise riots in Australian immigration detention centres. The chapter proposes that Australia's detention centres are ideal incubators for riots, that riots in this context are predictable and preventable, and that actions by Australian authorities are major contributory factors in the cause of riots.

The Story of One Riot: Woomera Detention Centre, August 2000

On 30 November 1999, a group of 140 asylum seekers was flown to Woomera and became the first group of people to be detained at the newly opened Woomera detention centre (JSCM 2000, 32). The facility had been converted from a disused military base to an immigration detention centre in order to cope with the increased numbers of asylum seekers arriving by boat. Initially planned to hold 400 people, the centre soon became overcrowded. The Joint Standing Committee on Migration visited Woomera detention centre on 28 January 2000, just eight weeks after it opened, and reported that the centre then held 936 detainees (JSCM 2000, 93), and by April 2000, that number had grown to 1500 (Whitmont 2003). Staffing and infrastructure lagged behind and tensions in the centre, among both staff and detainees, increased correspondingly. In June 2000, some 500 detainees broke the perimeter fence and walked into the town where they staged a three-day sit-in protest before returning to the camp (for more on this see Chap. 4). Following the break out, security at the detention centre was significantly tightened. Ibrahim, who was involved in the June 2000 breakout, reported that following that protest, an additional perimeter fence was erected with an exclusion zone between the two: 'They made the fence double now … and the new one that's higher, higher than the first one and stronger.' 'Courtesy fences' were established within the centre, creating compounds to enable easier management of future disturbances. Each separate compound could be isolated and people's movement within the centre restricted. A former Australian Correctional Management (ACM) employee testified to the People's Inquiry into Detention that detainees returning to the detention centre following the June breakout were greeted by officers in full riot gear, and that families were separated from each other: 'they had separated women from their children, they had separated husbands from their wives' (cited in Briskman et al. 2008, 165). The worker went on to explain that, 'from June 2000, the mindset of detainees was totally different' (cited in Briskman et al. 2008, 165).

The atmosphere in detention grew increasingly tense as more people arrived and few were processed. As early as January 2000, the Joint Standing Committee on Foreign Affairs, Defence and Trade (2001, 33) noted that 'the lack of any processing at the time of the Committee's visit had created obvious tension among the detainees.' This assessment is echoed by Department of Immigration staff at Woomera, ACM guards, medics and former detainees. Anthony Hamilton-Smith, then Department of Immigration Business Manager at Woomera detention centre, testified to the Human Rights and Equal Opportunity Commission (HREOC) that when he, 'arrived at (Woomera) in May 2000, none of the residents there had had a decision made in relation to their visa applications' (Hamilton-Smith 2002, para 8). Dr Bernice Pfitzner, employed by ACM as a doctor at Woomera, told the HREOC Inquiry that, 'the main cause of this stress was visas processing. The length of time taken was inordinately long and information given to applicants was almost non-existent. People were therefore suspended in limbo' (Pfitzner 2002, para 7). A former detainee told the People's Inquiry into Detention, 'we started to lose hope completely because we have noticed there is no single individual released from the detention. People had their nerves completely destroyed. People just lost their patience and they started to involve in demonstrations' (cited in Briskman et al. 2008, 164).

By July, some people had received visas and been released from detention, but more continued to come, processing was slow and the information flow to detainees remained inadequate. Issaq was involved in a series of protests leading up to the riot:

> Well, as I said, we started it peacefully, we just did the demonstration. I mean, for three or four weeks we used to go and sit in one place just to show our objections to what they do. But it wasn't getting across. There was a (Department of Immigration) manager sitting in there and laughing at us because our objection wasn't getting anywhere. It was as far as those detention and people who were in detention and it wasn't getting anywhere. (Issaq)

The protests began to escalate and at 2.00 p.m. on Thursday, 24 August 2000, approximately 100 detainees began marching around the centre chanting, 'We want our freedom.' According to an ACM report to the Department of Immigration, the group 'attacked the inner eastern courtesy fence' and threw rocks at staff (ACM report, cited in Morton 2002). Shortly after 5.00 p.m., the group was dispersed and the Centre Emergency Response Team (CERT) was 'stood down.' Later that night, a slightly smaller group of detainees resumed marching around the main compound, once again chanting for their freedom. The second protest lasted about an hour and a half before the protesters returned to their rooms and 'normalcy' was restored in the centre. The ACM report (cited in Morton 2002) concluded that 'this was a peaceful but vocal demonstration by the detainees.'

This protest was to become the catalyst for a violent clash between detainees and ACM guards just a few days later. Allan Clifton was the ACM Operations Manager at Woomera at the time and he told the *Four Corners* television program that he believed the subsequent 'riot' was caused by ACM's heavy handed response to the protest (Whitmont 2003).

The following day, all was quiet at the centre, but '[t]o assist in controlling potential trouble, ACM head office arranged the deployment of a ten person specialist CERT team from the Arthur Gorrie Correctional Centre to Woomera' (ACM report, cited in Morton 2002). ACM nurse Mark Huxstep described the CERT team's arrival:

> They were certainly something to behold. They seemed to be everywhere at once. They were dressed in dark blue overalls with like riot gear, and helmets, riot shields, batons, they had covers over their elbows and knees, they were

prepared for a full on conflict … it was just intimidating to witness it, and I was on their side of the fence. (Huxstep, cited in Morton 2002)

Woomera detention centre remained quiet for most of the following day, Saturday 26 August. Late in the afternoon ACM decided to 'extract' the suspected leaders of Thursday's protest from the main compound and take them to the management unit. Between twenty and twenty-five people were removed. ACM Operations Manager Allan Clifton reported that the detainees sent a delegation to see him to report that two people who had been taken to the management unit had not been involved in the protest and were being wrongly held. They asked for those two individuals to be released back into the main compound:

> Detainees raised with me that they believed that some of the people we had removed to Sierra Compound may not have been involved in the disturbance, and they were very unhappy about their removal to Sierra. They were, incidentally, also very unhappy with those who had caused the disturbance.
>
> I accepted that some of those removed may not have been involved in the disturbance and I wanted to release them into the general population. I negotiated with the detainees in the main compound and agreed to speak to my superiors to see if they could be released. I was of the view that the situation could continue to escalate if it was not handled carefully.
>
> I called head office and was told by the Detention Services National Operations Manager at the time, 'Fuck 'em. ACM does not back down, take them on.' I warned that there would be a riot if nothing was done, and I did not believe that we had enough staffing resources to handle the situation, but I was ignored. After I communicated the decision to the detainees, there was a riot with fires and extensive property damage. Several staff were injured during this incident (nil detainees were injured). (Clifton 2002, para 15)

Trevor Robertson was a guard at Woomera from 2000 to 2002, and shared Clifton's concerns that ACM's handling of detainees was inappropriate. He told Quentin McDermott of *Four Corners* that,

> 'Black Panadol' was the terms that the ACM jail officers would use for batons used on prisoners: 'oh he needs a bit of Black Panadol to calm him

> down.' 'Gas and bash' was the terms that the fly-in CERT teams would use, as they seemed to think that you would come in, blow [tear] gas on people and beat them and resolve the situation. (McDermott 2008)

ACM reports to the Department of Immigration state that at 2325 hours[1] on Saturday, 26 August, a group of approximately 100 detainees gathered in the main compound and began throwing rocks at staff and administration buildings (Morton 2002). A little before 0030 hours on Sunday, 27 August, a CERT team entered the compound and ACM reports that the team was met by organised detainees who 'had formed a defence line with barricades … and were rushing forward in waves' (ACM report, cited in Morton 2002). Mark Huxstep was in the medical building at the time, which was one of the buildings that detainees were throwing stones at, and he disputes this report. Huxstep told Tom Morton of ABC Radio National's *Background Briefing*, 'I didn't see any waves of detainees, they didn't seem to be very well organised from what I could see' (Morton 2002).

ACM became worried that the detainees would breach the perimeter fence and escape. ACM's Executive General Manager in Sydney was contacted and gave permission for tear gas to be used. Allan Clifton's report to ACM states that a water cannon was also used. The detainees dispersed and relative calm was restored for a few hours (Morton 2002).

Issaq remembers the night well and described the mood in Woomera. He said that detainees already felt frustrated about the lack of response to their earlier peaceful protests, but that ACM's decision to put suspected ringleaders in isolation in the management unit triggered the violence. He said the violence in August 2000 wasn't planned, but was a culmination of frustration, fear and rumour:

> The first violent clashing started when the officers started to just hand-pick a few people who knew they were organising all these protests. They started to hand-pick them, like in the middle of night just come and take them and put them in isolations, different places, because we had all these different isolations.

[1] The ACM reports all use the 24 hour clock, and the militaristic language is re-used here to assist in conveying the atmosphere at Woomera both before and during the riot.

> People just got frustrated and frustrated. There were rumours that they were being hit in there, they were being tortured in there. It just put on your anxiety and then you lose it. Then the next officers who comes to pick up someone, everyone else come to hit that officer and then you see all officers in riot gears and batons coming to control people and people with the rods and everything. Before you know it, it's in the news and they bring the water cannons and tear gas and it became a war basically, it became a war between two groups, detainees and officers. (Issaq)

The direct confrontation between guards and detainees ended in the early hours of Monday, 28 August, following the deployment of tear gas and water cannon. After this, both detainees and guards settled in for a tense night. ACM identified twenty-three detainees who it believed had been instigators of the night's violence. They quickly planned an 'op' to extract these twenty-three detainees, which was codenamed 'Operation Morning Glory.' The Department of Immigration was not notified of the planned action (Morton 2002). At 0500 hours, Woomera ACM staff and the CERT team from Arthur Gorrie Correctional Centre entered the rooms of the suspected ringleaders. According to the ACM report, 'five of the detainees were removed without incident, and then one of the extraction teams was attacked by approximately one hundred detainees, throwing rocks and attacking them with bed-posts, slingshots and other bed parts' (ACM report, cited in Morton 2002).

While ACM had been preparing for the early morning raid, so too had the detainees. Issaq explains that,

> you just respond to it. I mean every action brings a response and when they were coming in the riot gear that was our response. We didn't have riot gears, we didn't have gas but we could get an iron post out of the fence or there was lots of rocks around. That was our response to their action… (Issaq)

ACM guards withdrew from the compound and fired a second canister of tear gas into the crowd of protesters. The detainees dispersed to the perimeters of the compound and set fire to a tent at one of the internal compound gates. By 0700 hours, the protesters had re-grouped and begun attacking three of the perimeter fences. They also set two mess halls on fire. Detainees had made makeshift shields out of bed bases and positioned wheelie bins as barricades. They tore fence posts from the internal 'courtesy fence' and used these both to lever holes in the perimeter fence and as weapons in the confrontation with guards. The protesters managed to create a large hole in the eastern perimeter fence, prompting CERT teams to move in rapidly to prevent an escape. The ACM report (cited in Morton 2002) states that 'the situation resulted in hand-to-hand confrontation' and that at 0800 hours they again used tear gas on the protesters.

The violence and confrontations continued throughout the day, but by evening a negotiated calm had been restored. Moira-Jane Conahan, a nurse employed by ACM at Woomera and a witness to the riot, described the scene to a public meeting in June 2002:

> The riot of August 2000 was a horror that I never expected to see in my country. Water cannons and guards with body armour and guns, burning buildings, smoke and stones. The day after I watched the shell shocked families come wandering out of the rubble, their children skirting around the debris, the tears and apologies and the guards' recriminations started. I watched in disbelief as a loud roar shook the earth and sky and an airforce bomber flew low over the camp, practising manoeuvres, terrifying those war-shattered people. (Conahan 2002)[2]

Many witness accounts of the day from ACM guards and management, from medical staff and from detainees invoke images of a 'war zone.' This was the first time that tear gas and water cannons were used in a detention centre, but not the last. Over the next several years, tear gas and, less commonly, water cannons were used to quell riots in Curtin, Port Hedland, Baxter and Woomera detention centres. Although accounts of the August 2000 uprising in Woomera raised serious concerns about ACM's handling of the build-up to the riot and the riot itself, no public inquiry has ever been held. Tom Morton, from ABC Radio National, questioned the Department of Immigration about its internal investiga-

---

[2] The precise timing of the military fly over has not been confirmed, but in response to a question on notice Defence Minister Robert Hill confirmed that the Royal Australian Air Force (RAAF) conducted hundreds of aerial manoeuvres over Woomera between its opening in 1999 and 2002 (Commonwealth of Australia 2003, 13434).

tion into the incident. He was advised that an investigation had been conducted but that 'the findings of the report are confidential as they relate to the security and good order of the centre' (Morton 2002).

Many right wing commentators and 'shock jocks' discussed the riots as evidence of the detainees' inherent violence and criminality. A caller to talk-back radio told listeners 'they're used to being rather barbaric' (McDonell 2000). Roz St George, a Woomera local, told British newspaper *The Independent*,

> you can't convince me none of these people are a threat to national security. It was the World Trade Centre; it could be the Sydney Opera House next. They hate Australians and the women officers get abused for wearing shorts. Who do they think they are? This is not the Middle East. (Marks 2003)

The Immigration Minister rejected any criticism of the conditions in Woomera detention centre or ACM's handling of the riot and its build-up, laying the blame solely on the detainees and emphasising that their actions were criminal and had been planned and committed by 'people with no entitlement to be released into the Australian community' (BBC 2000). The Minister told the media that the rioters were people who had been through the refugee status determination process and found not to be refugees, and who were protesting against their failure to be granted visas (McDonell 2000). In fact, several of the rioters were later found to be refugees and released into the Australian community, including Issaq, whose testimony is included in this research.

Ruddock rejected any criticism of the conditions in detention, the length of time that people were being detained or the paucity of information given to detainees about their status. Glenn Milne, from *Sunday Sunrise* television program, proposed to the Minister that 'the root problem [was] the length of time that it takes to process applications,' to which the Minister responded 'well, it's not the problem' (Bath 2001). Instead, Ruddock talked about 'people who don't like the decisions accorded them,' people who are not refugees and who are 'non-compliant' (Bath 2001).

Explanations that focus on the cultural or pathological barbarity, criminality or simple 'otherness' of detainees do little to help us understand how or why riots happen in immigration detention centres. Professor Richard Harding, then Western Australia's Inspector of Custodial Services, observed after visiting Curtin detention centre in 2001 that, 'it is no coincidence that riots occur in a system that lacks accountability. We do not have riots in our detention centres because we have a riotous group of refugees; we have them because we run appalling systems' (Harding 2001).

Few, if any, asylum seekers engaged in direct protest action within the first several months of arriving in Australia. All those interviewed for this research, along with accounts of people's arrival recorded elsewhere (Hekmat 2010), indicate that asylum seekers typically feel a mixture of relief, hope and trust when they first arrive. While detention may be confronting and the refugee status determination process confusing, people's trust in 'the West' and Australia as a human rights respecting country, and their hope that they will be accepted and are at the start of a new chapter in their lives, is not readily shaken. This makes for a highly compliant population in detention. So what happens to shift this position of compliance to violent resistance?

The Structure of a Riot

Naming a 'Riot'

Defining a riot is a subjective exercise. There are significant disparities in legal, sociological and lay definitions of 'riot.' The British *Riot Act* of 1716 defines a riot as 'twelve or more people disturbing the public peace for a common purpose' (Wilkinson 2009, 330). Australia has no such federal statute (although some state jurisdictions do), but rioting is defined through common law as the gathering of three or more people who use violence in pursuit of common goals and cause alarm to a bystander of 'reasonable firmness and courage' (Butt and Hamer 2011, 516). Sociological texts are less specific about the minimum numbers involved, but refer to 'crowds,' 'mobs,' 'groups' or other terms denoting a large number of people in close proximity, collectively engaging in violent acts against other people or property, and typically include some reference to causal or contextualising factors (Horowitz 2001; Rudé 1964; Wilkinson 2009). Populist uses of the term also infer large numbers of people, violence, disorder and chaos, but are more likely to focus on the destructiveness of riot and rioters than to canvas potentially explanatory political, structural or historical factors.

The naming of an event as a riot is often a pejorative act, implicitly carrying a swathe of value judgements about the nature of the act(s), its legitimacy, the character of those involved and its generalised threat to society. Recent events in the Middle East involving large groups of people gathering in a common cause, shouting, throwing projectiles and engaging in violent confrontation with police or military have been discussed in Western media as 'the Arab Spring,' 'uprisings,' 'civil unrest' and 'popular upheaval,' implying a moral rightness to the same actions that, when committed by the urban poor in Detroit or Brixton, are clearly named 'riots.' Similarly, peasant riots in England in the mid-1760s are, from the vantage point of history, widely referred to as 'food riots,' implying that the methods used were violent and therefore questionable, but adding the descriptor 'food' links it to a socially just cause and introduces some sense of rationality and justification for the rioters' actions (Randall 2006).

Understanding Riots

Populist lay theories of riot typically explain the phenomenon through reductionist 'mob psychology,' which describes a group of disaffected people feeling charged emotions, causing them to become highly suggestible. In this understanding, the group is infiltrated by malicious or criminal individuals determined to create chaos and destruction for their own selfish gain (Waddington 2007, 38). The riot may be sparked by a trivial incident and is an entirely illegitimate reaction, evidencing the feeble herd-like nature of the participants and the pathological immorality or criminality of the leaders. Media reporting of riots is not entirely without blame in promulgating this view. Riots are generally reported within a framework of 'moral panic' and participants are portrayed as irrational hooligans and criminals hostile to society (Scraton et al. 1991, 115). In this framework, 'we' are the victims and 'they' are the threat. Negotiation and discussion with destructive and irrational delinquents holds no promise and, instead, strong-arm policing and a determined and uncompromising reassertion of state control is the only credible response.

This view of riot has roots in eighteenth- and nineteenth-century theories of riot and crowd behaviour. However, since at least the 1960s, modern social science disciplines have rejected univariate psychological explanations of riot as too simplistic to adequately capture or explain such a complex social phenomenon (Carrabine 2005; Horowitz 2001; Randall 2006; Waddington 2007). Riots have occurred in almost every society across several centuries. Rural peasants participated in a series of riots across England in the mid-eighteenth century. University students rioted throughout French, Italian and other European cities in the late 1960s, as did residents of the ghettos in several large American cities. Prisoners detained at Peterhead prison in Scotland rioted on several occasions in the late 1980s, while detainees in Australia's immigration detention centres rioted in the early 2000s and again in 2011, 2013 and 2014. Even a cursory glance at temporally and geographically disparate riot episodes exposes the weakness of pathologising explanations. The groups listed above are sufficiently distinct in their national, historical, religious, cultural, social and economic profiles to fundamentally unsettle explanations which locate the cause of riot entirely or even substantially within a 'riotous' individual or group. George Rudé, in his study of British and French riots between 1730 and 1848, cautioned against prevailing reductivist explanations of riot and instead emphasised the utter 'ordinariness' of the people who rioted. They were, he said, largely ordinary individuals with rational reasons to be involved (Rudé 1964).

Riots overwhelmingly display a similar core structure, whether occurring in a prison setting, an impoverished developing nation or a modern urban setting (Carrabine 2005; Horowitz 2001; Randall 2006; Waddington 2007). Differences in theoretical explanations of riot are largely a matter of emphasis rather than substance. Each theory cautions against reading the riot as beginning at the first point of violence and emphasises that riots are not random or spontaneous events, but rather have their roots in established antipathy and long-held grievances

(Horowitz 2001). The immediate 'trigger' is generally the 'final straw,' an incident that is read by the protesters as emblematic of ongoing injustice and that functions to crystallise people's shared grievances sufficiently to mobilise the group to action (Waddington 2007).

US President Lyndon Johnson established the National Advisory Commission on Civil Disorders (NACCD) in 1967 to examine urban rioting in a number of US cities. The Commission was chaired by Otto Kerner, Governor of Illinois, and had eleven members drawn from Democratic and Republican parties, police, the National Association for the Advancement of Colored People (NAACP), trade unions and business. The Commission looked at twenty-four civil disturbances in twenty-three cities, surveying police, participants, witnesses and experts. The Commission concluded that,

> disorder did not erupt as a result of a single 'triggering' or 'precipitating' incident. Instead, it was generated out of an increasingly disturbed social atmosphere, in which typically a series of tension-heightening incidents over a period of weeks or months became linked in the minds of many in the Negro community with a reservoir of underlying grievances. At some point in the mounting tension, a further incident - in itself often routine or trivial - became the breaking point and the tension spilled over into violence. (Participants experienced) ... frustration deriving from a perceived inability to change matters via the political system; an increasingly tense social atmosphere, involving a sequence of negative incidents between local people and the police; and finally, a triggering or 'precipitating' incident representing the 'final straw' ... within entrenched feelings of mutual hostility. (NACCD 1968)

Drawing on the work of several key riot theorists, including Waddington (2007); Horowitz (2001); Scraton et al. (1991); Randall (2006); Wilkinson (2009), and Lea and Young (1982), the following section presents an outline of the core structure of a riot common throughout the literature. The model identifies five general pre-conditions (deeply held grievances, no access to redress, generalised hostile beliefs, close proximity and communication, and breakdown in authority-community relations) and three immediate pre-conditions (the precipitating incident, communication and exceptional norm building, and mobilisation and escalation) for riots to occur, whether in a custodial or non-custodial setting. The model also includes an analysis of the 'critical importance of the state response to riots' (Wilkinson 2009, 336).

General Pre-conditions

Long- or Deeply-Held Grievances

Studies of hundreds of riots have identified that among groups who have engaged in rioting, there have been widely held long term or deep grievances generally arising out of persistent breaches of groups members' legal rights and/or unmet social and economic needs (Horowitz 2001; Waddington 2007; Wilkinson 2009). For urban African Americans, these grievances may include high unemployment rates, perceptions of over-policing, inadequate housing and generalised social exclusion and racism (NACCD 1968). For prison populations, grievances might include arbitrary use of force by prison staff, poor standards of food, over-crowding, poor hygiene facilities or arbitrary use of punishment and solitary confinement (Scraton et al. 1991). Ethnic riots require a privileging of an in-group's ethnic identity in contrast to an out-group, typically viewed as getting more favourable treatment, of causing the poverty or unemployment of the in-group, or as presenting a threat to the peace and lives of members of the in-group (Horowitz 2001). The critical element in each of these examples is that personal subjective experiences of injustice, inequality or discrimination are widespread among individual members of the prospectively riotous group. This shared experiential characteristic becomes important in forming a sufficiently strong collective identity as a basis for action. News of an infringement of a group member's rights (whether or not that individual is personally known), is readily assimilated and reinforces shared grievances and a belief in the immutable injustice of social relations.

Within a few months of arrival, it would be unusual for any person in detention to not have personal experience of their legal rights being transgressed, or their social, cultural or material needs being unmet, creating personally felt and shared grievances. Daily life in detention involved a myriad of minor grievances and frustrations around food, sleep, occupation, communication, and other issues. Detainees and former detainees have also reported frequent incidents of much more serious grievances relating to arbitrary use of solitary confinement and excessive use of force by authorities (e.g., see *Behrooz v Secretary, DIMIA* 2004).

Complaints about food were commonplace, both in terms of the rigid rules around eating times, which made it especially difficult for children who might be hungry outside of set meal times, and about the poor quality and lack of variety being seen as a reflection of the poor regard in which detainees were held. Of the food served in detention, Osman said 'if you offer it to animal, animal will reject it… The way you eat in your home, bring it to us.'

Life in detention followed a strict and spartan regimen. Each day was marked by three 'musters,' or head counts, when guards would confirm the presence of every detainee. Detainees were issued photo ID cards upon arrival and allocated a number. Detainees were required to carry these cards with them and present them at each muster and at meal times.

One of the regular musters was in the early hours of the morning (around 1.00 a.m. or 2.00 a.m.). Guards would enter the detainees' rooms, shine a torch on their face and loudly demand to see the ID card. While all musters were resented by detainees, the night time muster was particularly antagonising. Some six years after his release from detention, Mohammed remained offended by the intrusion:

> Very, very simple point I'm telling, very, very, and at night time when you're asleep they wake you up, put the torch in your eyes 'Where is your ID card?' Now fuck man… (Mohammed)

The practice of shining torchlight into the faces of sleeping detainees has been criticised by several bodies investigating conditions in detention, including the United Nations (UNWGAD 2002), Australian Human Rights Commission (HREOC 2004) and the Joint Standing Committee on Foreign Affairs, Defence and Trade (JSCFADT 2001). However, ACM and the Department of Immigration defended the practice as necessary for the security of the detention system and, in fact, the

Department of Immigration compelled detention centre staff, through its *Handbook to Guide Departmental Managers of Detention Facilities*, to

> … physically sight the detainee. If the detainee is covered with bedding staff must pull back the sheet/blanket so the detainee can be identified. (cited in HREOC 2004, 291)

Apart from attending meals and musters, there was little structured activity in detention. Schooling for children was sporadic and education for adults was almost non-existent. Some work was available within the detention centres, such as cleaning or assisting in preparation of meals, but this was very limited and poorly paid (HREOC 1998, 138–139; 2004, 606–607). The Australian National Audit Office (ANAO) identified that a 'major disturbance' was the 'chief security risk' in immigration detention and warned the Department of Immigration that the boredom in detention centres was a major factor heightening the risk:

> … the boredom and monotony of life in the (detention centre) has the potential to be the catalyst for problems amongst or with residents. Residents are considered to have far too much unproductive time in which to ponder, speculate and react to rumours as to their fate. (ANAO 1998, 47)

The ANAO recommended that the Department of Immigration introduce and expand work, education and recreation programs in detention in order to reduce the risk of a major disturbance. The Department did make some changes to the work program at Port Hedland, but there is little evidence that this important recommendation was adequately heeded in the planning or operation of detention centres following the increase in the detention population from 1999 onwards. Boredom and a lack of meaningful activity have been repeatedly identified by detainees, their supporters and official visitors to detention centres as an ongoing complaint (Briskman et al. 2008; HREOC 1998, 2004; JSCM 2000), leaving detainees too much time to discuss the thousand 'little cruelties' (Jureidini, cited in Briskman et al. 2008, 132) of daily life in detention and to share their grievances.

The use of solitary confinement and the use of force by guards was seen by detainees as arbitrary, with no transparent process for determining if each particular action was justified or not. Farshid witnessed a mother crying and becoming verbally abusive towards ACM and Immigration staff in Curtin IDC when she was told that her eighteen-month-old son could no longer have child meals and would now be allocated adult meals. The child had been crying for several nights due to hunger, but she was refused milk for him and told simply 'this is the guideline and we can't favour you.' The young mother became increasingly distressed and angry. Farshid intervened to calm her down and to speak to the guards on her behalf:

> When the ACM manager come, I didn't even sit with him. They say 'You again!' They say 'Take this bastard' and two officers grabbed me, just hauled me and lift me from the floor with two other officer. They just put me on chest and face and bang me on the floor and they hand cuff me with those rubber hand cuffs and they just hauled me like that. They didn't even listen to what I wanted to say. (Farshid)

The incident escalated further as other detainees witnessed Farshid's treatment and 'show[ed] some anger' (Farshid). Farshid doesn't know what happened next, as he was taken to solitary confinement and threatened with unspecified criminal charges. On this occasion, no riot erupted. Farshid continued to explain that what happened to him was commonplace and happened to many other detainees for minor or non-existent infringements. He spoke of another incident of excessive and unnecessary use of force:

> There were some people who were psychopathic, the way they acting, they enjoy that sort of torture. The day they beat a guy because he was asking for a sleeping tablet. I couldn't believe that the guy I knew would cry that loud under a punch. It wasn't a punch, but the way they putting him on the floor and squeezing his hand and he was crying so loud. I was thinking 'God, what is this guy thinking? Is he enjoying that level of torture? I mean, that level of crying noise?' (Farshid)

Baha'adin told of guards at Baxter detention centre taking people from their rooms in the middle of the night:

> They were so cruel what they were doing to us. They were taking us by force like middle of night when we were sleeping. For example, you see forty or fifty people they come to your room, forty guards, fully armed. They come to your room in the middle of the night at three or four in the morning, they take you by force. They put you in isolation room and when you are in isolation room you just feeling so frustrated, like you go crazy in there. It's just because you see four walls around you. It drives you mad you know… (Baha'adin)

Emad witnessed many similar incidents and said that 'we just saw some, a very hard line treatment and it was typical every day, every morning, every night.' Osman also complained the guards beat detainees 'often,' and that this would escalate the situation and usually lead other detainees to come to assist the person being beaten. He expressed his indignation and outrage at the guards: 'Listen to him. Don't beat him! So when we see him beaten … they have no right to beat us. My father never beat me. Even here, you don't beat your kids. So who did give you the right to beat him?'

The arbitrary use of power, whether through the use of isolation or excessive force, meant that detainees had little faith that the punishment they observed being meted out was warranted and, further, detainees could easily imagine themselves in that situation. This created strong solidarity between detainees, regardless of the individual detainees' personal or political relationships. Sayed said that seeing women and children in the same situation was particularly difficult:

> When the women and children were with us in isolation area, we get more upset because of that. And the things we heard. If we see someone used to cry a lot, we try to involve in that and calm down and do something you know. And it involve us because if human hurt, sometime we try to help each other. (Sayed)

Ibrahim summed up the mood in detention: 'We were always angry. Always angry. Getting angry playing dominoes. Seriously, we were always angry. Since the morning.'

No Access to Redress

Official channels for resolving long or deeply-held grievances must be absent, such as during racial segregation in the USA; inaccessible to members of the group, due to factors such as language, cost or prejudice; or perceived to be ineffective, such as through prison complaints systems. Typically, efforts by the group to gain redress through 'proper' channels, whether legal or political, have met with state indifference (Waddington 2007, 49). As 'normal' or 'legitimate' methods for addressing the groups' grievances are closed off, alienation from the existing social order grows and proposals by members of the in-group to launch other methods outside of the system such as protest, strikes or riot begin to gain traction.

If a detainee wanted anything other than that provided during meal times, he or she had to fill out a request form and lodge it with an ACM guard who would then forward the request to the appropriate person. Detainees were required to lodge request forms to access the telephone to call their migration agent, to request an appointment with a Department of Immigration officer to ask for news about their case, to request a pain-killer for a headache, to request an appointment with a dentist or to request a blown light bulb be replaced in their room. These written requests were very often not acted upon in a timely manner, sometimes refused, or, most commonly, ignored entirely. Hussein expressed his exasperation:

> For example when you've got a headache, a Disprin necessary for you. So to get a Panadol, and if you go there and say 'no, we won't give you' and you have to wait for one or two days. What you have to do? It's true. (Hussein)

More complex or expensive requests, such as to see a specialist, were even less successful. Mohammed was detained for four years and as his mental health deteriorated, he sought help: 'I applied more than 10,000 times to see the specialist for my mental. They never, ever bring anyone.' Ismail was detained for five years and during that time he 'used to write a lot of question and request for them. I had this much [*makes a sign with open thumb and forefinger*] request about different issues. All they answer "No," "we don't know" or ignore it. It didn't do anything.'

The cumulative frustrations of daily life in detention often led to protests. Most of these protests went unreported in the media. Osman told of a 'strike' that detainees in Port Hedland staged to get appointments with Department of Immigration staff. For a week, detainees refused to clean or remove rubbish: 'We did the mess, leave the rubbish, smell, oh, very very mess.' After a week of refusing to work, the Department of Immigration agreed to meet with detainees. Not all protests were successful though. Issaq described a daily 'sit-in' outside Immigration offices at Woomera, demanding access to telephones to call their families. At that time, there were approximately 1500 people detained in Woomera and everyone sat outside the Department of Immigration office for half a day. Their request was refused. 'They were bringing all these excuses that "we can't bring you a phone" and all this sort of thing. People got angry, people got frustrated.' ACM guards dispersed the crowd and people returned to their compounds feeling frustrated and angry. According to Issaq, this incident in April 2000 was the first in a series of protests, culminating in the mass breakout in June 2000 in which several hundred detainees marched into Woomera and camped by the public telephones for three days:

> That was the first protest and just for the phone which it became bigger and bigger and people decided, well, we have to do something and we broke out and went to a town and sat in the town… It wasn't because we wanted to get out, it was because we just wanted to use the phone. In there, there was one Telstra public phone that people started to call *1800 REVERSE* and call their families. (Issaq)

ACM and Immigration's indifference to the detainees' request for telephones escalated to a mass breakout from the detention centre.

Smaller protests and complaints were often greeted with a hardline response from ACM. Dissent was not tolerated. Those who were known or suspected of being involved in organising protests were routinely placed in isolation or 'management' compounds. Ibrahim explained:

> So Serena camp and India camp it was really awful punishment for anyone who start to make any violence. Well, to be honest, all the people who were transferred to this camp, they haven't been violent at all. They just were talking

about why the food is bad, why they not allowed to talk to our families. They just complain. Well, to complain that's not violence! So you don't even have the small right to complain. You don't have this right. You are here, you have to obey, you have to follow what we say to you and what we do to you. You don't have any right to say anything. Don't argue. Don't. Ever. Argue. (Ibrahim)

Detainees sometimes lodged complaints with ACM management and the Department of Immigration about guards' excessive use of force, but all participants in this research said that their complaints were dismissed without proper investigation. Mohammed said he complained about guards' treatment of detainees several times but,

never ACM, they never, ever, the supervisor never ever, or the head of ACM look at maybe some officer doing it wrong. Always support them. What happened, we complain from them and we go see DIMIA. We accept that DIMIA is the manager and see everything. But what DIMIA does is make it worse. (Mohammed)

He expressed his frustration at the Department of Immigration, which represented protests and riots in the media as entirely due to detainees being 'trouble makers,' and excluding any discussion of provocation or brutality by guards. 'Absolutely it was rubbish because we so many times, many, not one, two, three… one hundred times we saw different act' (Mohammed). Farshid tried writing to external organisations such as Australia's Human Rights Commission, the United Nations and Amnesty International. But all correspondence had to pass through the Department of Immigration's manager at Curtin IDC, who refused to post any complaint letters:

I was getting good in writing but he was getting good in just tearing. I was told by one ACM officer, the one that became a friend, she told me once 'In Australia don't talk, write things and just submit your written things with a witness and it should go somewhere. If you're talking they can deny that you said anything.' I was getting good at writing but he was getting good at tearing it up. (Farshid)

Flowing from his background in law, Emad believed in settling disputes through discussion and transparent processes. He spent his eight months in Curtin detention centre trying to mediate between detainees, ACM and Department of Immigration staff and urging detainees not to protest. He made no progress with management:

> I thought of communicating with the management, sending groups to them, asking for appointments, to see them and talk to them. But unfortunately most of my requests were ignored at that time. Actually, they didn't listen to even the most moderate way of thinking on the refugees' side. I don't know. I'm thinking of a manager as, even in the science of management, the manager always has options let's say, in negotiation skills. [But it was] just like being in an army unit. (Emad)

He also made no progress with detainees, who saw no hope in negotiation:

> Most of the people in the detention centre were laughing on my judgements that the law will rule in the end. They said 'Look, there is no rule of law here.' Because I believed in the rule of law, even when I was in Iraq, and I said there will be a time when the rule of law will govern all people, from the head of the states to the normal people. The refugees didn't believe in this, because what they saw around them is a very far behaviour, a very far, a very rude behaviour, very aggressive psychologically and physically to their human rights. (Emad)

Prior to the increase in boat arrivals between 1999 to 2001, an expert committee was formed by the Department of Immigration to advise it on managing risk at the Port Hedland detention centre. This committee noted that 'the more control detainees had over their daily activities and benefits, the better their behaviour,' and recommended that 'use of this strategy in the (detention centre) could aid compliance and security' (ANAO 1998, 46). In spite of expert advice that recommended increased areas for detainee autonomy and the inclusion of detainees in negotiation and decision-making where possible, the reality of the intransigence of management and refusal to engage detainees in even mundane decision-making processes was a common thread brought up throughout interviews for this research. Detainees saw that 'hardline' management was supported by the Prime Minister and Minister for Immigration, and all talked of the futility of negotiation.

Generalised Hostile Beliefs

Members of the prospective rioting group must share a generalised hostile belief about members of the out-group. This belief may be against the society from which they are estranged or subsections within it, typically the police or other institutions representing authority. Waddington (2007, 40) notes that studies of riots throughout Europe and the USA reveal a background of 'entrenched feelings of mutual hostility' between police and rioters. Horowitz (2001, 532), in his study of *The Deadly Ethnic Riot* also identifies a simmering hostility and apprehension among pre-riot groups, noting that any account of riot must incorporate emotion. Generalised apprehension enables the imputation of hostile intentions of members of the out-group towards the in-group to be quickly assimilated as credible and functions to prepare rioters for what participants will likely see as vigorous and necessary 'self-defence' (Horowitz 2001, 532–533, 528). This generalised belief will typically grow and spread throughout the group in the weeks or months preceding a riot episode. In the USA, the Kerner Commission highlighted that the periods leading up to the twenty-four riots it studied were marked by 'an increasingly disturbed social atmosphere, involving a sequence of negative incidents between local people and the police' (NACCD 1968, 6) and that these negative incidents were, in the minds of the local people, linked to the long-term grievances they collectively held. They were seen as evidence of the police's hostility toward them and fuelled an atmosphere of mutual hostility and distrust (NACCD 1968; Waddington 2007). It is this generalised hostile belief that crystallises during the 'trigger' event (discussed below).

There was a widespread belief throughout the detainee community that the ACM guards and Department of Immigration staff hated detainees and wanted confrontations. Hussein spent almost three years in Curtin and Baxter detention centres and he believed that 'some of them—they hate us, the officers.' He went on to explain that he believed that ACM intentionally selected people who were hostile to asylum seekers to work in the centres 'of course, they wanted some people… What sort of idea they had, it's really evil. I mean, a couple were alright, but most of them, they chose some people that are very tough against us. Maybe we call them as racists' (Hussein). Hussein's friend Mehdi agreed, and went further to say that the guards would provoke confrontations with detainees, 'all the time the officers they trying to make you angry to do something.' Detainees were frequently told that 'Australians' hated them and that they were not welcome (Briskman et al. 2008, 135; Fiske 2006, 222).

Detainees were often also aware of the wider political landscape and believed that they were being used as pawns in Australian national elections. They believed that they were meant to suffer, and to suffer very publicly, in order to deter prospective asylum seekers and enable the government to appear 'tough on immigration' to an uneasy electorate (for more on detainees' analysis of Australian politics, see Chap. 3):

> That was their policy for sure. They knew exactly what's going on in detention everyday. But they really didn't care. They wanted to make us frustrated more and more and more… The reason was because I reckon in that time when we came a lot of people they were coming to Australia and the policy was to show to other countries 'we don't want refugees anymore.' Actually, they used us as the victims to show to the people that the refugee come to Australia. I also put it in the other hand that that was quite racist from John Howard and Phil Ruddock, they done that. (Baha'adin)

Believing that their suffering was deliberate and was a political strategy to win votes upset detainees and served to reinforce feelings of hostility towards the government:

> Philip Ruddock used us a bit of a thing like 'they are dangerous people, they are terrorists' or 'they are criminals' and things like that. On the news actually he said that. I was very .disappointed with what he was saying about us. It really made us more angry and upset of what he said. (Baha'adin)

As well as the general hostility between guards and detainees, the arbitrary exercise of power, occasional forced removal (of which all detainees were afraid) and lack of communication with detainees created an atmosphere of high anxiety. The level of apprehension and tension among the detainees in all detention centres was consistently high. Farshid was struck by the atmosphere in Perth detention centre when he first arrived:

> I arrive in Perth at the detention centre and as soon as I got in I met some people who were totally traumatised and paranoid. They were thinking there are microphones everywhere and they were fearful to talk to one another and the only time they could talk freely was during their break time in their exercise time in the exercise yard. And every time one ACM officer in that period of time was coming to pick someone, everyone their hearts were racing because they didn't know what was going to happen to them. People were taken by forceful deportation or people were taken by force or manipulation and then someone else come and took them off for a simple thing like medical visit or a lawyer visit. (Farshid)

Several months later, Farshid too became highly suspicious of the government. 'I was at that time very suspicious about what was going on. I was really annoyed and suspicious. This is a lie, why does the government have to lie?' The cumulative effect of detention conditions was an apprehensive and hostile environment with 'sides' clearly bounded.

Close Proximity and Communication

Potential rioters need to communicate with one another to enable sharing of personal stories of injustice which facilitate the development of a collective identity based on shared experiences and oppression. The group needs to share analyses of their experiences and, in particular, to hold a shared belief about who is to blame for their oppression. The common analysis is produced through communication and relationships. These stories may be told and retold, enabling solidarity beyond personal relationships. The retelling of stories may include rumour, but heard within the generalised feelings of hostility outlined above, even unlikely rumours which accord with the dominant and growing beliefs of the disaffected group will be taken as true and can be instrumental in mobilising the group to action. Prospective rioters also need to be in close physical proximity to one another to enable a rapid response when a triggering event occurs (Horowitz 2001; Waddington 2007).

People in immigration detention centres are, by necessity, in close proximity with one another and have little else to do but worry about their applications and talk about events happening in detention. Osman described that, 'like for example, we are sitting, me and you and talking "we have to do something," and another guy come, and this guy join us sitting… It's just chatting and it becomes all, "OK, let's do it!"' Similarly, Shahin said that there was, 'no book, no magazine, newspapers, radio or TV you know. The people would come to my donga,[3] to my room and they would sit and tell stories, they would tell me stories. Sometimes I have heard the same story maybe fifty times.' This telling of stories and the absence of any meaningful activity or objective information about people's progress through the system heightened the sense of solidarity between detainees. It also established a fertile environment for rumours. Ibrahim said that the rumours escalated, particularly when groups were separated without explanation, 'because the rumours are everywhere now—they don't know about us, we don't know anything about them. So they start to talk, everyone talk in his version.' The removal of people to isolation compounds was particularly escalatory:

> I felt sorry for these guys. This situation in Serena Camp and India Camp was very awful. They took them by force. They force them to go there and keep them for about three weeks – alone! Imagine it! We already in trouble. I'm with people but I'm still feeling bad. What if I'm alone?! You can't imagine it. (Ibrahim)

Detainees worried about people who were taken to isolation. Having seen the force used to remove people from the main compound, it was a short step to imagine their fellow detainees being mistreated there. Issaq said that in the immediate lead-up to the first Woomera riots, 'there were rumours that they were being hit in there, tortured in there. It just put on your anxiety and then you lose it.'

Breakdown in Authority-Community Relations

The final general pre-condition for riot is a substantial breakdown in authority-community relations. Once the authorities are seen by the prospective rioting group as harassing and indiscriminate in their policing,

[3] A 'donga' is a transportable building.

then any action of the authority against any member of the group is seen as an offence against all and the likelihood of a collective response is greatly enhanced (Lea and Young 1982, 12). Waddington (2007, 49–50), in his *Flashpoint Model of Public Disorder*, notes that groups, including groups in authority such as police, develop their own cultures on the basis of shared conditions and experiences. As relations between the groups become more adversarial and confrontational, and as their understandings of certain events diverge, they begin to 'perceive each other in terms of fundamentally negative stereotypes,' and the stage is set for a trigger or flashpoint to ignite a riot. In the lead-up to riots and mass disturbances, the authorities, whether police, prison guards or detention officers, come to be seen as a substantially undifferentiated whole, to be exercising their powers unjustly, and consequently, are seen as powerful rather than authoritative. In his study of prison riots, Eammon Carrabine (2005, 898) observes that 'prisoners withdraw their consent for regimes they regard as unjust and morally bankrupt.' Maintaining legitimacy in the eyes of the detained, argues Carrabine, is crucial for avoiding riots in prisons. This legitimacy cannot be attained through legal or physical force alone, but through engagement, accommodation of reasonable requests, transparent and fair procedures and a range of other processes which build the moral legitimacy which underpins authoritativeness. When an authority is seen as illegitimate, prisoners are far more likely to riot and revolt.

Similarly, the behaviours of those in authority are shaped by collectively held perceptions of the group they are interacting with. When they hold a preconceived negative view of the group, they are likely to read actions by the group accordingly. This is heightened when media, politicians and other shapers of public opinion respond to the actions of the dissenting group in ways that frame their actions or demands as illegitimate, and that vilify the group or denounce their actions (Waddington 2007, 49). This serves to both reinforce the authority's negative view of the dissenters, thereby supporting overly strong and potentially escalatory policing actions, as well as reinforcing feelings of resentment within the dissenting group.

It is important to note here that members of the dissenting group often view their behaviour quite differently from those in authority. The dissenting group see their grievances and resulting actions as legitimate. A noisy protest involving marching and chanting or shouting may be seen by protesters as legitimate and peaceful action, whereas the authority may view it as a precursor to a riot and respond accordingly (Waddington 2007). A protest is more likely to escalate to riot when it occurs within a context of poor relations between the authorities and the dissenting group. Where the authorities and the group already hold mutually negative views of each other, each will read the other's actions through this lens and, if the authorities' response to the protesting group is seen as indiscriminate, brutal or disrespectful, the involvement of authority will likely be a causative rather than preventative factor (Waddington 2007).

The public representations of detainee actions by politicians and the media as being without legitimate basis and arising from their criminality and refusal to accept the outcome of a fair process has been well documented (e.g., see Klocker and Dunn 2003; Mares 2003; Pickering 2005). The Department of Immigration repeatedly referred to riots in detention as 'criminal activity' and attributed the cause of riots to failed visa applications. During a riot in Woomera in December 2001, a Department of Immigration media release stated that,

> this was not an unrestrained riot – it was a deliberate campaign of criminal activity to hold the Australian people to ransom in order to gain visas. (DIMIA 2001)

The atmosphere in detention became increasingly polarised. Detainees in all centres reported that the guards, and sometimes even Department of Immigration staff, told them that Australians 'don't want you, the people outside hate you, the people outside think negatively about you. You jumped the queue, you have no rights whatsoever' (Emad). Allegiance between detainees grew stronger as relationships with guards and Department of Immigration staff deteriorated. Baha'adin explained that 'we were kind of like a team when you were in detention. So we were like detainees and guards (were) like another thing.' The breakdown in relationship between detainees and guards dehumanised members of each group amongst members of the other. In an interview with *Four Corners*, several former guards spoke of how stressful their role was and how a culture developed among guards in which all detainees were viewed as threats and as the enemy. Carol Wiltshire, who was a guard at Woomera in 2002, told Quentin McDermott that she,

> … hated them. I honestly did. I hated them and I wanted to run them over. I just wanted to strangle them. I thought, you know, this is me, a compassionate person turning into an absolute animal, and that's how I felt though. (McDermott 2008)

Guards who showed kindness to detainees were derided as 'care bears' and risked ostracism from their colleagues (Briskman et al. 2008; McDermott 2008). The relationship between guards and detainees was not always hostile, but during the build-up to violent confrontations, indiscriminate and negative views of the out-group became more dominant. Another former guard, Trevor Robertson, described how in one fight with detainees at Woomera, he became so frightened that he was striking out at,

> … anybody that looked Asian by the throat and trying to seriously fucking hurt them. I was trying to kill people because I thought somewhere around there, there was a knife that was going to slip into my ribs or into someone else's ribs and that. (McDermott 2008)

Osman described how a peaceful sit-in in Port Hedland detention centre escalated to a physical confrontation between guards and detainees when guards tried to disperse the group and the group refused to move. He particularly noted that the guards approached the group indiscriminately and used actions against the whole group rather than particular individuals:

> One officer came in and hit with his leg the guy who was sitting there, not hard, more like a push. That's very bad in any culture. It's like animal or rubbish…. So what's gonna happen? This guy is sick mentally … mentally exhausted. So you don't do that action. So what happened? He [the guard] kick him and he [the detainee] come out and push the guard. He push the guard. OK '*he*' push the guard. You go to *that* person, not the people who are sitting in peace. So what happened that action there, we were sitting

> here – psht – they start using the [tear] gas. We were sitting, the action happened there. [The gas] stings and burns your eyes. So they use that things on us, we were just sitting, that's it. So what's gonna happen? You do this, and I have to do something, that's my right. So we stood up and we started pushing and we don't have any weapon except water. So we start using the water, because if they use the gas and you use the water it doesn't work anymore. So we start like, bring the hose, put water on them. (Osman)

The escalation to a riot involves a series of actions and reactions which serve to reinforce generalised negative and homogenising beliefs about the other group and the threat that they pose. These reinforced beliefs also shape the actions and reactions of each group. Riot experts advise that recognition of this pattern, leading to the maintenance of evidence-based action by authorities that is targeted only at specific individuals, as well as the maintenance of communication with leaders, are essential (Waddington 2007). However, there was little evidence of this in the lead-up to riots in Australian immigration detention centres by the private security companies contracted to run the centres.

Immediate Pre-conditions

Precipitating Incident: The Trigger

The conditions outlined above create the necessary environment for a riot to occur, and, in that sense, a riot is not a spontaneous event. The pre-conditions for a riot can endure for extended periods of time before resulting in riot, or may never culminate in a riot. However, when a specific triggering event occurs within this context that typifies the sort of injustices experienced by group members, it becomes imbued with signifiers for the oppressed group and can spark a riot. This trigger can be relatively minor in itself, but it will be read by the group as emblematic of their deeply-held grievances and serve to crystallise community sentiment to action.

Horowitz (2001, 544–545) observes that the group's reaction to the precipitant is 'to outsiders, startlingly disproportionate, *when the precipitant is considered as a one-time event,*' (emphasis in the original) but, he says, rioters are 'radical ontologists' and 'prodigious unifiers, who assiduously link together events in a single, unbounded chain and link targets in an indivisible group.' So too are politicians, media and society, as they homogenise 'rioters,' both across and within riot events occurring in different times, locations and social settings. Hundley's analysis of riot precipitants in American cities supports this proposition. He states that the 'significance of this event is that it immediately focuses the attention on an overt act of suppression that is met with open hostility, not because of the act itself, but because it is representative of a long history of such acts' (Hundley, cited in Waddington 2007, 42–43).

The triggering event may have no independent importance, but its importance lies in its capacity to carry the feelings of resentment, oppression and injustice of the crowd. Horowitz (2001, 522) notes that emotion is an important factor in riots and that the riot is a mixture of instrumental and impulsive violence, combining both reason and passion. The violence is instrumental because it responds to and seeks to change the unjust relationship between groups, even if only temporarily, and it is impulsive because it enables the discharge of built-up anger and aggression by the participants. Riot as protest, Horowitz (2001, 522–539) proposes, may convey a message to society and so have some communicative elements, but its immediate function and a benefit for rioters which ought not be excluded in efforts to understand riot, is its cathartic power. A riot is rarely a planned affair, but nor is it spontaneous. Rather, it is the culmination of the collapsing of long-term and proximate wrongs in a particular moment.

In many instances, the immediate trigger to riots in detention was the excessive and arbitrary use of force or solitary confinement by guards against detainees. Visa refusals, poor conditions, a lack of information about detainees' legal status, too much unstructured time and a generalised atmosphere of fear, anxiety and hostility form a crucial backdrop to the triggering event. Witnessing the misuse of power was a near daily event in detention, but in particular moments, this was sufficient to cause all the pre-conditions of a riot to coalesce and erupt.

Mohammed, having said he witnessed mistreatment of detainees 'a hundred times' without rioting, described the start of a riot. He and other detainees 'saw the officer bashing one detainee underage,' and felt compelled, 'to go support.' Detainees 'from Palestine, Iran, Afghanistan… Iraq, everyone knows what they have to do. Put the fire, put the pain.' The response from ACM was swift and brutal; 'ACM or DIMIA didn't come talk to us. They straight away put armed, … hot water machine and jump and start to kick out … they start to put the tear gas … suddenly they start bash, they didn't care, kids there, woman there, man, they start going everywhere.' Although Mohammed lamented the lack of communication or negotiation from Immigration or ACM, he also remarked that 'even honest with you, many of the detainees didn't come and mediate it, the people got so mental they want to broke and burn everything. "We are stop, please, enough, enough, stop."'

Similarly, Issaq told of the first Woomera riot and how people were taken, unjustly in the opinions of the detainees, to isolation following a non-violent protest, and that this provoked the detainees to retaliate against the next CERT operation. He spoke of people feeling 'frustrated and frustrated' and that CERT operations, alongside detainee rumours, 'just put on your anxiety and then you lose it.' A detainee involved in riots in Christmas Island detention centre in March 2011 told a similar story of a non-violent protest by detainees, followed by Serco (the private security contractor running Christmas Island IDC) deciding a 'show of force' was needed and organising what the detainee termed a 'snatch and grab' operation to remove twenty suspected ringleaders from the main compound:

> This not only did not help to calm the situation down, but created more anger and frustration among other detainees… Not surprisingly, other detainees responded to the arbitrary arrests, and broke into the high security Red Compound in an attempt to free the twenty people who had been taken away in handcuffs. It was then that the police used tear gas and fired beanbag rounds. (Anonymous 2011)

The detainee explained that police and Serco actions 'enraged the crowd, and some lost their control and started to cause property damage by setting some tents and canteens on fire and smashing CCTV cameras' (Anonymous 2011).

The precipitating incident in each of these examples was an occasion of perceived injustice against a small group of detainees which was witnessed by a larger group of fellow detainees. The incident served to crystallise anger and indignation sufficiently to mobilise the group to action.

Communication and Exceptional Norm Building

During and immediately following the precipitating incident, word is quickly spread and feelings of outrage, and perhaps fear, are shared. In the process of discussing the incident, it is important that prospective participants build a clear, shared understanding of where blame for this most recent (and prior) injustice lies. Information about the precipitating incident and prior incidents is communicated throughout the group and community. Smelser (cited in Waddington 2007, 40) noted that rumours can be powerful at this stage of immediate pre-riot and can 'distort reality' and 'short circuit' the normal paths to the amelioration of grievances. This shared assignation of blame, shared outrage and indignation at the latest affront and immediate communication facilitates the group's developing exceptional norms that will support and enable the rioting behaviour. Contemporary theories of riot accept that riots are not caused by 'riotous individuals,' but that, as rioting involves ordinary people transgressing social norms, participants need to understand their actions as justified and 'right' (Horowitz 2001; Rudé 1964). Social support and sanction is essential to the riot.

Horowitz's study deals with deadly ethnic riots, which differ substantively from riots that principally target property, but nonetheless, his analysis offers useful insights into the structure and anatomy of riot as a sharp departure from the 'norm.' Rioters, Horowitz (2001, 528) contends, seek justification for their actions and evidence of their 'rightfulness,' and they 'reason about justification, however cursory and faulty their reasoning may be.' A riot, he says,

> is not a wholly irrational affair … at the outset, their reasoning is not defective, … they get the facts of the provocation right.… What [they] get wrong are the facts about the facts: they exaggerate the significance of the

> precipitants, … they add false facts or exaggerated facts, rumours of … aggression, … poisoned water supplies… Rioters imagine themselves engaged in self-defence. (Horowitz 2001, 555)

Rioters 'view themselves as participating in something akin to military operations' (Horowitz 2001, 529). Once the situation is constructed as war-like, behaviours on both sides that are not normally accepted become permissible. The exceptional, temporarily at least, becomes normalised.

Most participants in this research used the analogy of 'war' to describe the situation in detention. Even those detainees who, throughout their detention, maintained that negotiation and non-violent resistance were the only acceptable courses of action, used war as an analogy. Shahin, whose story is partially told in Chapter 3, said that he 'accepted consciously that [he was] in a war,' and that this shaped his thinking throughout his twenty months in detention. Issaq expressed it more directly:

> … it became a war basically. It became a war between two groups, detainees and officers. You don't see any friendship in there any more you know. You don't care that officers were good officers. You see him as a person in riot gear with a helmet with batons and shots in his hand, and you don't care who he is. (Issaq)

Solidarity among detainees grew as people saw that actions against a fellow detainee could easily be used against them too. Osman explained that if a detainee was being beaten by a guard, he would go to their aid, even if he didn't know that person or the circumstances that lead to the conflict:

> Anyone! Anyone who are detainee. It doesn't matter if you are Iraqi, Afghan, no. No. We *are* detainee. We are detainee. If I hear that one African guy is under attack – I will go. Why? Even if he's done wrong, if he's done wrong, [it's] because he's sick, he's lost his patience. Listen to him. Don't beat him! So when we see him beaten, they have no right to beat us. (Osman)

Osman didn't distinguish between the unknown 'African guy' and himself. Rather, the transgression of the other man's rights was viewed as a transgression of his own rights.

In war, the sides are clear and polarised, every person is categorised as enemy or ally, and a different set of norms is developed. Sayed and Ismail discussed needing to rethink 'right' and 'wrong' in detention. Sayed used the analogy that in ordinary circumstances, it is wrong to steal, but that 'in extreme circumstances, for example if I am really, really hungry and about to die, I might steal the bread.' He said that although he may 'feel bad' about stealing, he thinks that in certain circumstances, acts normally prohibited can be justified or even necessary. Ismail agreed and added, 'and we knew that detention was wrong.'

Mobilisation and Escalation

Within this heightened state of threat and passion, someone must propose retaliation for a riot to develop. The proposal may be verbal or through a 'spontaneous' hurling of an object at a building or representative of authority. Dynamic leaders may emerge at this point who lead the action. These leaders may be long-term community leaders or simply the most persuasive speakers or actors present (Hundley, cited in Waddington 2007, 42). Most theorists agree that the state's response at this point is crucial in determining whether the disturbance escalates to violence or is dispersed. Hundley, Speigel, Waddington, and Lea and Young all concur that authorities need to be careful not to confirm the crowd's view of them as seeing the group as an amorphous whole (Lea and Young 1982; Waddington 2007). If police 'manhandle everyone in sight,' the situation is likely to become inflamed, and so authorities must be careful to discern which individuals within the group are engaged in violence and make arrests selectively and with the minimum use of force (Speigel, cited in Waddington 2007, 46). Hundley (cited in Waddington 2007, 43) recommends that authorities contact leaders within the community and 'furnish them with meaningful concessions to put to their constituents.' Indiscriminate arrests, excessive use of force and refusal to enter into negotiations are all likely to have escalatory effects (Wilkinson 2009). Similarly, public statements by politicians and other leaders which vilify the protesters and close off opportunities for political re-engagement will do little to avert violence or bring it to an early end.

Policing the Riot

In each of the riot episodes examined for this work, there was a build-up of smaller protests, followed by a 'zero tolerance' response by ACM, which then escalated through a series of actions and reactions, culminating in an explosion of violent protest.

The Woomera riot, explored in the opening pages of this chapter, describes detainees protesting 'peacefully' but 'vocally.' ACM then took suspected leaders of the protest into solitary confinement. Fellow detainees asked management to release two people who they considered to have been wrongfully punished. Their request was refused, a CERT team was flown in and detainees reacted with anger, attacking fences and property in the detention centre. When ACM attempted to execute a dawn raid the following day, detainees had armed themselves and attacked the CERT team. The riot lasted three days before calm was restored.

The anonymous detainee's account of the Christmas Island riot in March 2011 outlines a remarkably similar path of events (Anonymous 2011). In the months leading up to the riot, detainees participated in a series of protests, such as hunger strikes, lodging complaints with the Commonwealth Ombudsman and demanding meetings with Department of Immigration staff. None of these actions were successful, and so on 11 March 2011, up to 150 detainees broke out of detention in protest (AAP 2011a). Most returned the following day, but a second breakout of less than 100 detainees occurred on 13 March (AAP 2011b). Again, most people returned to the detention centre within twenty-four hours, although a group of approximately twenty people remained outside. The Minister for Immigration organised for a delegation to meet with the protesters and to discuss their concerns (Bowen 2011). According to a detainee, the negotiator was taking their concerns back to the Minister and the detainees had informed him that they would continue non-violent protests while awaiting a response (Anonymous 2011). Meanwhile, the Australian Federal Police (AFP) and Serco conducted a 'round up' of twenty suspected ringleaders and took them to Red Compound, a high security isolation block. That evening, detainees staged a noisy but nonviolent protest, waving white flags and asking about the whereabouts of the men who had been removed. The AFP responded to the protest by firing tear gas and bean bag bullets at the crowd. According to the detainee informant, 'this behaviour from the police enraged the crowd, and some lost their control and started to cause property damage by setting some tents and canteens on fire and smashing CCTV cameras' (Anonymous 2011).

A series of smaller protests were met initially by state indifference. The protests gradually escalated over a period of months until a particular protest event was met with 'strong-arm' and indiscriminate policing, which in turn escalated the detainees' actions. The process of action and reaction ultimately resulted in a riot.

In December 2002, detainees at both Woomera and Port Hedland rioted following a newspaper report that immigration detention centres were like 'five star hotels' and the Immigration Minister's complete rejection of a United Nations report criticising Australia's detention centres (Downer and Ruddock 2002; Penberthy 2002). Osman was in Port Hedland at the time, and said that detainees there protested by marching around the compound chanting, 'Philip Ruddock liar. Philip Ruddock liar.' Detainees saw a news report that night of protests and fires in Woomera. They also noted, with some bewilderment, that Port Hedland detention centre that night had only two guards instead of the usual ten:

> I was wondering why there is no people, just two. So other people who were very angry, very desperate, they took that opportunity. They smash and smash and smash and suddenly burn everything. (Osman)

Port Hedland detainees were angry about detention being likened to a five star hotel, but also were concerned about what had triggered the protests in Woomera. 'Something happen in Woomera, like why? Why?

Bad things more are going to happen to us. Everyone in detention, we are in the same boat' (Osman). Detainees were able to move between different compounds, and so they made their way to India compound and set it alight, 'because the India camp was bad memories for many people because it was the first place to be in detention and was isolation as well. So they burn it' (Osman). Memories of recent injustice, rumours of injustices in Woomera and apprehension about what might happen in Port Hedland, coupled with a lack of response and staffing from ACM, was sufficient to escalate an initially peaceful protest into fire and property destruction.

Sociological theories of police responses to riot state that it is important that police neither under- nor over-control an escalating riot. An under-reaction by authorities enables people to act with impunity and can encourage more people to become involved, whereas an over-reaction, such as sending in police with riot gear, horses or dogs before negotiations have been exhausted, is likely to be inflammatory (Speigel, cited in Waddington 2007, 45). The riots in Woomera in August 2000 and on Christmas Island in 2011 are examples of escalatory over-policing, while the Port Hedland riot of December 2002 appears to be the opposite. In each case, there is no evidence of ACM, Serco, the Australian Federal Police or the Department of Immigration engaging detainee leaders in any meaningful negotiations or being willing to accommodate any of the detainees' demands. A letter from the Secretary of the Department of Immigration to detainees during riots in Woomera, Baxter and Port Hedland detention centres in December 2002 reveals the government's belief that there was no room for negotiation with detainees. The letter bluntly advised detainees that,

> those of you currently in detention are there by your own choice because you are pursuing your cases through the Court system or because you are refusing to cooperate with arrangements to depart Australia. Your situation therefore, could not be any clearer. You can choose to bring your detention to an end at any time by leaving Australia. (DIMIA 2002)

The same letter also advised that detainees risked criminal prosecutions, that protest would only make their situation worse, that the destruction of detention centre property would result in them being 'accommodated in circumstances that are far less comfortable,' and that the Minister would refuse to consider any claims from people in detention until 'these disturbances cease.'

This *Message to Detainees* was released to the media along with a press release which stated that 'there have been ongoing discussions with detainees, to ensure that it is understood that criminal activity will be punished and disturbances are counterproductive to their cause' (DIMIA 2002). The Department of Immigration and the federal government continued to see the riots as a protest over visas and a result of detainees' bad characters. The government was unwilling to consider concerns about the conditions of detention. With no acknowledgement of any legitimate basis for complaint by detainees, good faith or meaningful negotiations cannot occur.

Conclusion

Using this model, Australia's immigration detention centres could be seen as almost laboratory incubators for riots. They contain a physically, politically, socially and culturally excluded group of people with deeply-held grievances, in close proximity to one another facilitating the development of generalised hostile beliefs. Detainees are more often than not portrayed homogenously and negatively in the media by politicians and social commentators alike. Guards are generally poorly trained and many hold indiscriminately negative views of detainees as a group. Official systems designed to address detainees' needs or complaints work poorly, if at all, and effectively put access to official redress for grievances beyond the reach of detainees. The close proximity of detainees and lack of meaningful activity to structure each day means that information and rumour circulates rapidly throughout and between detention centres. While some respondents in this research talked about some 'nice guards,' the relationship between detainees and guards, and detainees and broader Australian society could be characterised as substantially negative, marked by mutual distrust and suspicion. Detention centres are exceptional sites.

Their inhabitants are in a legal limbo, with limited rights and no national identity. They are between states, between statuses and between norms. And so detention centres also develop exceptional norms to guide behaviour, of both detainees and guards. All the pre-conditions for a riot are met and any number of mundane daily events can act as a trigger.

Breakouts, hunger strike, lip sewing and many other forms of protest may be read as strategies of detainees to evade, undermine or dialogically challenge the technologies of state power. Riot, however, is a different form of confrontation and communication. The message to be conveyed was an angry one, expressing a loss of hope in civil dialogue and functioning more as catharsis and retaliation. Riots occurred in Australia's immigration detention centres when 'sides' became polarised and issues oversimplified. Like hunger strikes, riots cannot be adequately read through a detached prism with clear delineation of the personal and the political, of emotion and reason. Nor can they be properly read through the actions of rioters alone. The riots in detention centres not only mark moments when fears and tensions in detention centres were heightened, but also moments of intransigence by the state or its representatives. The deployment of state power in detention was always met with resistance in some form. Riots made visible, in a most dramatic way, the struggle and conflict between asylum seekers and the state. Setting fire to buildings, tearing down fences or throwing stones at guards gave release to the anger and indignation of injustice. It was not the civil voice of Arendt's *homo politicus*, but the direct challenge and raw emotion of Foucault's criminalised, institutionalised, discredited, subjugated rising up to tear down the physical representations of their oppression.

Bibliography

Anonymous. (2011). A riot on Christmas Island: The detainee's version. *ABC Unleashed*, May 18. Retrieved May 20, 2011, from http://www.abc.net.au/unleashed/2717968.html

Australian Associated Press (AAP). (2011a). Asylum seekers break out of Christmas Island detention centre. *Perth Now*, March 12. Retrieved June 8, 2011, from http://www.perthnow.com.au (home page).

Australian Associated Press (AAP). (2011b). Second breakout on Christmas Island. *Sydney Morning Herald*, March 13. Retrieved June 8, 2011, from http://www.smh.com.au (home page).

Australian National Audit Office (ANAO) (1998). *Auditor General Report No. 32: The Management of Boat People*. Canberra: Commonwealth of Australia.

Bath, C. (2001). Philip Ruddock discusses current immigration issues. *Sunday Sunrise* Broadcast, April 8. Transcript. Retrieved March 9, 2011, from http://www.parlinfo.aph.gov.au (home page).

Bowen, C. (2011, March 18). *Update on ongoing Christmas Island unrest: Media conference*. Transcript. Retrieved June 8, 2011, from http://www.minister.immi.gov.au/media/cb/2011/cb162819.htm

Briskman, L., Latham, S., & Goddard, C. (2008). *Human rights overboard. Seeking asylum in Australia*. Melbourne: Scribe Publications.

British Broadcasting Corporation (BBC). (2000). Australian police battle immigrants. *BBC News*, August 28. Retrieved February 21, 2012, from http://news.bbc.co.uk/2/hi/asia-pacific/899166.stm

Butt, P., & Hamer, D. (2011). *LexisNexis concise Australian legal dictionary* (4th ed.). Chatswood: LexisNexis Butterworths.

Carrabine, E. (2005). Prison riots, social order and the problem of legitimacy. *British Journal of Criminology, 45*, 896–913.

Clifton, A. (2002). Statutory declaration. *Human Rights and Equal Opportunity Commission National Inquiry into Children in Immigration Detention*, July 1. Retrieved March 15, 2011, from http://www.hreoc.gov.au/human_rights/children_detention/submissions/clifton.html

Commonwealth of Australia. (2003). Parliamentary debates: Senate. *Official Hansard No. 8* (Tuesday, August 12, 13434). Canberra: Commonwealth of Australia.

Conahan, M. J. (2002). Transcript of a speech by Nurse Moira-Jane. *Chilout*, June 3. Retrieved March 8, 2002, from http://www.chilout.org/web_images/moira_speech.htm

DIMIA. (2001). Arson at Woomera detention facility. *Media Release*, December 18. Retrieved March 21, 2011, from http://www.newsroom.immi.gov.au/media_releases/421?page=64&

DIMIA. (2002). Message to detainees. *Media Release*, December 31. Retrieved July 11, 2011, from http://www.newsroom.immi.gov.au/media_releases/455

Downer, A., & Ruddock, P. (2002). *Government rejects UN report on arbitrary detention. Joint Media Release*, December 13. Retrieved February 21, 2012, from http://www.foreignminister.gov.au (home page).

Fiske, L. (2006). Politics of exclusion, practice of inclusion. Australia's response to refugees and the case for community based human rights work. *International Journal of Human Rights, 10*(3), 219–229.

Hamilton-Smith, A. (2002). Submission No. 282. *Human Rights and Equal Opportunity Commission National Inquiry into Children in Immigration Detention*, October 24. Retrieved March 15, 2011, from http://www.hreoc.gov.au/human_rights/children_detention/statements/hamilton.html

Harding, R. (2001, October 10). Prisons watchdog slams immigration detention centres, criticises lack of accountability. Retrieved March 21, 2011, from http://www.custodialinspector.wa.gov.au (home page).

Hekmat, A. K. (2010). Asylum seekers risk boats because it is the only option. *The Age*, December 27. Retrieved January 5, 2012, from http://www.theage.com.au (home page).

Horowitz, D. (2001). *The deadly ethnic riot.* Berkley: University of California Press.

Human Rights and Equal Opportunities Commission (HREOC) (1998). *Those who've come across the seas: Detention of unauthorised arrivals.* Sydney: Human Rights and Equal Opportunities Commission.

Human Rights and Equal Opportunities Commission (HREOC) (2004). *A last resort? National Inquiry into Children in Immigration Detention.* Sydney: Human Rights and Equal Opportunities Commission.

Joint Standing Committee on Foreign Affairs, Defence and Trade (JSCFADT) (2001). *A report on visits to immigration detention centres, 2001.* Canberra: Commonwealth of Australia.

Joint Standing Committee on Migration (JSCM) (2000). *Not the Hilton. Immigration detention centres: Inspection report, (September).* Canberra: Commonwealth of Australia.

Klocker, N., & Dunn, K. (2003). Who's driving the asylum debate? Newspaper and government representations of asylum seekers. *Media International Australia, 109,* 71–92.

Lea, J., & Young, J. (1982). The riots in Britain 1981: Urban violence and political marginalisation. In D. Cowell, D. Jones, & J. Young (Eds.), *Policing the riots.* London: Junction Books.

Mares, P. (2003). Distance makes the heart grow fonder: Media images of refugees and asylum seekers. In E. Newman & J. van Selm (Eds.), *Refugees and forced displacement: International security, human vulnerability and the state.* Tokyo: United Nations University Press.

Marks, K. (2003). Refugee camp children sew their lips in protest. *The Independent*, January 22. Retrieved March 21, 2011, from http://www.independent.co.uk (home page).

McDermott, Q. (2008). The guards' story. *Four Corners*, ABC Television, September 15. Transcript. Retrieved March 18, 2011, from http://www.abc.net.au/4corners/content/2008/s2365139.htm

McDonell, S. (2000). The queue jumpers. *Four Corners*, ABC Television, October 16. Transcript. Retrieved March 8, 2011, from http://www.abc.net.au/4corners/stories/s200031.htm

Morton, T. (2002). Worse than prisons? Managing immigration detention centres. *Background Briefing*, ABC Radio National, October 6. Retrieved March 19, 2011, from http://abc.net.au/backgroundbriefing/ (home page).

National Advisory Commission on Civil Disorders (NACCD) (1968). *Report of the National Advisory Commission on Civil Disorders*. New York: Bantam Books.

Penberthy, D. (2002). Revealed: The truth about how inmates are treated inside Australia's detention centres. Five Star Asylums. *The Daily Telegraph*, December 17. Retrieved March 1, 2011, from http://dailytelegraph.com.au (home page).

Pfitzner, B. (2002). Statutory declaration. *Human Rights and Equal Opportunity Commission National Inquiry into Children in Immigration Detention*, July 16. Retrieved March 15, 2011, from http://www.hreoc.gov.au/human_rights/children_detention/statements/pfitzner.html

Pickering, S. (2005). *Refugees and state crime*. Annandale: Federation Press.

Randall, A. (2006). *Riotous assemblies: Popular protest in Hanoverian England*. Oxford: Oxford University Press.

Rudé, G. (1964). *The crowd in history: A study of popular disturbances in France and England, 1730–1848*. New York: John Wiley and Sons.

Scraton, P., Sim, J., & Skidmore, P. (1991). *Prisons under protest*. Buckingham: Open University Press.

United Nations Working Group on Arbitrary Detention (UNWGAD). (2002). Civil and political rights, including the question of torture and detention report of the Working Group on Arbitrary Detention: Visit to Australia. *United Nations Commission on Human Rights (59th Session)*, October 24. Document E/CN.4/2003/8/Add.2.

Waddington, D. (2007). *Policing public disorder. Theory and practice*. Cullompton: Willan Publishing.

Whitmont, D. (2003). '…About Woomera.' *Four Corners*, ABC Television, May 19. Transcript. Retrieved March 8, 2011, from http://www.abc.net.au/4corners/content/2003/transcripts/s858341.htm

Wilkinson, S. (2009). Riots. *Annual Review of Political Science, 12*, 329–343.

Court Cases

Behrooz v Secretary, Department of Immigration and Multicultural and Indigenous Affairs. (2004). HCA 36; 219 CLR 486; 208 ALR 271; 78 ALJR 1056 (August 6, 2004).

7

Immigration Detention Globally

Previous chapters have focussed primarily on asylum seekers' experiences of Australian detention centres, but neither immigration detention nor detainee protest against it are uniquely Australian phenomena. Prior to the 1990s, immigration detention was used sparingly as an instrument of last resort. The 1990s, however, saw a rapid and substantial expansion of the use of immigration detention throughout Europe, North America and Australia, a trend that has continued in each subsequent decade. This chapter presents a brief overview of immigration detention capacity, operating frameworks, conditions and detainee resistance in Europe, North America and Australia.

Establishing an accurate picture of immigration detention globally is extremely difficult. States collect different statistics, or none at all, there is no central database for recording the detention of non-citizens (including none for the European Union) and states use different definitions of detention (e.g., many do not include detention in police cells) in gathering the statistics that are available (Access Info and Global Detention Project 2015, 4, 6–8). These deficiencies in reporting the use of immigration detention may arise in part from a lack of capacity in both state and international systems to maintain accurate information about detention.

L. Fiske, *Human Rights, Refugee Protest and Immigration Detention*,
DOI 10.1057/978-1-137-58096-2_7

Many states practicing detention, however, also have active interest in maintaining a degree of obscurity. Immigration detention facilities are, as this chapter will outline, among the sites in which human rights violations are most likely to be committed by liberal democracies. Immigration detention is, at the very least, inconsistent with the values and principles espoused by detaining states throughout Europe, North America and Australia, and the exposure of many of the practices it entails cause 'sovereign discomfort' for states promulgating human rights norms on other stages (Flynn 2013, 7). These inconsistencies and gaps in data make direct comparisons of detention practices impossible. Nonetheless, there is a clear global trend in the expansion of immigration detention, with insufficient structural safeguards which permit unacceptable conditions and practices targeted against people who have fallen outside the embrace of the state system.

All European Union (EU) Member States have immigration detention facilities of some form. The Council of Europe Committee on Migration, Refugees and Population estimated in 2010 that EU Member States had 235 dedicated immigration detention facilities with a holding capacity of 30,000 (CoE 2010, 7). By May 2013, this had expanded to 420 official immigration detention facilities with a capacity to hold 37,000 people (MEDU 2013, 19). This does not include those detained at airports, on ships, in prisons, police holding cells or other places of confinement. The USA currently has an immigration detention capacity of 34,000, up from 6785 in 1994 (Sampson and Mitchell 2013, 101). More than 477,000 people were detained in US immigration detention in 2012 (CMS 2014). In 2015, the USA expanded its capacity to detain families with children in specially designated detention centres by more than 3000 beds (HRF 2015, 2). As of 10 September 2013, Australia had a detention capacity in Australian-based facilities of 11,632 (DIBP 2013). Australia also funds the detention of asylum seekers at off-shore detention facilities in Nauru and Papua New Guinea which, in December 2015, were holding 537 and 922 asylum seekers, respectively (DIBP 2015, 4).

The EU, the USA and Australia are additionally supporting the expansion of detention beyond their borders to prevent the arrival of prospective asylum seekers. The EU gave Ukraine 30 million euros to build nine new detention centres, while the USA funds detention in Guatemala and Mexico (Sampson and Mitchell 2013, 101–102). Australia funds a growing network of detention in Indonesia, the most common departure country for asylum seekers travelling to Australia by boat (Nethery et al. 2012).

While barriers to the international movement of goods and capital have been progressively dismantled, the last twenty years has witnessed the development of an ever expanding carceral web to disrupt and deter the movement of people deemed undesirable.

Categorisation—Who Gets Detained?

This extensive web of detention centres is matched by complex webs of laws, policies and practices which govern who gets detained, in what material and legal conditions and for how long. Depriving an individual of his or her liberty is a profound sanction and, in liberal democracies, typically has robust laws and procedures governing its use. An order to imprison or detain an individual is to be made by a properly constituted body on the basis of law and the circumstances of each individual case. Increasingly, however, immigration detention decisions are made not according to individual characteristics, but according to categorisations of persons. Although the European Council's (EC) Asylum Procedures Directive states that asylum seekers should only be detained in particular circumstances and not simply because he or she is seeking asylum, in practice asylum seekers are often detained throughout the EU 'merely and precisely *because* they are asylum seekers' (Cornelisse 2010, 11).

European detention centres hold a mixed population of irregular migrants consisting of undocumented migrants, foreign nationals who have completed a criminal sentence and are to be deported and asylum seekers. These populations are not always distinct categories, with individuals moving through different categories at different times and frequently falling into more than one category simultaneously. Elspeth Guild notes that 'irregular migrant' is not a legally defined category, but rather a residual category of those people who do not fit prescribed criteria of lawfully recognised migrants (Guild 2004). This imprecision of legal definition allows politicians and media commentators significant latitude to shape social and public constructions of irregular migration, including, in recent decades, the conflation of irregular and 'illegal.' This uncertainty or imprecision facilitates states' exercise of power over certain people and distances individuals from both legal and political human rights protections, as the rising use of immigration detention attests. The importance of categorisation as an enabling process in detention and attendant rights curtailment was addressed in more detail in Chaps. 2 and 3. The imprecision also makes it difficult to clearly delineate the detention of asylum seekers as a discrete focus of analysis. As much as possible, this chapter focuses on the detention of asylum seekers.

Most EU Member States make some attempts to distinguish asylum seekers from other irregular migrants in law and policy; nonetheless, asylum seekers are subject to detention in all jurisdictions, sometimes for extended periods of time, and including vulnerable persons. In Hungary, asylum seekers are subject to detention for a period of between fifteen and ninety days. In practice, however, people who lodge an asylum claim from detention are typically detained for six months, the maximum duration permitted under Hungarian law (Global Detention Project n.d.). Malta's detention regime has been criticised for not distinguishing adequately between asylum seekers and other irregular migrants and for subjecting asylum seekers to mandatory detention alongside other categories of irregular migrants (UNHCR 2013; CPT 2013). A 2007 report commissioned by the European Parliament Committee on Civil Liberties, Justice and Home Affairs criticised Lithuania, Greece, Poland, Estonia and Cyprus for having no systems in place to identify vulnerable people in detention to ensure either that specific needs were met or that they were released from detention (STEPS 2007, 190). The report further observed that 'people who have been victims of torture, or other serious forms of physical, psychological, or sexual violence' are present in detention centres throughout Europe and noted 'serious failings' in care provided to such people in detention (STEPS 2007, 17).

In February 2015, the Greek government announced that it would end the practice of immigration detention and, in November 2015, the International Detention Coalition reported that between 600 and 800 people were detained, significantly lower numbers than at any time in the previous decade (IDC 2015). However, a number of factors make the situation in Greece unclear. Greek law has always exempted asylum seekers from detention, but in practice asylum seekers have routinely been detained and people in detention have been prevented from lodging asylum claims (Global Detention Project n.d.). Despite the announcement of a departure from immigration detention, key pieces of legislation which permit detention have not been repealed (IDC 2015) and as recently as July 2015, Amnesty International reported serious overcrowding in at least two immigration detention centres (Amnesty International 2015). The International Detention Coalition reports that its partners in Greece fear the government may reinstate widespread use of detention (IDC 2015).

Policy in the UK permits the detention of asylum seekers in its fast-track process, pending a decision to remove, those subject to a Dublin transfer and pending removal. Policy also states that vulnerable people such as pregnant women, people with serious medical conditions, children and survivors of torture should not be detained. In 2009, the NGO Bail for Immigration Detainees (BID 2009, 3) reported that 70 % of people in immigration detention were seeking asylum. Many vulnerable persons as defined by the UK Border Agency (UKBA) are among them and systems designed to alert authorities to the detention of vulnerable persons have been criticised as ineffective. An inquiry into the provision of healthcare at Yarl's Wood Immigration Removal Centre (IRC) in 2006 following a hunger strike requiring the hospitalisation and re-feeding of two women detainees noted that 'In both cases, routine rule 35 letters, notifying IND [Immigration and Nationality Directorate] where detention might be injurious to health were sent to the immigration authorities although there is no evidence that these produced any reaction. They spent eight and nine months respectively in detention' (HM Chief Inspector of Prisons 2006, 15). A review of the welfare of vulnerable persons in detention in 2015 found that many categories of recognised vulnerable persons are routinely detained, attributing their detention in part to failed communication systems between the detention centres and the Home Office, particularly concerning rule 35 letters (Shaw 2016, 109) and including a finding that,

> it is perfectly clear to me that people with serious mental illness continue to be held in detention and that their treatment and care does not and cannot

> equate to good psychiatric practice (whether or not it is 'satisfactorily managed'). Such a situation is an affront to civilised values. (Shaw 2016, 88)

As in Europe, US detention centres contain a mixed population of people unlawfully in the country, foreign nationals who are subject to removal orders following a criminal conviction and asylum seekers. Although the majority of immigration detainees in the USA are not seeking asylum, asylum seekers are nonetheless detained regularly and in significant numbers. Asylum seekers who self-report upon arrival and those who are found within 100 miles of a port of entry within fourteen days of arriving are subject to mandatory detention. Asylum seekers who apply after gaining entry may or may not be detained, subject to the decision of the officer to whom they report (CVT-TASSC 2013, 6). Asylum seekers who have had their claims refused and are subject to removal orders are also detained, including while they are pursuing legal claims to remain. Refugees who have arrived through the USA's off-shore program are required to apply for permanent residency after one year. Refugees failing to file the necessary papers in a timely manner may be subject to detention for periods of usually between four and six months, but sometimes in excess of one year (HRW 2010, 8–9). Human Rights First reported that over 10,000 asylum seekers were detained in US prisons and immigration detention centres in 2007 (2009, 1). Access Info and Global Detention Project reported in 2015 that the US government provided incomplete information pertaining to immigration detention and no information at all about the detention of asylum seekers (Access Info and Global Detention Project 2015, 32). That detention for 'arriving' asylum seekers is mandatory and that some decisions to detain are not reviewable by an independent body results in the detention of vulnerable asylum seekers for whom detention may be particularly difficult. The Centre for Victims of Torture estimates that 6000 survivors of torture seeking asylum were detained in the USA between October 2010 and February 2013 (CVT-TASSC 2013, 2).

Australia introduced mandatory detention in 1992. In 1994, the government extended its application to all 'unlawful non-citizens' and removed the statutory time limit. Australia detains people who have over-stayed their visa, foreign nationals whose visas have been cancelled under Section 501 of the *Migration Act 1958 (Cth)* on character grounds and asylum seekers. Rather than seeking to exempt asylum seekers from immigration detention, this group is the primary target and largest population in Australian detention centres. Asylum seekers arriving by plane with proper documentation who are immigration cleared may reside in the community while their refugee claim is assessed. Asylum seekers arriving without proper documentation, whether by plane or boat, are subject to mandatory detention regardless of age, gender, mental or physical health status, disability, flight risk or any other individual characteristics. Section 189 of the *Migration Act 1958 (Cth)* states that an officer (of immigration, customs, police or defence) who reasonably suspects a person may be an unlawful non-citizen *must* detain that person. This lack of discretion, alongside national security and criminalisation rhetoric from politicians, has assisted in creating an operational culture which prefers detention if in any doubt about a person's lawful immigration status, irrespective of any assessment of an individual's vulnerability. This has led to the lawful detention of thousands of people who might be exempt from detention in other jurisdictions and the wrongful detention of hundreds of Australian citizens and permanent residents (Palmer 2005; Commonwealth Ombudsman 2005).

Duration

The maximum duration of detention varies in different jurisdictions and has increased alongside the expansion of immigration detention. In 2008, the European Council issued the Returns Directive (2008/115/EC), which limits the maximum period of immigration detention to eighteen months. Intended to establish common standards across Member States, the Returns Directive has had mixed effects. Switzerland and Bulgaria reduced the maximum period of detention from two years and no limit, respectively, while the eighteen-month maximum set out in the Returns Directive facilitated Italy, Spain and Greece increasing statutory maximum detention durations (Parkin 2013, 14; Global Detention Project n.d.). The UK has not implemented the Returns Directive and maintains no legal limit on the duration of detention. Malta also has no maximum period set out in law, but as a matter of policy limits detention to eighteen months (Cornelisse 2010, 17). In most jurisdictions, asylum seekers released from detention may be re-detained and the clock 'reset.' Multiple periods of detention are not uncommon (STEPS 2007, 181).

Jesuit Refugee Service (Europe)'s report *Becoming Vulnerable in Detention* examining people's experiences of immigration detention in twenty-three EU Member States found that asylum seekers are detained for longer than other irregular migrants (an average of 106.8 days compared to 71.26 days) and that of people detained for between five and six months, 78 %, were asylum seekers (JRS 2010, 7 and 31). State practices of detention are at odds with policy statements and guidelines intended to recognise the right to seek asylum and to detain asylum seekers only as a matter of last resort and for the shortest possible time.

The USA also has no statutory limitation on the length of detention. Immigration and Customs Enforcement (ICE) reported statistics for the 2010 fiscal year that of 15,769 asylum seekers detained that year, 11,251 (71.35 %) were released within ninety days of detention with release rates trickling down to 110 people remaining in detention for longer than one year (ICE 2012, 44). The Centre for Victims of Torture reported that it interviewed a person who was detained for seven years (CVT-TASSC 2013). Human Rights First disputes ICE's methodology of calculating its statistics and reports that asylum seekers spend three times longer in detention than non-asylum seeking detainees and reports multiple cases of asylum seekers being detained for three, five and eight years (HRF 2009, 6, 94–95).

Australia has no statutory limit on the duration of immigration detention for people who arrive by boat and extended detention is commonplace. Peter Qasim, an asylum seeker from Kashmir, was detained for seven years before being released on a temporary Return Pending Bridging Visa (Kerr 2005). A great many people are detained for periods exceeding two years, including eleven of the fifteen participants in this study (five of whom were held for more than five years). As of 30 December 2015, over 400 people in Australian detention centres had been held for longer than two years (DIBP 2015, 11). People are released from detention when granted a visa, removed from Australia or released at Ministerial discretion. Apart from a brief period in 2012 when government policy was to grant Bridging Visas to asylum seekers and release them in to the community, successive ministers have only very rarely granted release from detention.

Harmful Effects of Prolonged Detention

The harmful effects of prolonged detention, particularly indefinite detention, have been well documented. Prolonged detention is causally linked to deterioration in both mental and physical health, prompting psychiatrist Patrick McGorry to refer to Australia's immigration detention centres as 'factories for producing mental illness' (Cresswell 2010). Jesuit Refugee Service (Europe) concurs and notes that detention in excess of ninety days is particularly damaging to people's physical and mental well-being, causing depression, anxiety and other disorders (JRS 2010, 34).

Dr Aamer Sultan and Kevin O'Sullivan published an article in the *Medical Journal of Australia*, in which they outlined four progressive stages of depression, revolt and ultimately psychosis in long-term detainees. Sultan and O'Sullivan's (2001) research was particularly distinctive because Dr Sultan was also a detained asylum seeker from Iraq who conducted the research with O'Sullivan, using a mix of participant-observer and survey methodologies (some of Dr Sultan's story is presented in Chap. 3). Their findings are supported by other studies in multiple jurisdictions which report significantly higher levels of depression, anxiety, suicidal ideation, post-traumatic stress disorder and a range of psychological and psychiatric disorders among people held in immigration detention (Arnold et al. 2006; Bracken and Gorst-Unsworth 1991; Elliot and Gunasekera 2016; Loff et al. 2002; Mares and Jureidini 2004; Newman et al. 2008; Silove et al. 2001; Steel and Silove 2001; Steel et al. 2004; STEPS 2007). A global review of studies into mental health and immigration detention published in the *British Journal of Psychiatry* reported that 'All studies found high levels of emotional distress among individuals who were in detention or who had been previously detained' and that 'the findings relate in part to pre-detention trauma experiences, in addition to detention itself having an independent adverse effect on mental health' (Robjant et al. 2009, 306, 310). An international literature review conducted in conjunction with the UK's Shaw Review in 2015 found that all studies, regardless of the country in which they were based or the methodology used, showed that immigration detention is harmful to detainees' mental health and further, that unlike studies of prison populations, 'there is no published account of improvements in mental health or wellbeing resulting from a period of immigration detention' (Shaw 2016, 310). Studies consistently show that, while pre-existing trauma is a relevant contributory factor, detention itself causes high levels of mental illness.

Conditions

The material conditions of detention vary enormously across different countries and between different detention facilities within each country. The European Committee for the Prevention of Torture (CPT) found the Granges and Frambois detention centres in Switzerland to be 'satisfactory' but criticised the 'carceral regime' which included detainees being locked in cells for most of each day (Global Detention Project n.d.). Detention conditions in Malta and Greece have been robustly criticised by a range of reputable bodies, including the United Nations Working Group of Arbitrary Detention (2010), the European Committee for the Prevention of Torture (2011, 2012, 2013) and international NGOs including Amnesty International (2013) and Human Rights Watch (2014).

The conditions in Greek detention centres are such that the European Committee for the Prevention of Torture (CPT) issued a Public Statement in 2011. The CPT reported that it had visited Greece ten times in eighteen years and that Greek authorities had consistently failed to act on CPT recommendations or to address serious criticisms of the conditions of detention (CPT 2011). In its 2011 visit, the CPT reported severe overcrowding (such that people were observed to be sleeping in the space between the shower cubicle and the ceiling in the Soufli Police and Border Guard Station), inadequate access to toilets and ablutions (one toilet and one cold shower for 146 detainees), poor ventilation, no access to outdoor areas and insufficient provision of food (CPT 2012, 13). In Tychero Police and Border Guard Station, the CPT reported that 'a third room which was exposed to the elements but which, despite freezing temperatures and snow, was still used to hold people overnight (for example, seven women from the Dominican Republic had slept on sheets of cardboard there the day before the delegation's visit)' (CPT 2012, 14). The report noted that 100 people were accommodated in a single room measuring thirty-five square metres. The CPT also reported multiple incidents of detainees being ill-treated by guards in Attica, Evros and Athens (CPT 2012, 12–13).

> In addition, several detainees alleged that they were beaten up in the so-called visits room, and the delegation observed bloodstains on the walls of this room. The Director of the centre initially denied the existence of the bloodstains but when they were shown to him he stated that they were caused by detainees committing acts of self-injury. Such an explanation is not convincing in the light of what the delegation found. (CPT 2012, 12)

In a 2009 visit to detention facilities in Malta, the UN Working Group on Arbitrary Detention (UNWGAD) was critical of the tents that had been erected to address accommodation shortages, noting that even with the tents, '…in the winter month of January… 59 inmates did not find a place to sleep' and slept in the toilets or outside (UNWGAD 2010, 13). When the CPT visited in 2011, the tents had been removed but 'the material conditions of detention were still appalling,' 'extremely overcrowded' and sanitary facilities 'were in a deplorable state' (CPT 2013, para 55). The CPT visit had been prompted by excessive use of force by soldiers and police in responding to a detainee protest in August 2011. Tear gas and rubber pellets had been used to quell the detainee protest. Twenty-three detainees were transferred to a prison, many of whom told the CPT delegation that they had been 'punched, kicked and struck with truncheons, mainly by soldiers *after* having been handcuffed' (CPT 2013, para 50, emphasis in original). A similar situation occurred at Safi Barracks in January 2005, in which police and soldiers were accused of using excessive force to respond to a peaceful demonstration (De Bono 2013, 73).

In December 2013, video footage of detainees being told to strip naked and then hosed with disinfectant outside in a detention centre on Lampedusa was released. The practice was defended by the camp manager as a necessary preventative treatment for scabies and other skin conditions (Squires 2013).

These examples of the conditions in detention and the treatment of detainees have attracted both public and monitoring body attention, perhaps because they represent particularly offensive excesses of immigration detention, enabled in large part by regimes with weak statutory accountability and oversight. Such events ought not to be viewed, however, as extraordinary, but rather as the logical extension of a regime in which dehumanising practices are integral to the daily routine and which operate in a politico-legal environment with poor accountability.

Immigration detention is an administrative measure, justified by governments as an instrument to manage immigration programs. There is, however, a growing body of criticism that immigration detention functions not as a bureaucratic management tool, but as a punitive instrument operating outside the reach of law (Garcia Hernandez 2014; Parkin 2013, 12; Wilsher 2012, ix). Many detention centres, particularly in Western Europe, the USA and Australia closely resemble prisons. Some (such as Christmas Island detention centre in Australia, Colnbrook in the UK and the El Paso Processing Center in the USA) are built from high security prison models with razor wire, high-tech surveillance, cells with fixed furnishings and thick metal doors. The daily regimen and operational culture in such centres emphasises security, with little attention to the rights and welfare of detainees.

Australian detention centres are surrounded by high fences or walls topped with razor wire, several have interior and exterior perimeter fences with monitored exclusion zones separating them. In several detention centres, there is a high degree of surveillance using a network of closed circuit cameras. Most detention centres are divided into separate compounds to enable greater control over detainees (JSCM 2000, 27). Each detention centre has 'management units' which are separate compounds or secure rooms in which people can be held in group or solitary isolation. Several research participants reported that 'management' was used as punishment following a protest or non-compliance with guards' instructions, or for management of suicidal or self-harming behaviour. In at least one instance, solitary confinement was used as a pre-emptive warning when a refugee was transferred to Curtin detention centre as a known trouble maker.

Detention centres are run as penal institutions, but with limited statutory or contractual safeguards for detainees. In 2001, Australia's Commonwealth Ombudsman conducted an *Own Motion Investigation into Immigration Detention Centres* and concluded that immigration detention entailed a 'loss of liberty … akin to the situation of prisoners,' but that 'immigration detainees appear to have lesser rights and are held in an environment which appears to involve a weaker accountability framework' without the 'full protection of the law' (Commonwealth Ombudsman 2001, 3). The United Nations Working Group on Arbitrary Detention concurred:

> At the end of its visit, the delegation of the Working Group had the clear impression that the conditions of detention are in many ways similar to prison conditions: detention centres are surrounded by impenetrable and closely guarded razor wire; detainees are under permanent supervision; if escorted outside the centre they are, as a rule, handcuffed; escape from a centre constitutes a criminal offence under the law and the escapee is prosecuted. In certain respects, their regime is less favourable (indeterminate detention; exclusion from legal aid; lack of judicial control of detention; etc.). Several detainees who had been in both situations told the delegation that their time in prison had been less stressful than the time spent in the centres. During talks with government officials it became obvious that one of the goals of the system of mandatory detention and the way it is implemented is to discourage would-be immigrants from entering Australia without a valid visa. (UNWGAD 2002, 18)

The training of new staff and management of the centres reinforce the penal nature of detention centres. Kjell Liljegren, a former prison officer and immigration detention centre guard told ABC's *AM* program in June 2005 that 'it was more obvious that they wanted to run the centres more like prisons than actual detention centres which are meant for administrative purposes only' and that 'most of the training was based on control and restraint' (ABC 2005). This sentiment is echoed by the words of another former guard testifying to the Peoples' Inquiry into Immigration Detention:

> I was once told at Maribyrnong 'You are the cat, they are the rat and don't forget that.' The general mindset is the same at Baxter. Officers are not told

that it's not against the law to apply for asylum. There is a lot of emphasis placed on control and restraint of people, but I felt that the biggest thing missing was the key that these people essentially haven't done anything wrong. (Briskman et al. 2008, 114)

People are subjected to multiple daily 'musters' or roll calls, including at least one at night when, in the time that participants in this study were detained, sleeping refugees would be woken by a light being shone in his/her face and a guard's loud voice (Briskman et al. 2008, 132–133; JSCFADT 2001, para 6.87; UNWGAD 2002, 13). A former detainee testified to the People's Inquiry that,

> One of the most difficult things for me too was that there were three different head counts. There was one at six in the morning, one at midnight and another at two in the morning. No matter who you are, even a baby, they will have to wake you up, you show your card or shout your number loudly. (Briskman et al. 2008, 132–133)

This practice was a requirement of the Department of Immigration, as outlined in its *Handbook to Guide Departmental Managers of Detention Facilities* which stated that staff must '...physically sight the detainee. If the detainee is covered with bedding staff must pull back the sheet/blanket so the detainee can be identified' (HREOC 2004, 291).

Little appears to have changed. In February 2014, a former guard reported that his training was conducted by a former prison guard who advised the new recruits that 'the only thing that's different is the clothes we let them wear' (Global Mail 2014) The former guard said that training retains an emphasis on physical restraint of detainees and that his colleagues 'had no understanding of what people had been through before they arrived in Australia' (Global Mail 2014). A leaked copy of the company's 2010 staff training manual confirms the strong emphasis on physical restraint and details multiple methods to cause 'medium to high level pain' deemed likely to 'compel compliance from un-cooperative subjects' (Crook 2012). The manual outlines 'principles in controlling Resistive Behaviour,' instructing guards to 'cause pain, stun, distract, unbalance' and to use a 'striking technique' to cause 'motor dysfunction' (Crook 2012). It would appear that a key recommendation of a 2005 inquiry that the Department of Immigration should 'ensure that as much emphasis is given to recruiting people with health and welfare training and skills as is given to custodial and security qualifications and experience' (Palmer 2005, xxviii) is yet to be implemented. The arbitrary use of force by detention centre staff and the lack of effective formal mechanisms for making complaints about their treatment in detention is a major catalyst for protests.

Both Australia and Malta have been criticised for the practice of addressing detainees by identification numbers rather than their names (UNWGAD 2002; CPT 2013, para 49), a practice which participants in this research all found particularly offensive and degrading. Osman conveyed his frustration at this practice by saying 'Oh God! I've got a name. Your donkey, er, your dog and your cat has got name. I'm human like you, don't call me by number.' The UN Working Group on Arbitrary Detention was critical of the practice as dehumanising and unnecessary. Its report contains a story of children being called forward by their numbers to receive donated Christmas presents and that during its own visit to detention centres, 'most of the detainees who came forward introduced themselves by their registration numbers' (UNWGAD 2002, 13). Ibrahim has attempted to escape the dehumanising effect of the practice by using humour. He laughed and said that since he will never forget his detainee number, at least he now has a secure password for various accounts.

The UK, Hungary and Australia have all been criticised for the unnecessary use of handcuffs when detainees are attending medical or other appointments outside the detention centre (HMIP 2014, 5; UNWGAD 2002, 18). Asylum seekers attending appointments outside detention centres in Hungary are 'escorted on leashes' in addition to handcuffs (UNHCR 2012, 17). In Australia, detainees sometimes remain handcuffed and under guard during the medical appointment and any period of hospitalisation (Briskman et al. 2008, 128–129). Some have refused medical treatment due to the indignity of being handcuffed.

Provision of health services inside detention centres is very often inadequate. Médecins Sans Frontières (MSF) has identified detention itself (particularly in substandard conditions including overcrowding, wet mattresses, broken windows and poor sanitation) as a causal factor in poor detainee health (MSF 2013). The CPT was critical of health services in several Hungarian detention centres, noting that there was no health care at Nyírbátor holding facility and that 'feldshers[1] working at the Budapest holding facility were also performing custodial tasks' (CPT 2010, 26). In Italy, the provision of healthcare in detention is mandated in the contracts with companies running the centres, but MEDU (2013) and MSF (2010) report many failings in delivery. In many centres, little more than first aid is available inside detention. The UK also mandates that healthcare services are provided in detention centres, but there have been some critical failings in recent years. Various reports have identified systemic issues around poor information sharing not infrequently leading to detainees being detained following identification of medical vulnerability under rule 35 (Shaw 2016, 100–107), not receiving essential medication, particularly when first detained or transferred between centres, 'inadequate staff training (particularly in relation to trauma) and insufficiently detailed policies and protocols' (HMIP 2006, 5). In 2012, the London Coroner's Court investigating the 2011 death of Muhammad Shukat, an asylum seeker detained at Colnbrook, found that staff failed to recognise the seriousness of Shukat's condition and consequently 'failed to call 999 soon enough, to administer CPR or have a working defibrillator available' (Taylor 2012). In Bulgaria 'to date, there have been no medical facilities, treatment or supplies provided by the state in the centres' (UNHCR 2014, 10).

Inadequate provision of health services in detention is a longstanding problem in Australia. Australia's Human Rights and Equal Opportunity Commission (HREOC) criticised the inadequacy of health services in detention in its 1998 report *Those Who've Come Across the Seas* (HREOC 1998). Similar criticism has been made by the Joint Standing Committee on Migration (in 2000 and again in 2005), the Commonwealth Ombudsman (2001), the Western Australian Inspector of Custodial Services (2002), and again by HREOC in 2004 (HREOC 2004). As recently as November 2013, doctors contracted to provide health services in detention on Christmas Island wrote a ninety-two-page letter to their employer raising concerns about 'numerous unsafe practices and gross departures from generally accepted medical standards which have posed significant risk to

[1] A feldsher is a health professional with qualifications higher than a nurse, but less than a medical doctor.

patients and caused considerable harm' (Marr 2013). In December 2013, a professor of obstetrics and gynaecology, Caroline de Costa, published an article in which she expressed serious concerns about health services for pregnant women and new-born babies in detention. She spoke of one woman whose baby was stillborn and another whose baby died in early infancy in detention. Both women had been turned away from the health clinic in Darwin detention centre in the days leading up to their babies' deaths (de Costa 2013). The Australian government has responded to a series of public statements by health and welfare workers criticising detention conditions by passing legislation criminalising the disclosure of 'protected information' by immigration detention service providers, punishable by up to two years imprisonment (*Australian Border Force Act 2015*, section 42). The UN Special Rapporteur on the Human Rights of Migrants, Francois Crépeau, postponed a planned official visit to Australia in 2015 owing to a 'lack of full cooperation from the Government,' specifically noting the government's refusal to provide assurances that no-one speaking to him would be prosecuted under the *Act* (UNOHCHR 2015).

Mental health services appear to be particularly inadequate in detention centres across Europe, the USA and Australia. In addition to detention itself being a major causal factor in the deterioration of mental well-being, a culture of disbelief is evident among detention centre staff and political and policy decision-makers. Australian detention centres have on-site medical and mental health services and many detainees are prescribed anti-depressant medication, but detainees report that they believe medication was dispensed in the interests of centre managers rather than individual detainees. Hussein explained:

> I mean they started to take something to the psychology hospital or something. You can see psychologists everywhere. They come in the compounds, everywhere. They're always there… and I don't mean they're looking after us. No. They were thinking they were finding ways how to stop the person of doing, making troubles or something. It's not how to make him well.

Some health providers also shared this view. Dr Dudley, a consultant psychiatrist who had provided services inside Baxter and its Red One 'behaviour management' unit, testified to the Federal Court that 'the primary function of Baxter (was) to incarcerate and the medical staff were there to ensure it occurs in the most efficient manner' (S v Secretary, DIMIA [2005] FCA 549 181). Detained asylum seekers in Hungary reported similar concerns to the UNHCR in 2012, saying that they were 'systematically given drugs/tranquillizers, resulting in some of them becoming addicted by the end of their detention term' (UNHCR 2012, 17). MEDU raised similar concerns in Italy, including 'the administering of certain types of psychoactive drugs by the managing authority without a specialized doctor on site' (MEDU 2013, 16).

The penal nature of detention centres, including razor wire, high surveillance and carceral daily regimens, contribute to a seeming inability of security staff at detention centres to recognise behaviour which is indicative of psychological distress and to respond within a framework of care (Briskman et al. 2008; HREOC 2004; Palmer 2005). Behaviour is interpreted through the prism of a prison, encouraging a pervasive culture of understanding suicidality and self-harm as 'bad behaviour' (Proctor et al. 2013, 730). The New South Wales Coroner, investigating three suicides in Villawood detention centre between September and December 2010 observed that 'in all three deaths, some of the actions of some staff were careless, ignorant or both' (Coroner's Court of NSW 2011, 11). There were eleven deaths (five confirmed suicides, three still under investigation and three from natural causes) in Australia's detention centres between July 2010 and December 2012 (Commonwealth Ombudsman 2013). The Border Crossing Observatory based at Monash University records 27 deaths in Australian immigration detention centres between 2010 and 2015 (Border Crossing Observatory 2016). The rates of self-harm and deaths in detention centres raise serious questions of the provision of health care in detention centres, and more fundamentally, of mandatory indefinite detention itself. As senior medics in Australia have pointed out, suicide and self-harm prevention 'interventions would have a limited impact on those facing prolonged indefinite detention' (Proctor et al. 2013, 730).

Less dramatically, but no less importantly, detainees and visitors report that boredom is a major issue with which detainees must contend. Opportunities for work, education and recreation are extremely limited, if available at all. The little structured activity that is provided is generally provided by volunteer groups and NGOs for very limited periods each week (BID 2009). Watching television is not uncommonly the only recreation available. In Greece,

> … detainees are not offered any activities. Instead, they are left to languish, with detainees spending their time either sleeping or in a state of idleness; they are not even given access to reading material, board games, radio or television. Further, in many of the facilities described above, the detention areas are so packed with people that they cannot even move around the room in which they are held. Moreover, they are not offered access to outdoor exercise. (CPT 2011, 21)

A lack of meaningful activity has implications for detainees' mental health and well-being, and has been identified in both Europe and Australia as a risk factor for facilitating protests (ANAO 1998, 47; STEPS 2007, 170).

Conditions in detention in the USA also raise serious concerns. Asylum seekers are detained in prisons or purpose-built prison-like immigration detention centres following penal regimes. Detainees are required to wear prison uniform jumpsuits, are often locked in cells for twenty-three hours per day with little or no access to outdoor recreation, are routinely handcuffed and sometimes shackled at their wrists, waist and ankles during transfers and are subject to up to five 'counts' daily (CVT-TASSC 2013; HRF 2009). Human Rights First reports regularly witnessing guards address detainees by their 'alien registration numbers' and any visits from friends or family are conducted through glass panels (HRF 2009, 20, 1). Newly-built detention centres are located in isolated areas with poor transport, making visits from friends, family or legal representatives difficult.

US detention centres have been criticised for the excessive use of force in many facilities. 'In 2005, ICE Headquarters rated (Port Isabel detention centre in Texas) as deficient because of its use of EMDDs—Electro Muscular Disruption Devices' (Immigration Detention Justice Centre 2014). In 2010, a court awarded $100,000 to an immigration detainee who was Tasered by officers while detained in Jefferson, Oklahoma (Porros v Barnes cited in AELE 2011). Health services in US detention have also been criticised as inadequate due to delays of weeks to see a medic, denial of more expensive treatments, poor confidentiality including having guards or fellow detainees present during consultations and a disparaging approach to mental health issues (Heeren 2010; Rabin 2009, 713–720). Garcia Hernandez (2014, 1349) notes that 'individuals in immigration confinement are frequently perceived to be no different than individuals in penal confinement.'

Furthermore, the conditions of detention in the USA significantly disadvantage asylum seekers in the refugee status determination process. Represented asylum seekers are three times more likely to be successful in their claims, yet 84 % of immigration detainees are unrepresented (CVT-TASSC 2013, 13). Detained asylum seekers have the right to legal assistance, but must find their own lawyer, make contact and fund this themselves. An audit of the immigration detention network by the Government Accountability Office in 2007 found 'pervasive' problems in the telephone system (GAO 2007, 10), with direct implications for people's capacity to contact lawyers and other supports outside detention. Furthermore, ICE often transfers detainees to other detention centres, often far removed from their legal representatives and support networks; between 1999 and 2008, there were 1.4 million transfers of detainees (Heeren 2010, 614).

Getting Out of Detention

Securing release from detention can be very difficult and, in some cases, impossible before a final determination of an asylum seeker's claims. In Malta, asylum seekers have a legal right to challenge the basis of their detention. In practice, however, the system is such that the United Nations Working Group on Arbitrary Detention reported that it 'is unaware of a single case in which a legal challenge to immigration detention was successful' and that 'migrants in an irregular situation do not effectively enjoy the right to habeas corpus' (UNWGAD 2009, 12, 11). The Working Group made similar findings of Italy's judicial review of ongoing detention, stating that 'the judicial review over detention in CIEs, while formally complying with the requirement in Article 9 (4) ICCPR, appears to be in most cases an empty formality' (UNWGAD 2010, 19). It further reported that it met several detainees who, upon expiration of the legal limits of detention time extensions, had been released and re-detained three and four times (UNWGAD 2010, 19). The UNHCR termed judicial review in Hungary 'ineffective,' noting that 'it is common practice for the court to issue decisions for a group of five, 10, or 15 detainees within 30 minutes, thus significantly decreasing the likelihood of a fair and individualized review' (UNHCR 2012 16). Detainees in Greece have limited grounds on which they can challenge their detention, but the restricted grounds for challenge, coupled with a lack of information about their legal rights, poor access to legal assistance and the conditions of detention make realising the right extremely difficult. The UN Working Group on Arbitrary Detention visited Greece in January 2013 and on the conclusion of its visit, questioned the efficacy of review (UNWGAD 2013). Most periods of detention in Greece come to a conclusion through an expiration of the mandatory maximum period of detention, a successful resolution of an asylum claim or removal from Greek territory.

The UK has several mechanisms which enable detainees to be released from detention including Temporary Admission, bail, grant of a visa and removal. Daniel Wilsher notes that the *Immigration Act 1971* permits rather than requires detention and that UK courts, drawing on a prior commitment to liberty as a fundamental right extending to all within the jurisdiction (not just citizens), have tended to interpret the *Immigration Act 1971* in favour of release when the purposes of detention (to effect removal or lawfully prevent entry) are not likely to be achieved in a reasonable time period (Wilsher 2012, 88–91). This is not always the case, however, as the case of *Saadi v United Kingdom* at the European Court of Human Rights (ECtHR) illustrates. The ECtHR found that 'administrative convenience' for authorities dealing with significant numbers of asylum seekers was a sufficient basis for Saadi's continuing detention (cited in Cornelisse 2010, 24–25).

In cases where detention is lawful, detainees may still apply for bail. However, Bail for Immigration Detainees (BID) reports multiple difficulties in the bail system. Poor understanding of their right to apply for bail, how the system works and a lack of access to legal assistance results in many people who may be able to get bail remaining in detention and many asylum seekers needing to lodge multiple bail applications before securing their release (BID 2009).

In Australia there is no formal, independent or reviewable process for asylum seekers arriving by boat to seek release from detention prior to a final determination of claims. The Minister for Immigration has the power to order the release of an asylum seeker into the community or an alternative form of detention. Except for a brief period in 2012, the overwhelming majority of asylum seekers are released from detention only upon a final resolution of their refugee claims. Section 196(3) of the *Migration Act 1958 (Cth)* states: 'To avoid doubt, subsection (1) prevents the release, even by a court, of an unlawful non-citizen from detention' other than for removal or deportation 'unless the non-citizen has been granted a visa.' Asylum seekers are not effectively able to challenge their detention (UNWGAD 2002).

Most asylum seekers detained in the USA are eligible to apply for release on parole, bond or their own recognisance. To be successful, applicants must meet a range of criteria including securing housing, demonstrating links with the community and posting a bond. The bond must be set no lower than $1500 and is often set much higher. These conditions can be difficult for asylum seekers to meet, particularly those who are mandatorily detained upon arrival and may have very limited support networks to assist them post bond or to secure housing (CVT-TASSC 2013, 6–7). Grants of parole to asylum seekers dropped from 41.3 % in 2004 to just 4.2 % in 2007 (HRF 2009, 1). Continued detention in the USA is not subject to regular review and can extend for several years (Heeren 2010).

Detention as Arbitrary and Lacking Safeguards

Immigration detention centres are becoming notorious as sites where human rights violations are most likely to occur in liberal democracies. As Cornelisse notes, 'The detention of immigrants is seldom a transparent practice: information concerning detention facilities is often not made public and many of these facilities are located in isolated places, and as such it has been difficult to raise extensive public awareness for the situation of immigration detainees' (Cornelisse 2010, 2). When challenged on the use of immigration detention, governments use a range of techniques to rebut criticism, citing the practice as necessary to manage immigration, secure borders and maintain sovereignty. When challenged on conditions or practices inside detention centres, governments too often respond by further restricting access to detention centres (prohibiting the media or NGOs that speak publicly from visiting), discrediting the informant (e.g., Italy prosecuted a journalist who falsified his identity to get detained and report from 'inside' [Cornelisse 2010, 2], while the Australian government commissioned research to discredit medical studies critical of detention [O'Neill 2008, 159]), or deploying criminalising discourses about detainees and presenting the fact of detention as a reasonable and necessary consequence of the detainees' own actions. Rarely do governments respond by taking steps to improve conditions or protections available to detained persons.

Immigration detention centres lack the statutory scrutiny and enforceable legal protections of other sites of detention such as prisons or mental health facilities (Parkin 2013, 12). This confluence results in poorly over-sighted and monitored sites holding people who are vulnerable to abuse due to their status as detainees, compounded by a lack of citizenship, social isolation and political environments in which there is greater political currency in sovereignty and 'crimmigration' than human rights.

Detainee Resistance

Detainees do not always passively accept these conditions. Prolonged or indefinite detention, particularly in poor conditions, sees increased rates of detainee resistance to their detention. Many non-violent, low-level acts of resistance such as non-compliance with directives, painting banners, writing letters or arguing with guards occur daily and usually go unreported. A cursory search reveals multiple incidents of immigration detainees hunger striking, marching, resisting and sometimes rioting against detention.

The UK's detention network has been marked by frequent protests. In 2007, more than 100 women undertook a hunger strike to protest poor conditions in detention and abusive treatment in Yarl's Wood (Conlon 2013). In 2005, a large number of detainees from Zimbabwe in pre-removal detention launched a five-week hunger strike successfully calling for a halt to forced removals of Zimbabweans (McGregor 2011). In late 2013, Isa Muaza, a failed asylum seeker from Nigeria, undertook a 100-day hunger strike from Harmondsworth detention centre which left him unable to see or stand (Press Association 2013; Dunt 2013). Muaza was protesting about the fact of his detention, his inability to follow a medically prescribed diet (for diabetes) and his prospective removal to Nigeria. After about ninety days of hunger strike, Muaza was assessed to be unfit to be detained and unfit to fly (Allison 2013). Nonetheless, he was deported from the UK on 18 December 2013 (Duncan Lewis 2013).

Riots are less common but far from rare. In 2002, just three months after the arrival of the first detainees, half of Yarl's Wood detention centre was razed by fire during a riot, triggered by detainees' perception of unreasonable conduct by security staff towards a fellow detainee (Shaw 2004). Detainees rioted in Harmondsworth in July 2004 following the suicide of a detainee. The riot had been preceded by a short hunger strike in May. A former detainee told the BBC that the hunger strike was about the quality of food and 'fears about abuse' from staff (Casciani 2004). The hunger strike was called off when authorities agreed to address detainees' concerns. The former detainee points to the July riot as evidence that 'nothing has changed' (Casciani 2004). Another informant said that 'some detainees are so scared they are ready to believe that some staff are quite literally going to kill them, especially when they witness a deportation turning violent' (Casciani 2004). Detainees in Harmondsworth rioted again in 2006. Detainees complained about long periods of detention and poor and sometimes abusive treatment. One man told the *Guardian* newspaper, 'The officers treated us very badly every day—they showed us no respect … You know, just because we are detainees does not mean we are not human beings or that we should not be treated with dignity and respect or that we do not have human rights' (Lewis and Taylor 2006).

Similar protests have occurred across Europe with riots in Greece, Hungary, Bulgaria, Malta and Italy. Detainees in Voenna Rampa detention centre in Sofia rioted following the death of a detainee (Sofia News Agency 2013), while fellow detainees at Harmanli in Bulgaria conducted a hunger strike in November and December 2013 (Černušáková 2013). In October 2013, a hunger strike in Bekescsaba detention centre in Hungary progressed to a riot the following month. Detainees were protesting poor conditions, deportations and slow processing of claims (Anonymous 2014). Maltese authorities were criticised for excessive use of force when the riot squad was sent in to respond to a peaceful protest in Safi Barracks detention centre in January 2005 (De Bono 2013). Safi Barracks have been the site of multiple protests by detainees, including a peaceful protest involving detainees marching, shouting and hanging banners protesting poor treatment by guards, bad food and being 'treated like animals' in February 2006 (Massa 2006). Five months later, 400 detainees escaped during a riot (Schembri 2006). The European Committee for the Prevention of Torture was critical of conditions in Safi Barracks and the response of authorities to another riot in August 2011 (CPT 2013).

Italy's detention archipelago has also been marked by multiple hunger strikes, escapes and riots, including revolts in Caltanissetta in November 2009, Bari in August 2010, Lampedusa in September 2011 and Modena in May 2012. In 2011, Turin's detention centre, which holds 210 people, recorded 156 cases of self-harm. MEDU (2013, 31) described Italy's detention centres as 'congenitally incapable of guaranteeing respect for human dignity and basic human rights' and criticised the network's arbitrary rules, ineffective complaints mechanisms, lack of information provided to detainees about their rights and how to effect them, high levels of suspicion between guards and detainees and indeterminate length of detention. In February 2014, more than a dozen detainees in Ponte Galeria detention centre in Rome had sewn their lips during a hunger strike protesting their lengthy detention (Sapa-AFP 2014).

Protests are frequently staged in US immigration detention facilities. In March 2014, between 750 and 1200 detainees went on hunger strike in the Northwest Detention Centre in Tacoma, Washington with a further mass hunger strike in Joe Corley Detention Centre in Conroe, Texas. Both groups were protesting the conditions of detention and deportations (Cohen 2014; Lewis 2014). At the same time, a group of thirty-eight Sikh asylum seekers detained in El Paso started a hunger strike in protest at their continued detention. The men had all passed their credible fear interviews and had documents establishing their identities, yet had not had the opportunity to apply for bail (Kreighbaum 2014). There have also been several reported riots and 'disturbances' at immigration detention facilities, including in Adams County, Mississippi in May 2012 (Fox News Latino 2012) and the Mira Loma Detention Center in California in April 2008 (Hennessy-Fiske and Gorman 2008). In 2007, children detained in Hutto Detention Centre in Texas successfully used the legal system to protest the conditions of their detention. The case was settled out of court when ICE agreed to a range of minimum standards, including children no longer being compelled to wear prison uniform, expansion of educational and recreational opportunities for child detainees and a prohibition on guards threatening to separate children from their parents as punishment for the child's behaviour (ACLU 2007).

Conclusion

Although a broad survey, the accounts presented here raise questions about the links between immigration detention and detainee protest. In-depth accounts of specific protests are difficult to access, often only being available in the public realm where an official inquiry into an incident has occurred. Such inquiries are usually conducted only when manifestly excessive force has been used by those authorities charged with ending a protest or where major damage has been caused to detention infrastructure. The accounts which are available, whether comprehensive such as through an inquiry, or less so such as through investigative journalist reports, display certain structural similarities between protests in different detention centres in different jurisdictions. Immigration detention centres are too often framed by arbitrary rules, and this arbitrariness seeps through the system down to interactions between detainees and guards. That in many cases, the initial decision to detain rests more on someone's categorisation as an asylum seeker than on an independent consideration of the facts and circumstances of a particular individual within a robust legal framework, likely sets the tenor for detention practices. Detainees speak of a lack of information and the frustration of not knowing when or how their detention will come to an end, of the poor material conditions in which they are detained, and of the alienating carceral regimes structuring each day. Importantly, protesting detainees speak of a lack of confidence in the formal systems and processes which govern their lives, from determining their eligibility for asylum through to resolving daily issues such as obtaining medicine for a headache. Cumulatively, the standards and conditions of detention convey to detainees a disregard for the dignity and worth of the person as an individual. The experience of immigration detention is fundamentally dehumanising. While detainee protest aims at certain material objectives, it also serves important existential functions, acting as a means through which detainees can reject the powerlessness and non-status forced upon them by the detaining state, and experience their own agency as an essential characteristic of human life.

References

Access Info and Global Detention Project (2015). *The uncounted: Detention of migrants and asylum seekers in Europe*. Geneva: Access Info Europe/Global Detention Project.

Allison, E. (2013). Home Office issues "end of life plan" to hunger-striking asylum seeker. *The Guardian*, November 16. Retrieved January 30, 2014, from http://www.theguardian.com (home page).

American Civil Liberties Union (ACLU). (2007). ACLU challenges prison-like conditions at Hutto Detention Center. *ACLU*, March 6. Retrieved May 5, 2014, from http://www.aclu.org (home page).

Americans for Effective Law Enforcement Legal Centre (AELE) (2011). Use of force against immigration detainees. *AELE Monthly Law Journal, 5*(1), 301–306.

Amnesty International. (2013). Malta. *Annual Report 2013*. Retrieved May 5, 2014, from http://www.amnesty.org (home page).

Amnesty International. (2015). Greece: Humanitarian crisis mounts as refugee support system pushed to breaking point. *Media Release*, June 25. Retrieved February 11, 2016, from https://www.amnesty.org (home page).

Anonymous. (2014). Testimony: Refugee riot in the closed detention camp Békéscsaba. *No Border Serbia*. Retrieved January 15, 2014, from http://noborderserbia.wordpress.com (home page).

Arnold, F. W., Beeks, M., Fluxman, J., Katona, C., & de Zulueta, F. (2006, March 2). Unmet medical needs in detention. *British Medical Journal Rapid Response, 332: 251*.

Australian Border Force Act 2015. (Commonwealth).
Australian Broadcasting Corporation (ABC). (2005). New Villawood housing project launched today. *AM*, ABC Radio National, June 9. Transcript. Retrieved March 23, 2009, from http://www.abc.net.au/am (home page).
Australian National Audit Office (ANAO) (1998). *Auditor General Report No. 32: The management of boat people*. Canberra: Commonwealth of Australia.
Bail for Immigration Detainees (BID) (2009). *Out of sight, out of mind: Experiences of immigration detention in the UK*. London: Bail for Immigration Detainees.
Border Crossing Observatory. (2016). Australian border deaths database. Retrieved February 12, 2016, from http://artsonline.monash.edu.au/thebordercrossingobservatory (home page).
Bracken, P., & Gorst-Unsworth, C. (1991). The mental state of detained asylum seekers. *Psychiatric Bulletin, 15*, 657–659.
Briskman, L., Latham, S., & Goddard, C. (2008). *Human rights overboard: Seeking asylum in Australia*. Melbourne: Scribe Publications.
Casciani, D. (2004). Harmondsworth: A life inside. *BBC News Online*, July 21. Retrieved January 30, 2014, from http://news.bbc.co.uk/2/hi/uk_news/3912699.stm
Center for Migration Studies of New York (CMS). (2014). Immigration detention: Behind the record numbers. *CMS News*. Retrieved March 13, 2014, from http://cmsny.org (home page).
Center for Victims of Torture, Torture Abolition Survivor Support Coalition, International (CVT-TASSC) (2013). *Tortured & detained survivor stories of U.S. immigration detention*. Washington: The Center for Victims of Torture, Torture Abolition Survivor Support Coalition, International.
Černušáková, B. (2013). Bulgaria: "Inhuman conditions" spark protest at refugee camp. *Amnesty International*, November 19. Retrieved January 30, 2014, from http://www.amnesty.org (home page).
Cohen, B. (2014). Immigrant detainees resume hunger strike at Washington state facility. *Reuters*, March 25. Retrieved May 5, 2014, from http://www.reuters.com/article/2014/03/26/us-usa-hungerstrike-immigrants-idUSBREA2P03X20140326
Commonwealth Ombudsman (2001). *Report of an own motion investigation into The department of immigration and multicultural affairs' immigration detention centres*. Canberra: Commonwealth Ombudsman.
Commonwealth Ombudsman (2005). *Covering statement by the Commonwealth Ombudsman to the Minister for Immigration and Multicultural and Indigenous Affairs Concerning Reports under s4860 of the Migration Act 1958*. Canberra: Commonwealth Ombudsman.

Commonwealth Ombudsman. (2013). *Suicide and self-harm in the immigration detention network*. Report No. 02/2013. Canberra: Commonwealth Ombudsman.

Conlon, D. (2013). Hungering for freedom: Asylum seekers' hunger strikes—Rethinking resistance as counter-conduct. In D. Moran, N. Gill, & D. Conlon (Eds.), *Carceral spaces: Mobility and agency in imprisonment and migrant detention* (pp. 133–148). Farnham: Ashgate Publishing.

Cornelisse, G. (2010). *Immigration detention and human rights. Rethinking territorial sovereignty*. Leiden: Martinus Nijhoff Publishers.

Coroner's Court of New South Wales (2011). *Findings in the inquest into the deaths of Josefa Rauluni, Ahmed Obeid Al-Akabi and David Saunders at Villawood Detention Centre, New South Wales, in 2010*. Glebe: Coroner's Court of New South Wales.

Council of Europe (CoE). (2010). *The detention of asylum seekers and irregular migrants in Europe*. Report by the (Former) Committee on Migration Refugees and Population, Doc. 12105. Strasbourg: Council of Europe.

Cresswell, A. (2010). Call to abandon "factories for mental illness." *The Australian*, January 26. Retrieved January 27, 2014, from http://www.theaustralian.com.au (home page).

Crook, A. (2012). Serco training manual: How to "hit" and "strike" detainees. *Crikey*, March 14. Retrieved February 20, 2014, from http://www.crikey.com.au (home page).

De Bono, D. (2013). "Less than human": The detention of irregular migrants in Malta. *Race & Class, 55*(2), 60–81.

De Costa, C. (2013). Inside the immigration detention facilities in Darwin: Breeding grounds for mental illness. *Crikey*, December 17. Retrieved February 15, 2014, from http://blogs.crikey.com.au (home page).

Department of Immigration and Border Protection (DIBP). (2013). *Immigration detention facilities*. Retrieved January 24, 2014, from https://www.immi.gov.au/About/Pages/immigration-detention-facilities.aspx

Department of Immigration and Border Protection (DIBP) (2015). *Immigration detention and community statistics summary. 30 December 2015*. Canberra: Commonwealth of Australia.

Duncan Lewis Solicitors. (2013). Isa Muaza removed to Nigeria after out-of-hours court appeal refused. *Media Release*, May 18. Retrieved February 15, 2014, from http://www.prweb.com/releases/2013/12/prweb11433293.htm

Dunt, I. (2013). Botched Isa Muazu deportation opens door to judicial review. *Politics.co.uk*, December 5. Retrieved January 30, 2014, from http://www.politics.co.uk (home page).

Elliot, E., & Gunasekera, H. (2016). *The health and well-being of children in immigration detention. Report to the Australian Human Rights Commission. Monitoring Visit to Wickham Point Detention Centre, Darwin, NT. October 16th–18th 2015*. Sydney: Australian Human Rights Commission.

European Committee for the Prevention of Torture (CPT). (2010). *Report to the Hungarian Government on the visit to Hungary carried out by the European Committee for the Prevention of Torture and Inhuman or Degrading Treatment or Punishment (CPT) from 24 March to 2 April 2009*. CPT/Inf (2010) 16. Strasbourg: Council of Europe.

European Committee for the Prevention of Torture (CPT). (2011). *Public statement concerning Greece*. CPT/Inf (2011) 10. Strasbourg: Council of Europe.

European Committee for the Prevention of Torture (CPT). (2012). *Report to the Government of Greece on the visit to Greece carried out by the European Committee for the Prevention of Torture and Inhuman or Degrading Treatment or Punishment (CPT) from 19 to 27 January 2011*. CPT/Inf (2012) 1. Strasbourg: Council of Europe.

European Committee for the Prevention of Torture (CPT). (2013). *Report to the Maltese Government on the visit to Malta carried out by the European Committee for the Prevention of Torture and Inhuman or Degrading Treatment or Punishment (CPT) from 26 to 30 September 2011*. CPT/Inf (2013) 12. Strasbourg: Council of Europe.

Flynn, M. (2013). The hidden costs of human rights: The case of immigration detention. *Global Detention Project Working Paper No. 7*. Geneva: Global Detention Project.

Fox News Latino. (2012). Gang started riot at immigrant jail, Mississippi Sheriff says. *Fox News Latino*, May 21. Retrieved May 5, 2014, from http://latino.foxnews.com

Garcia Hernandez, C. C. (2014). Immigration detention as punishment. *UCLA Law Review, 61*, 1346–1414.

Global Detention Project. (n.d.). Retrieved January 24, 2014, from www.globaldetentionproject.org

Global Mail. (2014). At work inside our detention centres: A guard's story. *Global Mail*, February 14.

Government Accountability Office (GAO). (2007). *Alien detention standards: Telephone access problems were pervasive at detention facilities; Other deficiencies did not show a pattern of noncompliance*. Retrieved February 18, 2014, from http://www.gao.gov/new.items/d07875.pdf

Guild, E. (2004). Who is an irregular migrant? In B. Bogusz, R. Cholewinski, A. Cygan, & E. Szyszczak (Eds.), *Irregular migration and human rights:*

Theoretical, European and international perspectives (pp. 3–28). Leiden: Martinus Nijhoff Publishers.

Guild, E. (2010). *Criminalisation of migration in Europe: Human rights implications.* Council of Europe Commissioner for Human Rights Issue Paper. Strasbourg: Council of Europe.

Heeren, G. (2010). Pulling teeth: The state of mandatory immigration detention. *Harvard Civil Rights-Civil Liberties Law Review, 45*(2), 601–634.

Hennessy-Fiske, M., & Gorman, A. (2008). Detention centre riot probed. *LA Times*, April 24. Retrieved May 5, 2014, from http://articles.latimes.com/2008/apr/24/local/me-briefs24.S2

Her Majesty's Chief Inspector of Prisons (HMIP). (2006, February 20–24). *Inquiry into the quality of healthcare at Yarl's Wood immigration removal centre.* London: Her Majesty's Inspectorate of Prisons.

Her Majesty's Chief Inspector of Prisons (HMIP) (2014). *Report on an unannounced inspection of Harmondsworth Immigration Removal Centre by HM Chief Inspector of Prisons 5–16 August 2013.* London: Her Majesty's Inspectorate of Prisons.

Human Rights and Equal Opportunities Commission (HREOC) (1998). *Those who've come across the seas: Detention of unauthorised arrivals.* Sydney: Human Rights and Equal Opportunities Commission.

Human Rights and Equal Opportunities Commission (HREOC) (2004). *A last resort? National Inquiry into Children in Immigration Detention.* Sydney: Human Rights and Equal Opportunities Commission.

Human Rights First (HRF) (2009). *U.S. detention of asylum seekers seeking protection, finding prison.* New York: Human Rights First.

Human Rights First (2015). *Follow-up shadow report to the United Nations Committee on the elimination of all forms of racial discrimination.* New York: Human Rights First.

Human Rights Watch (HRW) (2010). *Costly and unfair: Flaws in US immigration detention policy.* New York: Human Rights Watch.

Human Rights Watch (2014). *Greece: Human Rights Watch submission to the United Nations Committee against torture.* New York: Human Rights Watch.

Immigration Detention Justice Centre. (2014). *Port Isabel Detention Centre.* Retrieved May 4, 2014, from http://www.immigrationdetention.org

International Detention Coalition (IDC). (2015). Greece and Turkey—Countries at immigration detention crossroads. *Media Release*, December 1. Retrieved February 10, 2016, from http://idcoalition.org (home page).

Jesuit Refugee Service-Europe (JRS) (2010). *Becoming vulnerable in detention.* Brussels: Jesuit Refugee Service-Europe.

Joint Standing Committee on Foreign Affairs, Defence and Trade (JSCFADT) (2001). *A report on visits to immigration detention centres, 2001*. Canberra: Commonwealth of Australia.

Joint Standing Committee on Migration (JSCM) (2000). *Not the Hilton. Immigration detention centres: Inspection report*. Canberra: Commonwealth of Australia.

Joint Standing Committee on Migration (JSCM) (2005). *Report of the inspection of Baxter immigration detention facility and Port Augusta residential housing project, April 2005*. Canberra: Commonwealth of Australia.

Kerr, J. (2005). Free at last, but a prisoner still of his tortured mind. *Sydney Morning Herald*, June 21. Retrieved July 3, 2012, from http://www.smh.com.au (home page).

Kreighbaum, A. (2014). Detainees from India on hunger strike at El Paso ICE Processing Center. *El Paso Times*, April 12. Retrieved May 5, 2014, from http://www.elpasotimes.com (home page).

Lewis, P., & Taylor, M. (2006). What really happened at Harmondsworth? *The Guardian*, December 13. Retrieved February 16, 2014, from http://www.theguardian.com (home page).

Lewis, R. (2014). Immigrant detainees on hunger strike allege threats by guards. *Al Jazeera*, March 20. Retrieved May 5, 2014, from http://america.aljazeera.com (home page).

Loff, B. (2002). Detention of asylum seekers in Australia. *The Lancet, 359*, 792–793.

Loff, B., Snell, B., Creati, M., & Mohan, M. (2002). 'Inside' Australia's Woomera detention centre. *The Lancet, 359*, 683.

Mares, S., & Jureidini, J. (2004). Psychiatric assessment of children and families in immigration detention: Clinical, administrative and ethical issues. *Australian and New Zealand Journal of Public Health, 28*(6), 527–536.

Marr, D. (2013). Doctors reveal 'harmful' standards of medical care for asylum seekers. *The Guardian*, December 20. Retrieved February 15, 2014, from http://www.theguardian.com (home page).

Massa, A. (2006). Asylum seekers stage protest. *Times of Malta*, February 21. Retrieved January 30, 2014, from http://www.timesofmalta.com (home page).

McGregor, J. (2011). Contestations and consequences of deportability: Hunger strikes and the political agency of non-citizens. *Citizenship Studies, 15*(5), 597–611.

Medici Per I Diritti Umani (MEDU) (2013). *The CIE Archipelago. Inquiry into the Italian centres for identification and expulsion*. Rome: Medici Per I Diritti Umani.

Médecins Sans Frontières (MSF). (2010). Over the Wall: A tour of Italy's migrant centres. *Médecins Sans Frontières*, January 2010. Retrieved January 28, 2014, from http://www.unhcr.org/50a606bc9.pdf

Médecins Sans Frontières (MSF) (2013). Health at risk in immigration detention facilities. *Forced Migration Review, 44*, 11–13.

Migration Act 1958. (Commonwealth).

Nethery, A., Rafferty-Brown, B., & Taylor, S. (2012). Exporting detention: Australia funded immigration detention in Indonesia. *Journal of Refugee Studies, 26*(1), 88–109.

Newman, L., Dudley, M., & Steel, Z. (2008). Asylum, detention and mental health in Australia. *Refugee Survey Quarterly, 27*(3), 110–127.

O'Neill, M. (2008). *Blind conscience*. Sydney: UNSW Press.

Palmer, M. (2005). *Inquiry into the circumstances of the immigration detention of Cornelia Rau*. Canberra: Commonwealth of Australia.

Parkin, J. (2013). *The criminalisation of migration in Europe. A state-of-the-art of the academic literature and research*. CEPS No. 61/October 2013. Brussels: Centre for European Policy Studies.

Press Association. (2013). Failed asylum seeker returns to Nigeria. *The Guardian*, December 19. Retrieved January 30, 2014, from http://www.theguargian.com (home page).

Proctor, N., De Leo, D., & Newman, L. (2013). Suicide and self-harm prevention for people in immigration detention. *Medical Journal of Australia, 199*(11), 730–732.

Rabin, N. (2009). Unseen prisoners: Women in immigration detention facilities in Arizona. *Georgetown Immigration Law Review, 23*, 695–763.

Robjant, K., Hassan, R., & Katona, C. (2009). Mental health implications of detaining asylum seekers: Systematic review. *British Journal of Psychiatry, 194*, 306–312.

S v Secretary, Department of Immigration and Multicultural and Indigenous Affairs. (2005). FCA 549 (May 5, 2005).

Sampson, R., & Mitchell, G. (2013). Global trends in immigration detention and alternatives. *Journal on Migration and Human Security, 1*(3), 97–121.

Sapa-AFP. (2014). Moroccans sew mouths shut in Italy. *IOL News*, January 26. Retrieved January 30, 2014, from http://www.iol.co.za (home page).

Schembri, K. (2006). Dozens of asylum seekers believed missing as detention system "about to collapse". *Malta Today*, July 2. Retrieved January 30, 2014, from http://www.maltatoday.com.mt (home page).

Shaw, S. (2004). *Report of the inquiry into the disturbance and fire at Yarl's Wood Removal Centre*. London: Prisons and Probation Ombudsman, House of Commons.

Shaw, S. (2016). *Review into the welfare in detention of vulnerable persons a report to the Home Office. January 2016*. London: Home Office.

Silove, D., Steel, Z., & Mollica, R. (2001). Detention of asylum seekers: Assault on mental health, human rights and social development. *The Lancet, 357*, 1436–1437.

Sofia News Agency. (2013) Tensions at Bulgarian refugee camp rise after Syrian Man's Death Society. *Sofia News Agency*, November 21. Retrieved February 20, 2014, from http://www.novinite.com (home page).

Squires, N. (2013). Italy's "appalling" treatment of migrants revealed in Lampedusa footage. *The Telegraph*, December 13. Retrieved January 27, 2014, from http://www.telegraph.co.uk (home page).

Steel, Z., Momartin, S., Bateman, C., Hafshejani, A., Silove, D., & Everson, N. (2004). Psychiatric status of asylum seeker families held for a protracted period in a remote detention centre in Australia. *Australian and New Zealand Journal of Public Health, 28*(6), 23–32.

Steel, Z., & Silove, D. (2001). The mental health implications of detaining asylum seekers. *Medical Journal of Australia, 175*, 596–599.

STEPS Consulting. (2007) *The conditions in centres for third country national (detention camps, open centres as well as transit centres and transit zones) with a particular focus on provisions and facilities for persons with special needs in the 25 EU member states*. REF: IP/C/LIBE/IC/2006-181. Brussels: European Parliament.

Sultan, A., & O'Sullivan, K. (2001). Psychological disturbances in asylum seekers held in long term detention: A participant-observer account. *Medical Journal of Australia, 175*, 593–596.

Taylor, D. (2012). Detention centre failures contributed to death of asylum seeker, inquest finds. *The Guardian*, May 26. Retrieved February 24, 2014, from http://www.theguardian.com (home page).

U.S. Immigration and Customs Enforcement (ICE) (2012). *Detained asylum seekers fiscal year 2009 and 2010 report to Congress August 20, 2012*. Washington: Department of Homeland Security.

United Nations High Commissioner for Refugees (UNHCR) (2012). *Hungary as a country of asylum. Observations on the situation of asylum-seekers and refugees in Hungary*. Geneva: UNHCR.

United Nations High Commissioner for Refugees (UNHCR). (2013). *UNHCR's position on the detention of asylum seekers in Malta*. Geneva: UNHCR. Retrieved January 27, 2014, from http://www.refworld.org/docid/52498c424.html

United Nations High Commissioner for Refugees (UNHCR) (2014). *UNHCR observations on the current situation of Asylum in Bulgaria*. Geneva: UNHCR.

United Nations Office of the High Commissioner for Human Rights (UNOHCHR). (2015). Migrants/human rights: Official visit to Australia postponed due to protection concerns. *Media Release*, September 25. Geneva: UNOHCHR. Retrieved February 12, 2016, from http://www.ohchr.org/EN/NewsEvents/Pages/DisplayNews.aspx?NewsID=16503&LangID=E#sthash.SxXfY6sp.dpuf

United Nations Working Group on Arbitrary Detention (UNWGAD). (2002). Civil and political rights, including the question of torture and detention report of the Working Group on Arbitrary Detention: Visit to Australia. *United Nations Commission on Human Rights 59th Session*, October 24. Document E/CN.4/2003/8/Add.2. Geneva: UNCHR.

United Nations Working Group on Arbitrary Detention (UNWGAD). (2009). Promotion and protection of all human rights, civil, political, economic, social and cultural rights, including the right to development, report of the Working Group on Arbitrary Detention: Mission to Italy. *United Nations Human Rights Council 10th Session*, January 26. Document A/HRC/10/21/Add.5. Geneva: UNCHR.

United Nations Working Group on Arbitrary Detention (UNWGAD). (2010). Promotion and protection of all human rights, civil, political, economic, social and cultural rights, including the right to development, report of the Working Group on Arbitrary Detention: Mission to Malta. *United Nations Human Rights Council 13th Session*, January 18, 2010. Document A/HRC/13/30/Add.2. Geneva: UNCHR.

United Nations Working Group on Arbitrary Detention (UNWGAD). (2013, January 21–31). Working Group on Arbitrary Detention statement upon the conclusion of its mission to Greece. Retrieved February 20, 2014, from http://www.ohchr.org (home page).

Western Australian Inspector of Custodial Services (WAICS). (2002). *Report of an announced inspection of Roebourne regional prison April 2002: Report No. 14*. Perth: Office of the Inspector of Custodial Services. Retrieved February 21, 2012, from www.custodialinspector.wa.gov.au

Wilsher, D. (2012). *Immigration detention. Law, history, politics*. Cambridge: Cambridge University Press.

8

Conclusion

The accounts presented here are of events occurring in Australia, but it is unlikely they are uniquely Australian phenomena. While the details of legal and policy frameworks may differ between jurisdictions, the legal and political positioning of being a non-citizen, of being reduced to a state of 'naked humanity' and consequently falling beyond most protections of the rule of law, are core to the asylum-seeking experience. Immigration detention centres are not subject to the same monitoring and scrutiny as prisons, and administrative decisions to detain are not made with judicial oversight or the suite of protections available to those accused of criminal acts. Standards of detention infrastructure and treatment are poorly defined and rarely legally enforceable. Independent scrutiny and monitoring is lacking, particularly by bodies with statutory power. Consequently, people's experiences while classified as asylum seekers or detainees are too often dependent on charity (or lack thereof) and not right, and so are vulnerable to whim. As astutely articulated by Hannah Arendt more than half a century ago, the state of rightlessness means a world for the refugee in which 'privileges in some cases, injustices in most, blessings and doom are meted out to them according to accident and without any relation whatsoever to what they do, did, or may do' (Arendt 1958, 296).

L. Fiske, *Human Rights, Refugee Protest and Immigration Detention*,
DOI 10.1057/978-1-137-58096-2_8

Administrative immigration detention is one of the most profound ways in which that rightlessness becomes starkly visible.

Wherever prolonged immigration detention is practiced, detainee resistance to that detention can also be found. Despite the seemingly ever expanding use of detention and the ample supply of media stories about immigration detainees hunger striking, rioting or escaping, detailed accounts from detainees about life inside detention and why protests happen are seldom published. Events and actions are reported without the necessary explanatory speech of the actors, and explanations are instead provided by authorities. Immigration detention is justified as a non-punitive administrative procedure enabling states to achieve certain policy goals. Protest by detainees thus comes to be understood as further evidence of their non-compliant behaviour and disregard for the rules and laws of society.

This book was motivated by a desire to discover how detainees explained their own acts of resistance against immigration detention. While Australian news between 1999 and 2005 was near saturated with stories of self-harm, hunger strike, riot, escape and other protests in immigration detention centres, detainees themselves were only seldom heard. This was in part due to strategies of the government to distance, dehumanise and silence asylum seekers through policies such as mandatory detention and tight control of media and public access to detention centres. Detainees also had to struggle against more globalised hegemony about refugees which idealise feminised, passive and grateful refugees in distant camps reliant on expert Western intervention contrasted against criminalised, masculinised active asylum seekers seeking their own resolutions to displacement being represented as threats to the nation. Detainees were simultaneously engaged in struggles at once highly localised, and inextricably entwined with global hegemonies around refuge, sovereignty, terrorism and geo-politics.

To establish an independent voice against such a powerful backdrop is a necessary and difficult task. Detainees' actions are sometimes highly visual spectacles designed to ensure media coverage and draw attention to their existence. Many messages from asylum seekers in detention use a language of human rights to articulate their positions, drawing our attention not only to the problem of immigration detention, but also to the need to think about human rights not so much as a body of laws and treaties, but as a discursive tool. The words and actions of former detainees reveal the power of human rights as a discourse enabling strategic alliances between temporally and geographically disparate struggles against dominant hegemonies. Through a language of rights, protesters were able to draw upon the hard won moral legitimacy of other struggles such as Irish hunger strikers, anti-Apartheid activists or the US civil rights movement and in doing so, strengthen a reading of the situation that questioned the morality of the laws which sanction mandatory indefinite detention. Detainees were also able to forge links with refugee supporters outside detention and to assist in the growth of domestic opposition to the policy. The concept of human rights, however extensive or limited a person's knowledge of human rights laws, assisted in mobilising resistance to felt injustice.

A foundational struggle within human rights is the tension between universalism and state sovereignty, on the one hand, and between universalism and diversity, on the other hand. Arendt argued that ongoing uncritical acceptance of the proposition that human rights are universal was dangerous rhetoric. It was rhetoric because the existence of refugees and displaced peoples was proof positive of the utterly contingent nature of rights—rights exist only as a result of human decision within a political community both willing and able to guarantee those rights. She argued that conceiving of human rights as universal and as flowing from God, nature or abstract man is dangerous because it facilitates complacency rather than the active ongoing human engagement and commitment required to make human rights real. Leaving responsibility for human rights in the hands of the nation-state fundamentally undermined any realisable universality of human rights.

While Arendt argued against imagining that human rights are universal in application, she also stated that aspects of the human condition are universal: that we all have the capacity for speech and action, that we are all distinct and unique individuals who share a need to live in community and so are 'political animals.' A just society, for Arendt, was one in which members of the community make a decision to regard all members as political equals. Arendt's work sought primarily to understand totalitarianism and the Holocaust. From this she theorised that a loss of citizenship (belonging to a formal political community) was a loss of the 'right to have rights,' which she defined as the right to 'a place in the world which makes opinions significant and actions effective' (Arendt 1976, 296), something only possible in community as we are intersubjectively constituted. Without the right to have rights, any freedoms or benefits one might enjoy are a matter of charity or chance, not guaranteed or enforceable rights. A rightless person is reduced to 'simple humanity' and, she contended that the international community saw nothing compelling in the image of naked humanity being marched off to the gas chambers of the Holocaust.

Simple or naked humanity was, for Arendt, no basis from which to claim rights. Stripped of citizenship and other key markers of individual identity (such as names), asylum seekers in detention have only their naked humanity (including the capacities for speech and action) to use in their determination to restore their right to have rights; to be recognised as distinct beings and to gain admittance to a new political community. It is at this point, where Arendt's concern with totalitarianism and the Holocaust anchors her work to a specific historical event, that the work of Foucault can extend the potentiality of naked humanity and recognise a more fluid, fractured and dynamic flow of power, one which is untethered from monolithic sites such as 'the nation-state' and which engages and is engaged with by actual people.

Through Foucault's reconceptualisation of power as a force present everywhere and in all social relations, rather than as a finite commodity resting in certain sites and not others, detainees and asylum seekers are no longer powerless. They have *less* power than governments, but they are not *without* power. Human beings are socially constituted and therefore never cease to be engaged in social relations (whether directly or semiotically) and so remain discursive agents. It is a strategy of the more powerful to obscure, discredit, marginalise, suppress and even bury alternate knowledges and oppositional voices, but these efforts can never be entirely successful as, while power indeed produces and maintains hegemonic 'common sense' and 'Truth,' power also produces resistance. 'Power is everywhere,' Foucault contended, 'not because it embraces everything, but because it comes from everywhere' (Foucault 1976, 93). Detainees then, are not powerless objects upon which the state can exert its absolute power, but are less powerful subjects who both initiate and respond to encounters with the state and who are engaged in an unequal struggle for recognition and restoration of rights.

The creativity, courage and tenacity of detainee resistance to detention is not rooted in citizenship or any other legal status, but in a 'naked humanity.' Governments may see nothing compelling in this naked humanity, but detainees use their diverse and unique talents and capacities to resist governments' efforts to control the relationship between detainees and the polis, and to forge alliances and relationships with people outside detention. These acts force a place in the public sphere for detainee voices to introduce themselves, to explain who they are and why they are hunger striking, self-harming or burning buildings. In Australia, alongside frequent protests by asylum seekers in detention, refugee advocacy and solidarity networks grew. Formal members of the polis began to question government hegemony around 'boatpeople' and the purported need for immigration detention. By 2005, the dominant hegemony about asylum seekers was sufficiently unsettled that the government began to have divisions from within. Government backbenchers forced the government to withdraw draft legislation designed to further extend the government's power over detainees and instead, the government was compelled to introduce new policies which saw the release of children and long term detainees from detention centres. Australia's use of immigration detention, after a brief reduction, has grown again and protests by detainees and by supporters in the community have grown alongside it, focused particularly at the use of off-shore detention in Papua New Guinea and Nauru.

The words and deeds of detainees support a discursive and strategic universalism, fluid enough to allow for the richness of human diversity, yet sufficiently robust to empower local struggles and mobilise support and solidarity. A language of rights was used by detainees because it expressed their sentiments and beliefs (their incredulity and indignation at their treatment by the Australian state) and also had a number of effects. The ideal of human rights has a universal appeal and so a language of the same was able to build bridges and relationships between groups sharing little else in common, in spite of concerted efforts by the government to block such alliances. It also introduced a moral argument in contrast to the strict legality of detention, unsettling the power of the state and creating a space for unqualified and less powerful voices to make legitimacy claims. The realm of conscience (of detainees and the Australian people), relegated by modernity's eradication of ambivalence to the margins and to the private sphere, regained traction as a central concern in a heated public debate: is it *right* (as opposed to lawful) to treat people in this way?

Detainees interviewed here used their capacities for analysis, speech and action in creative and multiple ways. Dr Aamer Sultan used his medical training to scientifically document people's demise inside detention and then drew upon the power of the medical community to challenge a policy which so demonstrably goes against health and wellbeing. Shahin used himself: his writing, acting and speaking skills along with his energy and determination to tour *Refugitive* to audiences who might otherwise never meet a 'boatperson.' Through the immediacy of face-to-face encounters, he worked to dispel the government's national security and border crime propaganda. Escapees, seeking media coverage and to create a public voice by crossing the wires that demarcated their physical and political domain, inadvertently discovered the power of the Australian judicial system for establishing greater rights for themselves as charged persons and greater power for their testimony. Their words when spoken in a court of law could not be so readily dismissed.

Words alone were rarely enough, as hundreds of detainee hunger strikers understood. Realising that lacking formal political status, detainees' voices could be all too easily discredited and ignored, detainees used their bodies to insist upon a place in the polis. Issaq's testimony about the decision to sew his lips and to present this act in the public sphere through a doctor demonstrates a keen political awareness. Using one's body through hunger strike, lip sewing and self-harm is not, however, an intellectual act or a remote defence of principle. Embodied protests convey the interplay of political critique and intimacy of personal emotion. To attempt to understand detainee actions as arising from either personal despair *or* detached critique would fall into established binaries and present two-dimensional reductions of dynamic and multifaceted phenomena.

In looking at riot episodes, the roles of emotion and critique dramatically coalesce as people share stories, express outrage, form close bonds, and mobilise to impassioned and cathartic action. With civil speech and formal processes for resolution of grievances effectively closed off, detainee critiques of injustice fanned anger and indignation. Emotions in turn shaped critique, becoming powerful forces in need of release. State actions can inflame or diffuse escalating tensions, and in this, the Australian government and private contractors fell into uninformed populist understandings of riot. In their struggle for power, recognition and rights, detainees used their bodies again, but this time, unlike the hunger strikers who used their bodies to make visible the obfuscated violence deployed against them by the state, detainees used their bodies to directly confront and fight the state itself and to tear down the physical representations of state power.

Detainee testimony about protest also revealed the multifaceted purpose or function of protest. Sometimes aimed at achieving particular immediate or distant goals (such as gaining access to a telephone or establishing a detainee voice in the media), protest also played an important existential role for detainees—it was often only through resistant or subversive acts that detainees could experience their agency, the capacities of independent speech and action essential to the human condition and which distinguish us from 'beasts and gods' (Arendt 1958, 22). I am grateful to Ismail who expressed this so eloquently in my first interview when he explained that if he,

> … didn't do those things, nothing different between me and this table. With me? I got a soul. I got a mind. I got thinking. While this table … of course, I wouldn't stay like that.

Regardless of any material, political or semiotic outcome of protests, resistance was inevitable because detainees remained human, retained agency and were engaged in socially constituted power struggles.

The struggles are ongoing. Australia remains resolutely committed to mandatory indefinite immigration detention even following several preventable deaths and credible evidence of systematic sexual assault, including against children, and at a cost of more than $1.1 billion in 2015 for its off-shore detention centres in Papua New Guinea and Nauru alone (Commonwealth of Australia 2015, 42–44). The UK Home Office reported that 30,423 people were detained over the course of 2013 (UK

Home Office 2014). In the USA, the Department of Homeland Security (DHS) secured $1.84 billion for its detention operations for the 2014 fiscal year. This sum will fund 34,000 immigration detention beds at a cost of over five million dollars per day (NIF 2013).

The practice of immigration detention is growing and spreading globally. Michael Flynn of the Global Detention Project traces the developments of immigration detention, with US practices at the root and European nations, Australia and New Zealand adopting and extending similar practices, each learning from the other (Flynn 2014). Detention is being expanded and pushed further from the reach of law, to territories outside the EU, the USA and Australia where it is harder still for non-citizens to establish rights. The growing reluctance of European Member States, Australia, Canada and North America to meet legal obligations arising from the Refugees Convention and international human rights law make the task of revisiting the moral and philosophical foundations of human rights as a mutual guarantee between people ever more urgent. Asylum seekers and refugees, with their experiential knowledge of the state of rightlessness, particularly inside immigration detention centres, have much to contribute to this discussion.

While this book makes no claims of presenting the Truth, it uncovers sufficient repetition of discursive patterns (both between participants in this research and between detainees and activists in struggles elsewhere) to establish that detainees, like other oppressed peoples, critique their political environment, and that explanations of resistance cannot be properly understood only through narrations from detached experts. The testimony of former detainees gathered during this research provides useful insight not only into an alternate record of events in Australia, but also into how human rights can be conceived and mobilised. A discursive universalism enhances opportunities for alliances across constructed divides, while also allowing for a diversity of manifestations of human creativity as infinite as the situations in which people are placed.

Governments may want passive, silent asylum seekers upon whom they can project their own narrative as acts of sovereign power, but 'naked humanity,' of both asylum seekers and citizens, cannot be erased. We humans are always speaking, acting subjects and will always initiate, challenge, subvert, resist and rise up in the insistence upon a place in the world where our opinions are significant and actions effective.

Bibliography

Arendt, H. (1958). *The human condition* (2nd ed.). Chicago: University of Chicago Press.

Arendt, H. (1976). *The origins of totalitarianism*. Orlando: A Harvest Book, Harcourt Publishing.

Commonwealth of Australia. (2015, May 26). *Official Committee Hansard. Senate Legal and Constitutional Affairs Legislation Committee. Estimates.* Canberra: Commonwealth of Australia. Retrieved February 1, 2016, from http://www.parlinfo.aph.gov.au (home page).

Flynn, M. (2014). How and why immigration detention crossed the globe. *Working Paper No. 8*. Geneva: Global Detention Project. Retrieved May 2, 2014, from http://www.globaldetentionproject.org (home page).

Foucault, M. (1976). *The history of sexuality, Volume 1* (R. Hurley, Trans.). London: Penguin Books.

National Immigration Forum (NIF). (2013). *The math of immigration detention. Runaway costs for immigration detention do not add up to sensible policies.* Washington, DC: National Immigration Forum. Retrieved May 8, 2014, from http://immigrationresearch-info.org/report/other/math-immigration-detention

UK Home Office. (2014, February 27). *Immigration statistics, October to December 2013*. London: Home Office. Retrieved May 8, 2014, from https://www.gov.uk (home page).

Appendix: Details of Interview Participants

Name or pseudonym (interview date)	Length of detention	Locations of detention
Aamer Sultan (22/02/09)	Three years, six weeks	Villawood IDC
Baha'adin (16/02/09)	Five years	Curtin IRPC Baxter IDF
Emad (26/02/09)	Eight months	Curtin IRPC
Ibrahim (20/01/09)	Seven months	Woomera IRPC
Ismail (11/01/09)	Five years	Curtin IDC Perth IDC Baxter IDF Casuarina Prison Glenside Psychiatric Hospital Broome Police Station cells
Issaq (21/02/09)	Three years, eleven months	Woomera IRPC Port Hedland IRPC Villawood IDC
Mehdi (15/02/09)	Five years	Curtin IRPC Baxter IDF

(*continued*)

L. Fiske, *Human Rights, Refugee Protest and Immigration Detention*,
DOI 10.1057/978-1-137-58096-2

(continued)

Name or pseudonym (interview date)	Length of detention	Locations of detention
Mivan (15/02/09)	Five years	Curtin IRPC Baxter IDF
Mohammed (25/02/09)	Four years	Perth IDC Port Hedland IRPC Villawood IDC Roebourne Prison
Osman (18/01/09)	Three years, four months	Port Hedland IRPC Baxter IDF
Salah (15/02/09)	Two years, nine months	Curtin IRPC Baxter IDF
Farshi Kheirillapour (25/02/09)	Three years	Perth IDC Port Hedland IRPC Curtin IRPC Roebourne Prison Casuarina Prison
Sayed (11/01/09)	Six years	Perth IDC Casuarina Prison
Shahin Shafaei (17/02/09)	One year, eight months	Curtin IRPC
Tariq (19/02/09)	Eleven months, then escaped for three years, then five and a half months	Woomera IRPC Maribyrnong IDC Baxter IDF

Index

A

L. Fiske, *Human Rights, Refugee Protest and Immigration Detention*,
DOI 10.1057/978-1-137-58096-2

Printed by Printforce, the Netherlands